BOOKIE
GAMBLER
FIXER
SPY

ED HAWKINS is an award-winning sports journalist. He has twice been named the Sports Journalists' Association's Sports Betting Writer of the Year. This is his second book.

BOOKIE
GAMBLER
FIXER
SPY

A JOURNEY TO THE HEART
OF CRICKET'S UNDERWORLD

ED HAWKINS

BLOOMSBURY

LONDON · NEW DELHI · NEW YORK · SYDNEY

First published in 2012 by
Bloomsbury Publishing Plc
50 Bedford Square
London WC1B 3DP

This paperback edition published 2013

www.bloomsbury.com

ISBN 978 1 4081 6996 4

10 9 8 7 6 5 4 3 2 1

DISCLAIMER: This is a work of non-fiction. However, some names/identities
have been changed to protect the author's sources.

A CIP catalogue record for this book is available from the British Library.

Typeset in ITC Galliard by seagulls.net

Printed and bound in Great Britain by CPI Group (UK) Ltd, Croydon CR0 4YY

CONTENTS

AUTHOR'S NOTE

The aim of this book is to get under the fingernails of the bookmakers, punters and fixers who seek to corrupt cricket, and to expose – in minute, gory detail – how they might have done it in the context of one extraordinary match, which could be set for infamy.

Due to the sheer number of allegations encountered, it was not the intention to prove or disprove corruption in certain matches or by certain players. However, it was impossible not to attempt to delve into the one game in particular, and it will soon become clear why.

Nor was it the intention to give the complete account of cricket's historical relationship with corruption. Hansie Cronje, the South Africa captain who embarrassed the game with his corrupt ways, has only a walk-on role. The central characters are those who operate today in India's underworld.

Some names and places have been changed to protect the identity of those who spoke, who worry that a knock on the door from the mafia is a possibility. The two central characters of this true story, Parthiv and Vinay, met me, and talked, without knowledge that this book was being written.

On two occasions – in February 2011 and October 2011 – I travelled to India to undertake research, visiting Delhi, Mumbai, Bhopal and Rajasthan. But my research into match- and spot-fixing began in the summer of 2009.

In India one lakh equals 100,000 rupees, or £1,200; one crore equals 100 lakh, or £120,000.

Ed Hawkins, North London, May 2012

PART ONE

IN THE BEGINNING ...

CHAPTER 1

'THERE IS NOTHING NEW UNDER THE SUN'

Oxford Street, London. Late September 2010. The browsers, bargain hunters and tourists fill the pavements in their hordes. The windows of their basilicas – Niketown, Topshop, Benetton et al – reflect a thousand eager faces a minute. To stop and be swallowed by the greedy throng is to risk a bruising to the knees from the swinging of oversized shopping bags or to the ribs from the jutting lenses of daytrippers' cameras.

If you are ever unfortunate enough to find yourself carried along by this wave of consumerism on London's busiest street, do try to dig in your heels, hold back the tide, accept the inevitable bumps and barges and reflect. For this is the incongruous, somewhat surprising setting for the first and, it was hoped, last act of the story of match-fixing in cricket.

Where Oxford Street and Argyll Street meet is a small bureau de change. Apt really. More than 150 years ago it was the site for the Green Man and Still pub, an establishment notorious for being the place where cricketers would meet bookmakers. Money would change from one grubby hand to the next for fixes. And somewhere along this stretch of retail gluttony, which runs east to west from the landmark of Centre Point's reach-for-the-skies tower to the green tranquillity of Hyde Park, is a clothes shop owned by Sanjay Chawla, the bookmaker who was recorded by Delhi police fixing matches with Hansie Cronje, the disgraced South Africa captain, in 2000.

The Cronje affair was the darkest of times for a sport thought to be the most noble. When the scandal broke, cricket was considered to have lost its virtue. Whether it had any to start with is debatable. Cricket and betting have a long, rich history, having been snug bedfellows since 1646, the earliest reference to gambling on the sport: a court case concerning the non-payment of a wager made on a game at Coxheath in Kent on 29 May of that year. The stake? Twelve candles.

In the early 18th century, cricket was financed by the aristocracy for the precise reason that they could gamble on it. Every match that was considered important, whether it was a first-class game or a single wicket competition, was played for money. Newspapers of the time did not report the scorecards and results of these contests, but did record the odds and who won the wager. In 1744 the first set of laws for the game were drawn up, specifically to settle gambling disputes.

It was in those days of yore that cricket was first introduced to what could be considered the precursor to the spot-bet: the act of betting on a happening other than the match result. In 1757, Lord March, a compulsive gambler, won money by putting a letter inside a cricket ball and persuading cricketers to throw it to one another over fixed distances. He had wagered that he could propel a letter a certain distance in a certain amount of time. Then there was the 4th Earl of Tankerville, who had such faith in his gardener's metronomic ability as a bowler that he bet £100 – a huge sum in those days – that he could land the ball on a feather. He duly did so.

So cricket, riddled with the spirit of gambling, was ripe for corruption. It was in a book called *The Cricketer's Fields*, written by Reverend Pycroft, that this foul play was first laid bare. Pycroft frequented the Green Man and Still and became close to a number of players. For the taped mobile telephone conversations between Cronje and Chawla, read the conversation Pycroft had with an anonymous player about the fraternisation of cricketers with bookmakers, tricksters and blacklegs.

'All the names I had ever heard as foremost in the game met together, drinking, card-playing, betting and singing at the Green Man,' said the player. 'No man without his wine and such suppers as three guineas a game to lose, five to win could never pay for long.' Pycroft included these quotes in his book and in doing so published the first account of corruption in cricket. The year was 1851.

Pycroft had an interview with Billy Beldham, the Surrey batsman who in 1997 was named as one of the hundred greatest cricketers of all time by John Woodcock, the esteemed former cricket correspondent of *The*

Times. But Beldham too fixed a match, trying to make up for money lost in a previous fix that had gone awry, telling Pycroft: 'Matches were bought and matches were sold and gentlemen, who meant honestly, lost large sums of money, till the rogues beat themselves at last. Of this roguery, nobody ever suspected me.

'Hundreds of pounds were bet upon all the great matches, and other wagers laid on the scores of the finest players. And that too by men who had a book for every race and every match in the sporting world – men who lived by gambling.'

The anonymous source and Beldham reveal the key ingredients of fixing: greed, poverty and drink, of which the Green Man had plenty. Cricketers would be bought booze by the bookmakers, loosening their tongues and inhibitions before suggesting they throw a match for money. 'The temptation was really very great – too great by far for any poor man to be exposed to,' said Pycroft's contact. 'What was easier than for such sharp gentlemen to mix with the players, to take advantage of their difficulties, and to say, "Your backers, my Lord this, and the Duke of that, sell matches and overrule all your good play, so why shouldn't you have a share of the plunder?" – that was their constant argument – serve them as they serve you.'

The Cronje of this era was a player called William Lambert – some say Pycroft's chief source – who was found guilty of match-fixing and banned from playing at Lord's for life. Lambert was described by Arthur Haygarth, another notable player of the time, as 'one of the most successful cricketers that has ever yet appeared, excelling as he did in batting, bowling, fielding, keeping wicket, and also single wicket playing'. *The Cricketer's Fields* coined the phrase 'it's just not cricket' and its revelations forced the MCC to act. Bookmakers, who previously could have been found sitting under the pavilion, ready to take a gambler's money, were banned from Lord's. The Green Man and Still became a parcel office for the London and North-Western Railway.

Cricket unravelled in similar fashion during the 1990s. It began in 1990 when Mukesh Gupta, the bookmaker who would furnish India's Central Bureau of Investigation (CBI) with damaging information on the depth of corruption, first became involved with the India player Ajay Sharma.

Gupta (who was eventually cleared of all criminal charges by the Delhi High Court in February 2011 in relation to the Cronje match-fixing scandal) would meet Mohammad Azharuddin, the India captain, in 1995. A year later Azharuddin and Cronje would both allegedly take bribes from the man known as 'MK' during reciprocal tours between South Africa and India. Elsewhere, Pakistan was conducting its own inquiry into corruption claims about Salim Malik, the former captain who received a life ban for match-fixing in 2000 that was later lifted by a local court of Lahore in October 2008. And in Australia, it had emerged that Shane Warne and Mark Waugh had been fined for taking money from a bookmaker.

But it was the Cronje case which compelled. It was not clear how Sanjay Chawla became involved with Cronje, but Clive Lloyd, the manager of the West Indies team, claimed to have seen him in a VIP box during his team's tour to South Africa in 1998–99. When Delhi police released the Cronje tapes, recorded during the Pepsi one-day series in March 2000, Chawla was a key figure. A sample from those tapes reads as follows:

Sanjay Chawla: 'Is [Pieter] Strydom playing?'

Hansie Cronje: 'Yes he is playing. Yeah.'

Chawla: '[Nicky] Boje?'

Cronje: 'Boje is playing.'

Chawla: 'And who is playing? [Herschelle] Gibbs?'

Cronje: 'Gibbs and myself.'

Chawla: 'Yeah, what about anybody else?'

Cronje: 'No, I won't be able to get any more.'

Chawla: 'You won't be able to get more?'

Cronje: 'No.'

Chawla: 'OK, just tell me. But you have only four with you and not anybody else?'

Cronje: 'No.'

Chawla: '[Lance] Klusener and no one?'

Cronje: 'No, no, impossible, impossible. They were saying that they were already doing Cochin. The other guys are already angry with me because I have not received their money you know.'

Chawla: 'But I told you I have already given him altogether 60.'

Cronje: 'OK.'

Chawla: 'And tomorrow I can deposit the money in your account, it is not a problem because of the time difference. Tomorrow itself I can deposit the money.'

Cronje: 'OK. Everything is fine. Spoken to Gibbs and to [Henry] Williams and Strydom. Everything is fine.'

Chawla: 'And how many runs for Gibbs?'

Cronje: 'Less than 20.'

Chawla: 'Less than 20?'

Cronje: 'Yeah.'

Chawla: 'And if you score 270 it is off?'

Cronje: 'OK, and financially the guys want 25. They want 25 each.'

Chawla: 'All right, OK.'

Cronje: 'So that's 75 for those three and what can you pay me? I do not know how much you pay me.'

Chawla: 'You say.'

Cronje: 'If you give me 140 for everybody.'

Chawla: '140 altogether?'

Cronje: 'Yeah.'

Chawla: 'OK, that's fine.'

Cronje: 'All right. So we definitely are on.'

Chawla: 'OK, and one last thing I want to ask you, you know just in case India bat first and if they get out for less than 250 and when you come to bat in the second innings, is it possible you could ask Gibbs to? His wicket? ... Maybe we can get out of it.'

Cronje: 'OK.'

Chawla: 'And just in case India is all out for less that 250 if they bat first.'

Cronje: 'OK, I will tell him.'

Chawla: 'Yeah.'

Cronje: 'I will tell him.'

Chawla: 'And because if he starts scoring so early then we won't be able to get out of it.

Cronje: OK. Not so early in the first five or six in the Indian innings.'

Chawla: 'Yeah.'

Cronje: 'OK.'

On the basis of such evidence Cronje was banned for life in October 2000, following South Africa's King Commission. Gibbs and Williams were banned for six months, Boje and Strydom, who under oath both denied ever having been involved in fixing, were both exonerated. A month later the CBI published its report following the allegations made by MK Gupta. Azharuddin and Ajay Sharma were banned for life, Manoj Prabhakar and Ajay Jadeja for five years. The ICC still hold Azharuddin's ban although a high court in India ruled it illegal. Jadeja was eventually cleared by the Delhi High Court. Also in 2000, Pakistan's Qayyum Report was released. Life bans for Salim Malik (although his sanction was later overturned by a Lahore court in 2008) and Ata-ur-Rehman (his life ban was lifted by the ICC in November 2006) followed, while Wasim Akram was fined and barred from captaining his country. Rehman was later allowed to play again from 2007. The purge was complete. Apparently for the second time in its history, cricket had cut out the cancer.

Does it need to perform emergency surgery for a third time? This was the question I had on my mind when I stood outside that small bureau de change, the ghosts of the Green Man sending a chill down the spine. Billy Beldham's parting shot to Pycroft was ringing in my ears, too: 'What has been will be again, what has been done will be done again; there is nothing new under the sun.'

The sport was reeling. The International Cricket Council (ICC) had just suspended three Pakistan players, Mohammad Amir, Mohammad Asif and Salman Butt, on corruption allegations relating to spot-fixing. A *News of the World* investigation had alleged the players, at the behest of an agent called Mazhar Majeed, bowled no-balls at pre-determined times during the Lord's Test against England that summer. Lengthy playing bans for each of the men followed and, for the first time, cricketers were convicted in a court of fixing, or to use the legal parlance, 'conspiracy to accept corrupt payments, and conspiracy to cheat at gambling'. Butt, the former Pakistan captain, was sentenced to two years and six months, Asif got a one-year jail sentence and Amir, his fellow bowler, six months. Majeed was sentenced to two years and eight months.

As a gambler and cricket fan I wanted to know more of how corruption in cricket worked, who the bookmakers were, how and where they operated, what markets they bet on, how players were targeted, what they were promised and how they were paid. How was a fix set up? How was money actually generated from a fix? Was it bookmakers manipulating odds? Was it punters placing bets? The spot-fixing case involving the Pakistan players had not answered any of these questions. There were confusing and contradictory elements of the case which set off a desire to understand more about a historic, thriving corrupt industry – a sort of personal version of *The Cricketer's Fields*.

Sanjay Chawla could perhaps provide answers to my questions. Originally from Delhi, Chawla had lived in London since 1993, running his garment shop. He had learned the trade from the family business which had been set up in 1953, originally in Jangpura. Year by year it had grown, until by the end of the century more than 25,000 shorts, trousers, jackets and pullovers were being produced on a daily basis. His store, apparently, was inauspicious, selling cheap non-Indian clothing. 'The ambiance of the store does not give the impression of Chawla being a man who can trade in thousands of pounds,' it was said at the time of the Cronje case.

So on that Oxford Street afternoon I went door to door, seeking him out at each of the shops which best matched the description. 'Does Sanjay Chawla work here?' Eleven times I asked the question, most of the time receiving a shake of the head or blank stares. Twice I was told to 'wait here' as the assistant went to the backroom from where I believed Chawla would materialise. But he did not. The worker returned with a blank face and I was on my way.

Two weeks later I came across Chawla's mobile telephone number. It rang three times before an irritated voice answered.

'Hello, Sanjay? … Sanjay Chawla?'

'Yes, who is this?'

I explained who I was and that I wanted to talk to him about cricket and betting.

'You've got the wrong number,' he said and hung up.

Chawla has never spoken of his past, apparently sleeping in his car to avoid reporters. I sent a text message a day for about a week, hoping he would agree to 'meet for ten minutes for a coffee'. He did not reply.

Of course, I was being lazy. I thought a stroll down Oxford Street on a pleasant late summer day would satisfy my curiosity. In reality I would have to undergo a more arduous journey, one to the heart of cricket's underworld. In the end I believe I got the answers to my questions and a lot more besides.

I hope this book will explain how corruption in cricket works and that the answers to my questions will interest the reader as much as they have interested me. I've met with India's illegal bookmakers, stayed in their homes, eaten with their families, watched them take bets, been coerced into giving them information which could have landed me in trouble with the ICC's Anti-Corruption and Security Unit (ACSU), received details about fixes before they have happened, drunk beer at TGI Friday's with one of India's most infamous punters, had sweets and chai with a fixer who pleaded his innocence, met the Delhi police who interrogated Mohammad Azharuddin and spoken with spies in Pakistan's intelligence agency. After all of it, I will never watch a cricket match in the same way again.

CHAPTER 2

FEAR

It was a typically balmy January evening in 2003 in Dubai's Al-Karama, a quiet, well-to-do residential suburb in the old town. From across the jostling water of the creek, where five-star hotels loomed over less auspicious neighbours, came the gentle sound of revelry; the faint holler of laughter from the businessmen celebrating plots for a super city to rise from the desert dunes and the amiable patter of the tourists they hoped to lure for years to come.

The merrymakers didn't hear the gunshots. Twenty were fired, drowning the kisses of cue ball on colour in the snooker hall of the Indian Club, a members-only sports and fitness club which, boasted its website, was 'synonymous with a certain standard'. Blood pumped from the skull of Sharad Shetty, darkening the green baize of the table to a dirty auburn. He had been shot from point-blank range by two men.

Shetty was taken to Sheikh Rashid hospital, where doctors declared him dead on arrival. The killing had been ordered by Mumbai underworld boss Chhota Rajan. It was the culmination of an eight-year mafia war with his rival Dawood Ibrahim's infamous D-Company gang, of which Shetty was a deputy. In reprisals that could have been straight out of the Godfather trilogy, the adversaries had traded body bags: racketeers, goons, lieutenants.

But Shetty was the greatest prize. The original slumdog millionaire, he hailed from the squalor of Jogeshwari, a seedy suburb to the south of Mumbai, where the pitiable locals use historic Hindu caves as toilets. Growing up in the chawls – the tenement blocks stacked five high and 20 wide, offering a single room and no sanitation – Shetty had started out as a jeweller. He graduated to smuggling gold with Ibrahim in 1979. Flesh trading, drug trafficking, protection rackets and hotel deals followed.

Yet muscle, murder and misappropriation were not why Shetty would gain infamy. When the Mumbai newsmen reported how the bullets ripped into his body, leaving him slumped in the resinous mixture of felt and his own blood, they described not another gangland assassination, but the slaying of India's greatest match-fixer. It was two months before the 2003 World Cup in South Africa.

The timing was not a coincidence. Chhota Rajan, who admitted to ordering the hit – 'I killed Sharad Shetty' – in a 2011 interview in *Tehelka*, a weekly news magazine, had plotted with twin objectives: to gain revenge on Ibrahim and to loosen D-Company's vice-like grip on match-fixing ahead of a tournament expected to be worth more than £500 million to India's illegal gamblers. With Shetty dead, Rajan would be able to get a foothold in the market.

Shetty and Ibrahim had attended cricket matches in Sharjah from 1989 to 1991. The ICC's ACSU now recognises that one-day games played there are thoroughly tainted by fixing. It was where D-Company cut its teeth. Fittingly, like the gambler who steadily grows his staking balance to a sum sizeable enough to turn professional, the D-Company duo did the same. In the run-up to the 2003 World Cup, Shetty was the kingpin. He never wrote anything down, preferring to memorise key information. So the telephone numbers and contact details of the cricketers, particularly from India and Pakistan, bookmakers and gamblers, his pawns in the fixing game, were lost when he was murdered, meaning Ibrahim would have to start again.

Shetty was named in the 2000 CBI report into match-fixing, commissioned following the scandal involving Hansie Cronje, and the CBI had considered issuing an international arrest warrant for his involvement: 'His hold over bookies and punters was total,' a Mumbai police official said at the time. Yet his specialism was matches between India and Pakistan. 'The approximate turnover for a match between the subcontinent rivals was close to £25 million and that's where he got most of his ill-gotten gains. His commission was huge.'

India and Pakistan were slated to meet in Pool A of the 2003 tournament and Shetty had been expecting a pay day like no other. More than

£60 million was eventually gambled in the illegal market on the contest in Centurion, Pretoria, which India won by six wickets.

With the fixer dead and the market seemingly fragmented, it was perhaps not surprising that before a ball had been bowled, Lord Condon, the director of the ACSU, bragged: 'I'm absolutely confident that the World Cup in South Africa will be the best and cleanest there has been. We're all determined to do that. There will be a sensible but stringent security regime in place, which will act as a major deterrent to would-be corruptors. If there are people out there who think they are going to target the World Cup, they had better think again.'

The problem for Condon was that Ibrahim and Rajan remained, both energised by that murderous night in Dubai. Ibrahim's grubby fingers had to be nimble to retain some sort of hold, Rajan the same. It is telling to compare Condon's confident prediction in 2003 with what he said in 2010 when he left his post: 'I can't give it a clean bill of health because I just don't know.'

The problem for cricket today is that Ibrahim and Rajan are still around. Just as Mumbai parents eschew the Boogieman, warning disobedient children instead that 'D-Company will come and get you', cricketers who have crossed either gangster's path dread what could happen to them if they misbehave. They didn't hear the shots that killed Sharad Shetty either. They didn't see the blood. But fear seeps from one end of the cricket spectrum to the other as a result of the killing. The sound of leather on willow, synonymous with the sport since time imme-morial, has been stifled by the thud of notes landing on the bookies' cash desk and the echo of gunfire.

It was why Zulqarnain Haider, the Pakistan wicketkeeper who refused to be involved in corruption, scarpered from his team's visit to Dubai in 2011, casting terrified glances over his shoulder after receiving death threats from fixers. It was why Hashan Tillakaratne, the former Sri Lanka Test captain, kept quiet after suggesting match-fixing involving his country's national team since the mid-1990s. Even the everyday India cricket fan knows the consequences for crossing Mumbai's dons. A friend who hails from the city told me: 'Whenever I see those sort of guys coming, I fill my pants.' It was a crude description, admittedly, but one that matched the recurring theme of underlying menace, no matter who you asked.

For the purposes of this book, I asked a lot of people where I could find India's betting fraternity and how I should approach them. The answers I received made it transparent that anyone who wanted to talk to the bookies of India, walk with them and understand their work, would do so with dread in their heart. At every turn I was warned off these shadowy, underworld figures: 'They won't talk, and you don't want to talk with them.'

The former West Indies fast bowler Michael Holding, whose moniker Whispering Death struck fear into the hearts of opposition batsmen, was unequivocal. 'They're not people to get messed up with, man,' he said in that unmistakeable Jamaican burr. 'Hell, I've never met them, seen them, nothing … but I know they're not playing games. It's serious crime stuff.'

When Holding talks, it is wise to listen. Something of a statesman of the game, having travelled the world since his retirement in 1989, he has made a career as a television analyst who refused to be cowed by convention. He calls things as he sees them, no matter who it upsets.

It was Holding, on commentary duty for Sky Sports at the time, who first suggested something was awry when Hansie Cronje declared against England at Centurion in 2000, a Test match which will forever be tagged 'infamous' after it was revealed that Cronje had taken money from a bookmaker to engineer a result. Cronje enticed Nasser Hussain, the England captain, who was oblivious to his opposite number's motives, into agreeing to both teams forfeiting an innings and chasing a target on the final afternoon after rain had disrupted play. 'When this happened I said: "If this was in Asia we would all be talking about bookmakers." The producer that day was straight in my ear: "How can you back that up?" My fellow commentators shared such sentiments. They thought I was talking rubbish, possibly because they were naive about gambling,' remembers Holding.

Murali Krishnan was another friend who counselled against attempts to make contact with the bookmakers. Murali had for 20 years been investigating India's crime gangs, specialising in match-fixing. He had reported and written exposés for *India Today* and *Outlook India*, two leading magazines. 'I don't think that side of things is for you,' he said, toeing the party line. 'Not nice people. You walk in there and, I tell you, they won't trust you and that is not a good scenario. You understand that?'

Indeed. Fear was the immovable roadblock on a journey to the subcontinent. I didn't really want to find India's bookies. In the end I had little choice. They found me.

CHAPTER 3

'YOU WANNA FIX A MATCH?'

In its education programme to warn cricketers of the dangers of match-fixing, the ICC's ACSU advises that potential corruptors will first try to be their friend. They will enquire about their health. They will ask about hobbies and, lo and behold, share the same. They will express admiration for their work and, in most cases, offer a gift as an expression of their respect.

The cricketer, vulnerable to boredom and loneliness on the international or domestic treadmill, is often flattered by the interest. Emails, texts, Facebook messages and tweets can be exchanged. 'There's no harm here,' thinks the player, 'Parthiv/Vinay/Jamal is a nice guy.' There is no ulterior motive; he just wants to be friends. Right? Wrong.

What the player doesn't know is that Parthiv/Vinay/Jamal is an illegal Indian bookmaker. Why would they? Those who move in the shadowy circles of India's criminal underworld are masters of the subtle arts, the manipulation, the swindle. It is a skill inherent to their trade. The ACSU call it grooming – an unpleasant term.

So I was not surprised when I found out that three 'friends' I had been conversing with on Twitter proved to be bookies: Parthiv from Mumbai, Vinay from Bhopal and Jamal from Delhi. One of them was always asking 'how are you mate?' and they sure loved cricket, just like me. More than that, though, they loved gambling. That was the clue.

I was an obvious 'target'. My Twitter account was @cricketbetting, a useful marketing tool I thought to boost internet 'hits' on stories I wrote as a freelance cricket journalist. My specialism was betting on the game and as a tipster I was fortunate to have developed a reputation as a shrewd student, although the only true requirements for successful betting are a devotion to statistics and an apathy for emotion.

Before a match, mostly internationals, I would post a link on @cricket-betting to a betting preview that would analyse the strengths and weaknesses of the respective teams, the pitch and weather conditions, the match odds and the form of individual batsmen. When the game was under way, tweets would be composed on much the same topics, advising on potential wagers, and predictions on what would happen next. It was, essentially, a free tipping service. And although one could argue that 'even a stopped clock is right twice a day', a healthy number of followers were attracted.

Parthiv was one of the first few hundred. From his profile picture – wearing a leather jacket and shades, coolly leaning against a door frame – and the language he used, words like 'bro' and 'dude', it was clear that he was young, possibly in his early twenties. He would reply to most tweets, trying to garner more information, and if I was not posting updates, he would take it upon himself to ask for some. 'What's your view on the game bro?' 'How many runs is too much to chase here dude?'

During the long, cold nights of England's 2010–11 Ashes tour in Australia, when the action on my television screen was no guarantee of warding off sleep, Parthiv could be relied upon to keep the eyes open, asking question after question about players and match scenarios. The Ashes, which England won 3–1, proved to be a profitable series and Parthiv was fulsome in his praise of my work. He wanted to buy me a gift to show his gratitude. 'My friend works in electronics store … I send u iPad. Plse accept as a gift for your tweets. U r great m8.'

Vinay was more circumspect and, in fact, it was rare that he would make contact more than once a week. He was not interested in 'in-game' advice, but was keen to hear about pitch and weather conditions. I provided him with internet links to weather radars and the details of a gambler in Australia who specialised in making money on the fluctuations of odds caused by players scurrying for the pavilion when the heavens opened.

What Vinay was most keen on, though, was the Duckworth-Lewis method, the mathematical equation devised by two professors to calculate a team's innings runs in a one-day international halted by rain or bad light. 'What is D-L target?', 'How do I work out D-L target?' and 'I think I worked out D-L target. It's 216. Is that right?' Vinay's messages slowed to a trickle once I had sourced for him some software that was able to answer such queries at the push of a button.

Jamal was the opposite of Vinay. He was a pest and rude, too, demanding opinions and answers in bad English. His messages were sprinkled with expletives and he had, presumably, failed to work out how to switch off the CAPS LOCK key on his keyboard so he was forever shouting. 'WHO WIN THIS FUCKING GAME? U SAY NOW. THX.' Jamal did not elicit many responses. 'WHY U NO REPLY MESSAGE? I SHIT HEAVY LOSSES. HELP.'

It was not until the summer of 2010 that Parthiv, Vinay and Jamal revealed their trade. Until then they had appeared to be enthusiastic, if not obsessive, gamblers searching for an edge to win money off their local illegal bookie. It had never crossed my mind that, in fact, they *were* the local illegal bookie.

For months before this revelation, I had been attempting to investigate the possibility of corruption in cricket and trying to better fathom how the Indian industry operated. With little success, it must be said. Like many cricket supporters, I had believed that corruption in the game had largely been eradicated; the scandals of Hansie Cronje and Mohammad Azharuddin being a nadir for the sport. The ICC's ACSU had been set up – the first body of its kind across all sports – and cricket seemed to be a sport that had admitted its problem and was doing everything to repair a battered reputation. Prior to the spot-fixing case involving Pakistan, there were four instances which demanded a rethink.

The first was Lord Condon, the first head of the ACSU, claiming that the introduction of Twenty20 cricket – specifically the Indian Premier League (IPL), which launched in 2008 – had reinvigorated the corruptors. Condon, still in service, said in the summer of 2009 that the 'hit and giggle' format represented the biggest challenge to the integrity of cricket for ten years. He blamed a cocktail of party atmospheres, entertainment, cricket and celebrity. He may as well have added, in the case of the IPL, disparate groups of players signed to franchises to whom they had no loyalty or sense of belonging.

A canvassing of British bookmakers for thoughts on corruption, particularly in the IPL, seemed a sensible place to test Condon's theory. Of the ten oddsmakers/traders/executives that I surveyed, seven believed that cricket still had issues with corruption. From watching how markets move, flow of money – and obviously the games themselves – there were concerns in particular over the Indian Cricket League (ICL), a Twenty20 predecessor of the IPL, which was deemed in the opinion of one bookmaker to be too 'unpredictable to bother betting on'. The IPL was also of much concern, while there was also a strong belief that elements of Test matches and 50-over matches were 'not quite right' with regard to particular betting markets such as session runs.

'The tosses were fixed' was a consistent but misleading quote regarding the IPL edition of 2009 and two firms stopped taking bets on the 'which team will win the toss' market. One leading bookmaker identified three matches in that competition that produced irregular betting patterns on the toss. 'It was not the volume of money,' said one bookmaker's spokesman, 'but the fact that these were first bets on new accounts opened in the last few days. These new customers had four-figure bets and they won every time.'

'It's extraordinary because it was not a bet over which team will bat or field first, but the 50-50 toss of a coin,' added another. 'Three days in a row we had a request for a team to win the toss from Indian customers and each time they were correct.'

The notion that a British bookmaker would see actual evidence of fixing, in terms of betting patterns, is indeed out of the ordinary. The legal market is an annoyance for those who are fixing elements of a game for the simple reason that licensed bookmakers would (or should) immediately notify the Gambling Commission of suspect betting patterns and the account details of gamblers responsible. The paper trail is clearly visible: size of the wager, who placed it, address, telephone number, email address, IP address. The number of bets struck suggests that the information was such common knowledge that it filtered through to those who had nothing to do with Indian bookmakers and could most comfortably be explained by the fact that *the majority of 'tosses' took place before they were televised*. Information would leak out which could allow gamblers to take advantage of unsuspecting (British) bookmakers. In the case of the IPL toss results, it should be clear that instead of 'player corruption', this is evidence of an old-fashioned gamble by customers.

I spoke to Michael Holding, that pillar of reason, expecting him to dampen enthusiasm for a potential story. Instead he was forthright. 'It's never been away,' he said. 'There's far too much money to be involved for it to go away. And I don't know what the ACSU officers are doing, besides staying in five-star hotels and flying business class all around the world. It's a holiday for those folk.'

Finally, I arranged a meeting with a senior figure of the ACSU during the World Twenty20 tournament in England. We met at the Park Lane Hilton in London. I revealed concerns about fixing in the IPL and passed on the information about the tosses. The officer gave up little in return, apart from a sense of confusion. One minute he would be saying that 'once these guys get their hooks into a player, they can't escape ... all kinds of threats are made' and the next he was claiming that the World Twenty20 tournament would be clean. 'We're confident on that; I don't have suspicions about the teams taking part.'

Aside from the temptingly salacious nugget that he believed 'one in three' matches in international cricket to have been fixed on the Asian subcontinent from the late 1980s to mid-1990s, I was unsure what to believe. The sense of contradiction heightened when he asked whether any British bookmakers might have 'any idea' of which players might have been fixing. 'Can you find out any names?'

That summer of 2009 there was no appetite in the media, however, for a 'the fixers are back, they've never been away' story. The only chance it had of seeing the light of day was when an Australia player reported he had received an approach from a man suspected to have links to an illegal bookmaker in the bar of the Kensington Royal Garden Hotel after the Lord's Ashes Test in July. To this day a gambling associate insists that the man making the approach was his father, who had had one too many sherries and was having fun at the player's expense. Galling then, that the following summer match-fixing was back to the top of the agenda as the three Pakistan players – Salman Butt, Mohammad Asif and Mohammed Amir – were exposed by the *News of the World* for taking money to arrange no-balls during a Test match at Lord's.

I took to Twitter to see if the social network could link me up with some Indian bookmakers, asking contacts whether they knew of any who were willing to talk and if they could put me in touch. Parthiv, as was his wont, was first to reply: 'I work for a bookie … I thought I told u. U wanna fix a match?' Jamal was not far behind: 'I BIG BOOKIE HERE IN DELHI. TELL ME WHAT U NEED MAN.' And finally Vinay: 'We can't talk on here but email me and I explain everything for you.' Another user contacted me with a telephone number for a bookie in Dubai, but when I phoned him he refused to talk. Two more sent messages saying they could help, but nothing materialised.

I suspected that had I asked whether Jamal was an astronaut, he would have replied: 'I BIG ASTRONAUT HERE IN DELHI. TELL ME WHAT U NEED MAN.' So I asked Parthiv and Vinay – who, reassuringly and importantly, confirmed that they knew of each other's operations – what they thought of Jamal. 'Not a proper bookie,' Parthiv said. 'I have blocked him so many times.' 'Stay away from him, he not right,' Vinay said.

There was a tacit understanding that Parthiv and Vinay would answer my questions about how the bookmaking industry worked, and for the World Cup and the following summer for India's visit to England to play four Test matches, five one-day internationals and a Twenty20, I would provide them with statistical previews, pitch data (average innings scores, toss statistics) and weather reports.

A quid pro quo was inevitable, although both wanted more than statistics. Parthiv kept suggesting I use the Twitter account to provide his bookmaking business with customers, offering me a percentage in return. It was not something I was interested in and I kept delaying discussions about 'our biz opportunity'.

Vinay had business ideas of his own, too. He wanted to set up a webcam at each Test and one-day international venue in England and then charge bookmakers in India to subscribe to the feed. The man was infatuated with the weather. 'Lot of money in this,' he said. 'You can be my agent there.' Again, I was lukewarm and was eventually able to distract him with stories about how it would be impossible to get a licence for the cameras and the ECB would object. 'You pay them money,' Vinay said. I told him that bribery in England, and my experience of it, was limited.

Details of the information that I gave to Parthiv and Vinay, and the possibility of a 'biz' deal with the former and being an 'agent' for the latter are relevant because they provide an insight into the favour culture in India. It is very much a 'you scratch my back, I'll scratch yours' society – a neat reply for when, often, I was asked 'yes, but why would these bookies talk to you?' There was always a strong sense that you had to offer them something in return.

So talk they did as the start of the 2011 World Cup, hosted by India, Bangladesh and Sri Lanka in February and March, approached. As appeared to be the custom of the ICC before their showpiece event, an official made a statement about how the tournament would be corruption-free. Just as Lord Condon had boasted that the World Cup in South Africa eight years previously would be the 'cleanest there had been' it was left to Haroon Lorgat, the chief executive of the ICC, to allay any fears. He said he was confident that it would not be tainted, a fantastic swank given that a few months previously his organisation had meted out bans to the three Pakistan players for their part in the spot-fix scandal at Lord's.

'I am confident [the World Cup will be free from corruption] for two reasons,' Lorgat said. 'The main one is that the vast majority of players are honest players. They do play the game in the spirit that it should be played. They are not seeking to make gains out of untoward means.

'Secondly, we are alive to what could come to the fore in terms of corruption. We have measures in place, and people forget we had been tracking this [the Pakistan spot-fix affair] long before the *News of the World* had broken the story. I am satisfied we will have measures in place at the World Cup. We will increase capacity because we realise things do change.'

Soon after Lorgat made this statement he is said to have addressed captains of the international teams due to take part in the World Cup and, when asked what was being done to stop corruption, it is understood he became rather flustered and admitted: 'We don't have enough power, we can't stop it, it's very difficult, we've hired one more person.'

Indeed, the World Cup appeared to be a fixer's dream. The uncompetitive nature, and length of the tournament – 49 matches, only two fewer than the previous edition – provided the perfect environment for spot-fixing, the manipulation of specific elements of matches rather than the overall result. With Test nations playing apparently meaningless games against ICC Associate member countries – Ireland, the Netherlands, Kenya, Zimbabwe and Canada – the fixers were energised at the prospect of tempting the big teams into spot-fixes in matches which they knew they should comfortably win, regardless of skulduggery. The format of the tournament, as it transpired, was heavily weighted in the favour of the top teams and England still managed to qualify for the next stage despite defeat by Ireland and Bangladesh.

Parthiv and Vinay were convinced there would be foul play. 'It is the spot-fixing or fancy fixing,' Vinay said. 'Sometimes we will get a call about something happening, other times we watch for when a batsman changes gloves or the 12th man comes on. That is the signal.

'It is always happening. We are used to it. Last year there was a game I remember so well because it was blatant. We got a call saying there would be three continuous wides in the 15th over and it happened.'

Parthiv agreed with Vinay and to corroborate his point of view he arranged for me to speak with someone he called 'Big G'. Big G was Parthiv's boss, a Mumbai bookie who employed him to do all the menial tasks of bookmaking, like taking the bets and paying customers. Big G had been a bookie for 30 years and had started out when there was no television coverage of overseas tours. He would rely on radio reports to settle bets when India were playing in foreign climes. 'He knows the biz,' Parthiv said, 'absolutely inside out. He is keen to talk to you.' We arranged a Skype call and Big G wasted no time in pouring scorn on Lorgat's assertion.

'It cannot be corruption-free,' he said, matter-of-factly. 'We know some of the players and some of the officials and they are there to make money, too. We try to get some information from the curator [the groundsman], but they are difficult to get because they are paid by their boards, but we have other contacts.

'It will be innings runs and brackets [ten-over session runs]. Most probably they will be fixed. They're the main things because the first-round matches are too weak. There are teams like Canada and the Netherlands playing against the top nations, so that market will be the best. Say India v. the Netherlands will be an easy game for corruption because India can't possibly lose and they can afford to go a bit slower when they are batting to fix innings runs or session runs, the brackets, you know.'

I asked him whether he was concerned that he could lose money because of corruption. 'Not much I guess, because at some level the match has been corrupted. We know this. We are used to it. There are many ways you can see it. First you need to have some players, ex-players, commentators, officials, you just need some contacts and that's it, you fix a match. You get a brief idea on that.

'People are fixing more of Test matches, not exactly to fix a match but you can get a clue on pitches, whether it has been damaged by the curator or trimmed, or if the weather has a crucial role to be played.

'I know I cannot be a victim of the fixing because we know our punters personally. Betting is absolutely illegal so we have to trust everyone. All the transactions through cash. We know their contacts, how powerful they are ... if a fix is on we will have been told about it and if not we know if this person comes and tries to bet we know that a fix is on. The money tells you where the fix is.

'We don't know how many games will be fixed. Nothing can be judged right now. We can make it out when the tournament starts. But it will be happening, there is no question. If it doesn't happen it's very shocking for us.

'The worst teams? That would be Pakistan, no doubt in that ... They are big into fixing.

'The ICC have a very strict security at teams' hotels and the ground, which makes it risky for us, but we manage it and even the police are corruptible in India. It doesn't really make it more difficult for us. At some level we have a contact with players, the evening of the game, we have their cellphone numbers. That's how we come to get the info.'

'That's how we come to get the info' was the sentence that I kept repeating in my head throughout the group stages of the tournament.

Parthiv, tweeting via the direct message button, was free and easy with this 'info'. Twice he sent me details of matches which he claimed had seen spot-fixing:

8 March (in-game) – Pakistan v. New Zealand
'My sources in Dubai say NZ win.'

Parthiv was secretive of his sources in Dubai. He would never give a name. Here he had a one-in-two chance in getting this call right. But at least the information was received in the first two hours of play. Batting first, New Zealand scored more than 90 runs in the last four overs. They won by 110 runs. It seems inconceivable, however, that Pakistan would agree to fix a match and then lose by such a huge margin. The ICC's ACSU received no reports of anything untoward and the PCB also rejected the notion of wrongdoing.

10 March (in-game) – Sri Lanka v. Zimbabwe
'Seems [it was] planned to not pass the innings runs [quote] of SL
… it was around 350.'

Sri Lanka were not supposed to score more than 350. An interesting one, particularly as I had placed a wager myself on Sri Lanka scoring more than 350. They appeared to be cruising to such a total – and that's what made me place my bet. But from the 15th over they became rather lazy in their strokes, the run rate dropping below five an over, and it did not go above five until the 25th over. Their innings ended at 327. In mitigation, Sri Lanka's statistical weakness was their struggle to accelerate as an innings progressed, and again, the ICC's ACSU received no reports of anything untoward.

The only 'fixing' information Vinay offered was that a suspected bookmaker had been spotted in the India dressing room during their match against the Netherlands in Delhi on 9 March. India won the match by five wickets.

This was widely reported by Indian media. Pradeep Agarwal, who had been accused of attempting to fix matches in the 2008 edition of the IPL, was filmed sitting on the balcony of the India dressing room. Following an investigation, the ICC's ACSU issued the following clarification: 'Pradeep was appointed as the official local liaison officer for the Indian team by the DDCA (Dehli District Cricket Association) and it is only on the invitation of the team manager that Pradeep was provided a temporary visitor pass for access to the PMOA (players and match officials area).' Agarwal's status as a bookie is media speculation, and match-fixing allegations against him have never been proven.

Australia's group match against Zimbabwe had also come under the scanner. The *Times of India* reported that a source close to the ACSU had revealed they were investigating the slow start by Brad Haddin and Shane Watson, the Australia openers. They had scored 28 runs in 11 overs and 53 in 15 overs in the match at Ahmedabad on 21 February. Australia won by 91 runs. Naturally the Australian team rubbished the newspaper's claim, as did the ACSU, who denied any investigation and were adamant that the two Australia players had no case to answer.

On 22 March, the newspaper reported that Mumbai police had 'busted' a match-fixing ring involving three men from Dawood Ibrahim's gang. The D-Company trio's phones were tapped by police, according to the newspaper, to have made calls to Nairobi, London and Nagpur with details of spot-fixing.

These despatches from Parthiv, Vinay and various media outlets would have made for depressing reading had Big G not warned that corruption would be ever-present in the group stages. As he said, there could be no harm to a team's chances of winning a match by spot-fixing innings runs or runs in the first ten overs. 'If it doesn't happen it will be very shocking for us,' he said.

As the group stages were left behind and we moved into the knockout stages – matches that teams could not afford to lose – Parthiv's information line dried up and he went quiet. Until the afternoon of 30 March.

CHAPTER 4

SCRIPT

It was George Orwell who wrote that sport was 'war minus the shooting'. He penned this thought in December 1945, two years before the Pakistan state existed and seven before they met India on a cricket field. Orwell had a habit of being ahead of his time and that quote could have been accredited for Indo-Pak contests, which have become famed as the most bitter and intense rivalry in world sport.

The animosity of these clashes is often born from the absence of conflict. When the two are able to play against each other, it usually means they are not at war, so the desire to give the other a beating on the sporting field rather than the battleground stirs extreme nationalistic fervour, the like of which the rest of us can never truly understand.

The two have known partition, three wars, deep-rooted suspicion, animosity, Jammu, Kashmir, ceasefires, terrorism, a nuclear arms race, diplomacy and attempted reconciliation. Still they do not get along. India and Pakistan have suspended cricketing relations four times, the last of which came in the wake of the 2008 Mumbai terrorist attack, which was co-ordinated from within Pakistan and carried out by Pakistanis.

So when India were drawn with their 'neighbours from hell' in the semi-final of the 2011 World Cup, the world held its breath, fearing the potential for another chapter to be penned in a bloody tale. Never before had they met in a game of such magnitude. The victor would not merely claim dominance in the region in a sport with which both countries were obsessed, but also that their culture, religion and politics were superior. It was 'win the battle, win the war'. It was a war which had been fought before: the protagonists were slightly different, the ideology the same. In the 1920s, when India was subjugated by Empire, an annual quadrangular tournament was played between a team of Hindus, Muslims, Parsis and the British. The motivation for beating the British was to prove that 'our way of life is superior'.

The Punjab Cricket Association Stadium in Mohali, a suburb of the city of Chandigarh in north-west India, just 150 miles from the Pakistan border, was the front line for the latest skirmish. It was not long before The City Beautiful (Chandigarh's nickname) became The City Bastion, the numbered sectors which divided it increasing the sense of a military area. A no-fly zone over its skies was ordered, an exclusion cordon set up around the stadium and bomb-disposal robots patrolled the streets. Two Chandigarh policemen were ordered to eat three meals a day with the Pakistan team, testing food for poison. Battalions guarded the team's hotel. Snipers were on roofs. There were body searches, for civilians and the military.

The two governments behaved as if they were the best of friends. Manmohan Singh, India's Prime Minster, and Yousuf Raza Gilani, the Pakistan Prime Minister who had declared a half-day holiday at home, announced that they would sit and watch the match together in the stadium's VIP area. Sonia Gandhi, the head of the Congress Party, which was part of the ruling coalition, also got a ticket. There were only 35,000 available and the black market buzzed. Tickets were changing hands for as much as US$1,500 and police arrested people selling their tickets on eBay for vastly inflated sums. Those who would not be at the game made sure they would be in front of a television screen. India's parliament was to shut early at 2.30pm and a big screen was put up in the halls of debate. It was reported that Mumbai's taxi drivers, a relative army, would take the day off and businesses asked employees to start at 7am, promising they would be allowed to 'down tools' in time for the first ball. It was a match to stop a subcontinent as much as it was to split one.

What of the players? Ah yes, the players, on whose shoulders rested more than a billion hopes. MS Dhoni, the India captain, was introspective and quiet in his press conference, for which he arrived late. Shahid Afridi, the Pakistan captain, a joker, appeared to enjoy the temperature in the pressure cooker. He was full of bonhomie. 'Why, don't you like it?' Afridi laughed when asked why Pakistan were not training.

Afridi also played statesman. 'I think it is a great sign for both countries that the politicians are attending together,' he said. 'Sport, especially cricket, always brings these two countries together.' Yuvraj Singh, the India all-rounder, called on a higher power: 'We are doing the best we can and leaving the rest to God. No point saying it will be a normal match. You all expect us to win, the whole country expects us to win.'

What of the fixers? Surely they would get no change from such a game. Of course they wouldn't, said Rehman Malik, Pakistan's interior minister. 'I gave a warning that there should be no match-fixing,' he said. 'I am keeping a close watch. If any such thing happens, we are going to take action.' He was 'sure the team has very clean members', although he felt moved to give some friendly advice. 'Practise, sleep early at night and wake up at the proper time. They should dedicate themselves to Pakistan for the match. There is a lot of excitement about the India–Pakistan clash in the World Cup semi-final. There is a lot of love for cricketers and we hope they will win the game for us. We expect they will not disappoint the people.'

And what of the bookmakers? The *Times of India* quoted a Delhi-based bookmaker thus: 'Indian team is the favourite and people are betting big bucks on the Men in Blue. For every one rupee on India, the [win] rate is 60 paise and for Pakistan it's 1.55. India has never lost against Pakistan in a World Cup match and that's the reason the rates are high on Pakistan.' Below the story, in the comments section online, a reader called Nathan, from Bangalore, wrote: 'Why waste money 'n time in conducting and watching these matches, instead we can ask these bookies to write the script before itself and hand it over to the players to enact it ...'

Cynic or optimist, Indian or Pakistani, Hindu or Muslim, patriot or nonpartisan, it was a match not to be missed, if only to sneak a voyeuristic peek at the curious collision of sport and a schism. The television audience was expected to reach more than one billion, to make it the most watched cricketing contest in history.

The quixotic mix aside, it promised to be a thrilling occasion for the cricket enthusiast. The India team included the much-vaunted batting talents of Sachin Tendulkar, the deity known as the Little Master,

Virender Sehwag, an opening batsman of the explosive capability of a delinquent left alone in a fireworks factory, and Yuvraj Singh, who had previously taken six sixes from a Stuart Broad over in a Twenty20 match. They were up against a Pakistan outfit that excelled with the ball. In the tournament each wicket Pakistan had taken had cost them 19.95 runs to India's 29.14. Their economy rate was also superior. India's batsmen, however, averaged six runs per wicket more than Pakistan. It was a competition of contrasts in every respect.

It made for a mouthwatering betting heat, too. India were the favourites by dint of home advantage and a head-to-head record against their rivals in the country which had seen them win 17 of the 26 matches. The betting preview I wrote, dispatched as ever to Vinay and Parthiv, disregarded such statistics and focused on which side was more likely to hold their nerve under incredible duress and the importance of the toss. An excerpt read like this: 'On the face of it a good batting wicket and a very fine batting line-up gives India, who are 1.62 (5-8), an advantage against 2.58 (8-5) Pakistan. But a closer study makes it difficult not to reckon that MS Dhoni's side are poor value.

'To back them purely because they have better batsman would appear to be folly. India had the better batting against England in the group stages on a good surface, but they didn't win.

'And in 2007 in Mohali they had the better batting line-up against Pakistan. They still lost though, as Pakistan chased 322. It was Pakistan's second win at the venue in two attempts.

'The bottom line, however, is that the prices are wrong. We think India should be about 1.75 here. Their lack of penetration with the ball – only Zaheer Khan will worry Pakistan – and the toss bias (five sides out of 15 have won batting second under lights) means we have no option but to side with Shahid Afridi's men.'

Such unequivocal support for Pakistan could be explained simply by adhering to the golden rule of betting: value. One should not wager unless it can be proved that the odds are incorrect and in this case they most certainly were. The advantage for teams batting first made sure of that. With such a heavy prejudice against the team batting second, the two sides had to be closer in the betting because, after all, the toss of a coin is a 50-50 call. It is quite normal for match-odds markets to disregard such important statistics, however.

As it transpires, MS Dhoni wins the toss and chooses to bat and Pakistan immediately start to look like a bad bet. After the inevitable flesh pressing as both sets of players meet the two prime ministers and the national anthems, India exert their superiority. Sehwag is starting fires all over the field. He warms his hands with a four off the third ball of the match and then takes 20 off Umar Gul's second over – three fours coming from the first, second and fourth balls, whipped through the leg side. From the fifth and sixth, which was also a no-ball, Sehwag hits through the off side for boundary fours. The blue touchpaper is lit and Pakistan are burning.

As is tradition for the biggest of cricket matches, I am joined by Cherrene, an old friend, barrister and aspirant expert on the game for the purpose of impressing her father and Uncle Percy, who could be classed as 'cricket tragics' from Sri Lanka. Cherrene, despite her bloodlines, is fiercely patriotic of her upbringing and the mood in her house could be tense if England were meeting Sri Lanka: her father and Uncle Percy being of the 'anyone but England' mindset.

Cherrene had a habit of making jokes about the Tebbit test, the brainchild of the Conservative MP, Norman Tebbit, who argued that people of ethnic minorities in Britain should support the England cricket team rather the team from their country of ancestry. 'Uncle Percy would definitely have failed the test,' she would say, 'by telling Tebbit to bugger off.' Cherrene could be relied upon as stellar company for any cricket match. She always brought top-quality biscuits and her thirst for information on the game was rarely sated. 'What exactly is a leg-spinner?' 'What's a six-three field?' 'Say that again about so-and-so messing up his bowling options, Uncle Percy will be most impressed.'

Cherrene has missed the start of the match, living up to her reputation as a bad timekeeper. As Sehwag brutalises another Gul delivery to the boundary, her arrival is signalled by the aggressive sound of the buzzer, perfect timing as if the chastened bowler had come up with a foolish answer in a quiz show.

'Oh, Sehwag's going well, isn't he?' she says. 'Very impressive. Of course, I thought India's batting would prove too strong for Pakistan's bowling, it's something of a classic contest, I suppose, in that the teams are best in the tournament at the two respective disciplines.'

'Have you been reading *Wisden*?'

'No … Uncle Percy again. I thought I might be able to fool you with that one.'

By the time Cherrene has taken off her coat, which has sheltered her from a wet north-London spring day, Sehwag has fallen leg-before to Wahab Riaz. 'At least it's not Tendulkar,' Cherrene says. 'They'd all start committing suicide if it was.'

Over our first cup of tea, Cherrene is keen to find out the latest from my 'mafia friends' in India. I tell her I'm not sure they are quite as bad as that, but I reveal some of the 'fix details' that Parthiv has sent through for the group matches and the information exchange that was occurring.

'Well, that's the way it works in India. You have to give to receive, don't you? A friend of the family lived and worked there for a few years and he had dreadful plumbing problems in his bathroom. A plumber would come to fix it and then within a few weeks it would break again. Finally he worked it out when he told a colleague what was going on. He had to give the plumber a back hander. Sure enough, the next time he came around, this guy said: "Can you make sure it stays fixed this time?" and gave him extra. It's a bloody disgrace. You should be careful, though, they're probably trying to groom you or something.'

'The aim is to continue with the information exchange and hopefully go out there to see how they work because no one really knows in this country,' I say.

As we chat away, the wicket of Sehwag has done little to check India's progress. After the tenth over they are 73 for one with Tendulkar moving on to 23 from 25 balls. It is ominous from the batsman. Every run he scores is met with shrill cries of delight that pierce the ears even thousands of miles away. As the scoreboard ticks over, a country is edged closer and closer towards hysteria. India's idol is slaying the evil-doers. It is the perfect scenario, particularly when Tendulkar is reprieved after a leg-before decision is referred and he is given not out. The volume needs to be turned down.

'Is this match fixed then?' Cherrene asks.

'No way. They'd never dare fix a match like this. Far too important. Blood on their hands, Chezza.'

'Yes, I s'pose so. Even Pakistan aren't that stupid,' she says, referencing the spot-fixing scandal of the previous summer against England at Lord's.

Barely have the words passed Cherrene's lips when Tendulkar, rocking onto the back foot, slaps a short ball from Shahid Afridi into the hands of Misbah-ul-Haq at midwicket. Misbah, falling towards the ball like sap blown by a strong gust of wind, allows the chance to break through his fingers.

'Oh my God,' Cherrene laughs. 'They're bloody throwing the match!'

'No, no,' I say. 'They've never been able to field. Very hard chance, too.'

By the time Tendulkar is out, 15 short of the century that a nation craves, he has been dropped a further three times. With each chaotic miss, Cherrene becomes more and more excited, shouting at the television for Pakistan being 'bloody useless' or 'unbelievably foolish!' and then turning to me and teasing 'I thought you said it wasn't fixed?' Every time I repeat my line about them being bad at fielding, a joke that does not wear off.

Following Misbah's drop, the veteran Younis Khan puts Tendulkar down. Skipping in the air to pluck the juicy cherry from the tree, he has the morsel in his grasp for a second before it falls to the floor, spoiled and rotten. Kamran Akmal is next. A thick outside edge cannons off his gloves. 'What did Tendulkar eat for breakfast ...' asks Rameez Raja, the commentator, 'buttery fingers?' The third comes courtesy of Umar Akmal, brother of Kamran. 'What on earth is happening out there?' writes the Cricinfo ball-by-ball commentator. 'Tendulkar tried a whip-pull to midwicket, popping the ball in the air ... Umar Akmal is there for the shot at a wide midwicket, times the jump and gets both hands to it, and it pops out! Hafeez is fuming; Afridi is utterly disconsolate. That's the fourth drop!'

Later, Kamran Akmal allows an edge from the bat of Dhoni to escape him to take Pakistan's dropped catches count to five. That clanger was sounded on the second ball of the 42nd over. For the purpose of this tale it would be beneficial if, my suspicions suddenly aroused, I contact Parthiv to ask the question 'what on earth is happening out there?' Certainly Cherrene is goading me to phone my 'mobster friends'.

Instead another six balls pass and, with the innings winding down and Cherrene off making more tea, I check emails, news sites, Facebook and, finally, my Twitter account. My timing was slightly off, but only just. Ten minutes previously, Parthiv had sent a message:

> Bookie update ... India will bat first and score over 260, 3 wickets fall within the first 15 overs, pak will cruise to 100, then lose 2 quick wickets, at 150 they will be 5 down and crumble and lose by a margin of over 20 runs*

'Chezza,' I called out. 'I think you better have a look at this.'

'What is it?'

'A bookie has messaged me. He's sent me a script of what is going to happen.'

'Oh, this is extraordinary! Let me read it ... oh good God! How many have India got?'

India are approaching 260. At the start of the final over they are 256 for seven. Bowled by Wahab Riaz, it goes dot ball-wicket-single-single-wicket-two. India close on 260. Cherrene is beside herself. I urge calm.

'Hang on a sec, he said more than 260. The proof will be when Pakistan bat.'

'Oh, this is amazing!'

Indeed it was. Parthiv had been correct twice previously when he had messaged with information about a fix during a game. But he had not sent anything as detailed as this. I checked the scorecard. He was wrong about India losing three wickets in the first 15 overs and his prediction was out by a single run for a total of more than 260. This would be enough to exonerate India from wrongdoing. The information for Pakistan's innings was more thorough ... 'pak will cruise to 100, then lose 2 quick wickets, at 150 they will be 5 down and

---

* Of allegations about corruption in this match, Haroon Lorgat, the ICC chief executive, stated: 'The ICC has no reason or evidence to require an investigation into this match. It is indeed sad for spurious claims to be made which only serve to cause doubt on the semi-final of one of the most successful ICC Cricket World Cups ever.'

crumble and lose by a margin of over 20 runs'. Had this been received from anyone other than an Indian bookmaker it would be considered a wild guess.

I email two gambling associates, including Geoffrey Riddle, a journalist, sharing Parthiv's script and telling them that I expect Pakistan's innings to unfold exactly as he said. Parthiv had form, I write, for accuracy. The responses I receive are laden with expletives, expressing dismay that there could be any doubt about a World Cup semi-final between two such bitter rivals. Both of them, of course, tell me they have placed big wagers on India to go on to win the match.

Feelings of excitement at the start of the match have now morphed into ones of nerves, dread and bewilderment. Cherrene is tense, too. She sits forward on the sofa, knees together and holding a cushion to her chest. She says she hopes that Parthiv's message proves to be wrong.

'He has been right twice previously,' I tell her. 'He can't keep getting it right. I'm sure his information must be wrong sometimes. Law of averages and all that.'

As Pakistan's innings begins we are both gripped by a feeling of surreal fear. Not the usual fear that a fan holds in his heart when watching a sporting contest: the feeling of not knowing whether his team will succeed, fail horribly or acquit themselves with pride so he too can feel proud; the one which ties the stomach in knots and makes the heart beat faster, reverberating against the rib cage. It is an anxiety of a totally different kind inspired by the feeling that what is being played out in front of our eyes is planned, while desperately hoping that it is not. The stomach turns; the heart sinks.

'It could all be over very quickly, Chezza,' I say reassuringly. 'Pakistan could be two down for nothing and then they won't be cruising to a hundred.'

'Yes, there is that,' she says.

Kamran Akmal, the Pakistan opening batsman, hits the first ball and the last ball of the first over of the reply for four. Cherrene and I exchange worried glances. The first of many I suspect. We are not put out of our misery early as, thanks to Akmal's dashing blade, Pakistan start well. At the end of the eighth over they are 43 for no loss, scoring at a rate of 5.37 an over.

'Well, they are certainly cruising at the moment,' Cherrene says.

'Do you think that would stand up in court?' I joke.

Akmal is the first wicket to fall. Attempting to crash a square drive through point, he is undone by a slower ball from Zaheer Khan and he guides the ball into the hands of the fielder. The score is 44 for one. Asad Shafiq joins Mohammad Hafeez at the crease. Their progress is serene and the clatter of wickets that we hope for does not materialise. Hafeez is out in the 16th over. The Cricinfo commentary describes his wicket: 'What was Hafeez thinking? Again, yet again, a lovely 30 to 40 and he has combusted. He went for a paddle sweep, yeah a paddle sweep, to a full delivery outside off stump and edged it to Dhoni. Oh dear. Pressure? Or overconfidence?'

Pakistan steady the ship. A cliché it may be, but one that has a double meaning in this context. With Shafiq and Younis Khan they are cruising. Off the fifth ball of the 23rd over, Shafiq turns the ball off his pads to take two runs and bring up Pakistan's hundred. Their run rate is 4.34. They require a further 161 runs from 27 overs. There is no doubt they are going well.

'OK Chezza,' I say, 'They have got to a hundred pretty easily but this is where it gets interesting.'

'Yes, read the next bit of the script.'

'It says: "Pakistan will cruise to 100, then lose two quick wickets." Hold on to yourself. This is where we get an answer whether this thing is accurate or not. There can be no quibbling about "two quick wickets".'

The next over is to be bowled by Yuvraj Singh. Younis takes a single from the first ball. Cherrene and I breathe a sigh of relief. So too after the second, third and fourth balls of the over, which are negotiated without alarm.

'I reckon if they score 20 runs before a wicket falls we can forget about the script,' I say.

'Hope so,' Cherrene replies as Yuvraj trundles in for the fifth ball. Our collective breath is held again as the ball is released ... Shafiq steps away from his stumps, trying to direct the ball towards third man ... he misses and it knocks his middle stump out of the ground.

'Bowled him! Yuvi! Yuvi! Yuvi!' shouts Mark Nicholas, the television commentator.

'Another magical breakthrough,' says Rameez Raja.

'Uh oh,' says Cherrene.

'One more,' I say, 'And we might have a fix.'

Ten balls later it is Yuvraj again who, with more of a spring in his stride, jumps into his elegant, high left-arm action. The ball is full and tempting to drive. Younis Khan is tempted. He throws his hands at the ball but as he does so his right leg, his back leg, flies from under him, as if tethered by a rope which someone has suddenly decided to tug sharply. Off balance and now reaching, trying to right himself in the shot, the ball hits high on the bat. It is miscued horribly. Up in the air, straight into the hands of mid-off. Pakistan are 106 for four. They have added six runs. They have lost two wickets in ten balls. A swift demise. Rapid. Quick.

'Well, that was depressingly predictable,' I say.

'This is just dreadful, dreadful, dreadful,' Cherrene says.

An email from Geoffrey Riddle arrives. 'Amazing info!' Another contact telephones me. He says he can't believe what he is seeing. 'It's like I'm watching a replay, knowing the fall of the wickets and the result.' Cherrene has gone very quiet. She gets up to make tea.

It is a blessed relief that we have a relative hiatus until the next action, according to whoever the director of this game is, takes place. I try to reassure Cherrene that it still could all prove to be wrong. Pakistan are only four wickets down and could comfortably recover to win the match and book a final spot in Mumbai. At the end of the 27th over they are 112 for four. Umar Akmal and Misbah-ul-Haq are the batsmen. The script tells us that we cannot expect more than two wickets until Pakistan have reached 150.

The tension has dissipated now. The dread that we felt earlier about this fearsome tale coming true has been replaced by a disheartening acceptance. Cherrene and I sit glum-faced as we watch the pictures from Mohali, a doom-laden contrast with the supporters in the stadium, who wave flags and leap and shout as the match unfolds. They are still able to retain the joy of a contest which is unique in its standing in the cricket world. Unique to us for a different reason.

It is in a daze, rather, that we watch the match continue, as if waiting to be awoken again by an alarm bell as Pakistan approach 150. Umar Akmal and Misbah-ul-Haq are rebuilding Pakistan's innings, and with each over they survive, keeping the wickets column showing four and with each run they move closer to 150, we become more alert. Eight runs away from 150 – 'at 150 they will be five down' – the fifth wicket falls. It is Umar Akmal who is out, getting himself into a most unedifying muddle against the spin bowling of Harbhajan Singh. The confusion is matched on my sofa.

'I just don't believe this is happening,' Cherrene says. 'Uncle Percy is going to be furious.'

With the script accurate – Pakistan reach 150 off the second ball of the 37th over – the 'crumble' begins immediately. Abdul Razzaq is the sixth Pakistan batsman out one ball later. Despite the shots of India fans biting nails and clasping their hands in prayer, the television commentators begin to dissect Pakistan's performance: 'strange way of batting' ... 'poor shots' ... 'batsmen unaware of urgency'. Younis Khan and Misbah come in for particular criticism. Younis scored 13 off 32 balls, a strike rate of 40.62. Misbah scored 17 from the first 42 balls he faced, playing out 27 dots. During this period Pakistan's required run rate jumped from 6.07 to 8.45. During the 74 balls in which Younis and Misbah were at the crease together, 30 runs were scored.

Shahid Afridi is the seventh Pakistan wicket to fall, with the score on 184. Pakistan are, indeed, crumbling to 'lose by a margin over 20 runs'. When Afridi skies a catch to Virender Sehwag off Harbhajan Singh, Ravi Shastri, the former India captain-turned-commentator says: 'These are baffling tactics from Pakistan.' Rather than referring to the shot which Afridi played, Shastri is wondering why Pakistan have not taken the final powerplay – five overs when fielding restrictions are supposed to allow batsmen like Afridi, who is considered more dangerous in such situations, to score runs more freely and easily. Pakistan take the powerplay in the 45th over with Misbah and Umar Gul, the bowler, at the crease. When Misbah hits a four in the 48th over, Mark Nicholas, the hyperbole in his voice reduced to a befuddled whine, says: 'That's the reason we can't fathom why it [the powerplay] was not taken earlier.' Misbah takes

14 off the over. 'If he can produce these shots, why didn't he produce it earlier on?' Rameez Raja says.

India win by 29 runs. Misbah is the last wicket to fall. For the first time in the broadcast, we see a shot of the two prime ministers of India and Pakistan. Sat together, they applaud politely, their emotions inscrutable. Azhar Mahmood, the former Pakistan all-rounder, working as an analyser for Sky Sports says: 'Two terrible innings from senior Pakistan players Younis and Misbah. There was no panic.' Nick Knight, once an England one-day international opening batsman, agrees: 'I'm at a loss to explain those two innings.'

Cherrene starts to pack up her things. 'You've stolen Christmas,' she says. 'I'm never watching a game with you again.'

Later, reports emerge from Lahore that a 20-year-old Pakistani has committed suicide because of his team's loss. George Orwell, perhaps, was wrong.

PART TWO

DIARY FROM THE UNDERWORLD

CHAPTER 5

BOOKIE

Vinay does not fit the stereotype of the Indian bookmaker. He does not emerge from the shadows and, instead of skulking through the lobby doors of a hotel in Bhopal, he bounds in. His smile is broad and genuine, his handshake warm.

'Great to meet you,' he says. 'How are you enjoying it here?'

This is not what one expects when meeting someone from one of the largest criminal fraternities in India. There are estimated to be up to 100,000 bookmakers in the country. Enemies of the state and the supposed scourge of international and domestic cricket, their modus operandi is, reportedly, violence and intimidation.

Certainly I had been gripped by apprehension. Taking an early-morning flight from Delhi to Bhopal, the capital of Madhya Pradesh, the state known as the Heart of India, it had gnawed away that I was travelling into the unknown. Apart from Twitter messages, emails and the odd phone call to Vinay, when both of us found it difficult to comprehend what the other was trying to say, I had no idea who he really was. I could not even be sure that he was a bookmaker, let alone trust him.

My mood had not been helped by advice from Murali Krishnan, the investigative journalist from Delhi. When I told him of my plans, his face creased with concern. 'Be smart. Couple of friends of mine had a beer, slipped a tablet, drugged and robbed. So trust your instincts. Don't take any shit.'

After checking in at 8am, I lay on my bed and fretted over whether I had been horribly naive. My cellphone was ringing constantly. It was Vinay, wanting to know where I was staying. Having finally summoned some courage, I told him and then waited nervously in the lobby with the strains of pan-pipe music only adding to the unease. So you can see it was a relief to be welcomed in such a bright, genuine manner.

Vinay, wearing an Armani shirt and expensive-looking sunglasses resting on the top of his black hair, chuckled at his reputation. 'My dad didn't want me to become a bookie,' he says. 'He was upset. But that's because it's illegal here, not because I'm beating up persons or fixing matches. Bookmaking is a good business. Shadowy? No, it is quite clear. I would say it is the fairest thing.'

I ask him whether, as per his invitation, he has the time to explain exactly how the bookmaking industry works. He flinches. 'Of course,' he says, before lowering his voice. 'But not here. We could get in trouble if people overheard, so we can go somewhere private.'

In the lift to my hotel room, Vinay explains how he became a bookmaker: 'I had a friend, he was a bookie. I used to go to his shop when I was at school. I was 21. At that time in India everyone doesn't know the computers. I was OK at computers. He asked me to help with his computer. There was a software problem. I repaired that.

'After that he asked me whether I could design a software for him for his bookmaking. My father did not like this. He didn't want me to become a bookie. He said it was illegal. He was in the service industry, a sales manager. Cement industries. He said, "You can't do that." My friend approached my father and said, "I'm not making him a bookie, I am just learning computers from him." My father says, "OK, for 15 days, OK?" "It will not even take 15 days," my friend told him. But those 15 days are still going!

'After that we became partners. But we had a big loss. You see, other bookies took some of our bets because we don't have all that money. Sometimes bookies share bets. This bookie took 35 per cent of one of our bets, but he didn't pay us back, so we didn't have the money for our customers. But we had to keep our reputation in the market. We have to pay. We have to pay from our home. After that I started my own business. I started with just 100 rupees. I had five customers. Only five. Then it rose to 135. Up, up, up.'

While setting up his laptop and juggling two mobile phones – he changes his number every three weeks to avoid detection by police – Vinay explains how he makes 50 lakhs (about £60,000) a year from his bookmaking business, which has more than 200 customers. The average wager is one lakh (£1,200). He takes customers only on recommendation. This is uniform with the rest of the Indian industry, he tells me.

'You see, you wouldn't find it easy to get an account with a bookmaker because you don't know a local person. I don't know you, so I don't give you a credit account. Almost all of the accounts are credit accounts. It is all based on trust that the punter can pay and the bookmaker can pay, whoever wins. Maybe for you or someone new, we would take a cash advance and then, once you are trusted, we can give you a credit account.

'It works the same way when I have to pay my customers their winning monies. They have to trust me. If they do not trust me I have no business. This is the same throughout India. We all get along. Nicely, nicely. No rowing, no fighting.'

I allow myself a wry smile at an industry, maligned for malevolence and mistrust, apparently operating with honesty and integrity.

'You are surprised?' laughs Vinay. 'This is business. The customer comes first.'

Vinay has four offices dotted around the region, each with two people recording and writing down the wagers next to the name of the customer, who might use a nickname like 'K-Man' or 'Indian'. There are no betting slips. Each bet is struck via cellphone. 'Everything is recorded so there can be no dispute. We can play the bet back to the customer and we can show them in black and white. Dispute is very unusual, though.'

Once a customer is accepted, he will be given a number to call a telephone commentary service. A voice continuously relays the odds. This is called the bhao line.

'So we can have a room with 120 mobile phones all set up,' Vinay says. 'They are each capable of conference calling, and 600 customers are connected to one phone. So you can see how it spreads across the country with similar bookmaker operations around the country – 600 times 600, times 600, and so on and so forth.

'These phones are all connected to the bhao line. This is a man who is sitting in the same room as the mobile phones that are linked to his microphone, where he continuously reads out the live match odds. When the match starts [the first one-day international between India and England in Hyderabad on 14 October] we can listen and you will hear for yourself.'

Customers are paid the next day, without fail, using the hawala system.

'No bank transfers because we don't pay tax,' Vinay says.

The hawala system is glued by trust. That word again. It is a simple system. Money is transferred via a network of hawala brokers, often family members, or hawaladars. But the money does not, in fact, go anywhere, either physically or electronically, and the system can be defined by the term: money transfer without money movement. A customer will approach a hawala broker in one city and give a sum of money to be transferred to a recipient in another city. The hawala broker calls another hawala broker in the recipient's city, gives instructions of the funds and promises to settle the debt at a later date. All parties are given a code or password and at the start and end of the process, the broker charges a small fee. All money is paid out from the same pool that they take in.

'Ya, we use hawala,' Vinay says. 'The customer has to pay 300 rupees [£3–£4] per lakh [£1,200] for each cash transaction if they win. This is payable to me, the bookie.'

I ask Vinay how 'big' a bookmaker he is in the market. 'Oh, I am first-tier bookmaker. Do you have a pen and paper and I will explain?' The hotel stationery and complimentary pencil are pressed into action. Vinay starts to draw a family tree-style diagram. At the top he writes 'syndicate' followed by tentacles reaching out below to five 'first-tier bookmakers'. Below them are the second-tier bookmakers, followed by the third tier and so on. They are ranked by the number of customers they have. At the bottom are the customers.

'This second tier is a chain of about 50,000 bookies,' he says. 'The betting syndicate is a group who want to take big bets from all over India. They open up their prices, they tell the world what their prices are and the world bets on their prices. It means they are uniform. They post the prices and after that they put their prices up or down on the amount of money they get. If they get money on India they decrease the price.

'When the betting syndicate opens the prices to the general public, they want to bet. It means the betting syndicate are saying to them: "What would you say?" The general public does not know what the prices should be. He doesn't know whether it is a good price to back or lay, so he puts his money down.'

'Who is at the top of the syndicate?' I ask him.

'They are in Mumbai,' he says. 'All of them. At present. But when the matches start, they go to different parts of the country because in Mumbai at the moment they are very strict. The police. It is very risky. They don't want any trouble. We have to use Blackberry Messenger to communicate with each other because the police might intercept. I'm worried sitting here now with you. Mobile phones, laptop, cricket on television. This does not look good if the police knock on your door.

'The syndicate won't meet you. They won't trust you. Because I am outside, I can see you here. Jayanti Malad and Shobhan Mehta are syndicate heads. They will pick up my call within a single ring, but if you call them they won't.'

Vinay's anxiety over the police is not without foundation. At the time Malad, who Vinay describes as 'Delhi's biggest bookie', is 'on the run' after two of his associates were arrested for accepting bets on the Champions League Twenty20 tournament, which was won by Mumbai Indians. They were Indore-based bookies operating from a rented flat in Andheri, a surburb of Mumbai. Police confiscated 2.5 lakhs (£3,000), laptops, 20 SIM cards, mobile phones and voice recorders.

'Jayanti has been absconding since the arrest of his two associates. We have intensified our search for him,' said a crime branch officer.

Malad's real name is Jayanti Shah, but the best-known Indian bookmakers remove their surname in favour of the town or suburb from which they operate. Shobhan Mehta, for example, is known as Shoban Kalachowki, a suburb of north-central Mumbai. Vinay is not yet notorious enough for a surname change.

'You have to understand that bookmaking in India is based on a tiered system, like arms reaching out, far and wide. It is like a food chain. The syndicate could be based in Dubai, London or New York. They set the odds and the rest follow. Every bookie is connected. I show you.'

Vinay's laptop whirs into life. He logs on to a website called unicel.in, which allows him to send hundreds of SMS messages at a time. 'You see, I put the odds in here for the markets and then I send them to all the bookmakers. They send them on to other bookmakers. And so on. This is how the customers get the odds, you see, all the way from the top of the syndicate. This is a very important part of how we work ... I will include your phone when I send this.'

Seconds later my phone beeps and I have the odds for three markets in front of me. India are 86–89 favourites to win today's first one-day international against England in Hyderabad, the 'lunch favourite' is priced at 45–47 and 'lambi' at 276–280. These are what are known as 'forward bets', markets which close as soon as the match starts. In traditional bookmaking parlance they are known as ante-post wagers because they are not updated ball by ball. The live match betting, which is updated, is the second type of market and will include a new set of match odds, lambi and brackets.

'Lambi' is the term used for innings runs. The quote of 276–280 is not odds, but a spread on the number of runs that will be scored. Both teams are quoted and punters have the option to go over or under the runs quote: 'I think India will score less than 276' or 'I think India will score more than 280'. Brackets, which are only available when the match is underway, are the amount of runs scored in ten-over segments and are an estimation on the number of runs scored. Again, gamblers are betting on whether the team will score more or fewer than the spread given by the bookmaker. The odds for these over or under markets are 9–10 (bet £10 to win £9).

'If a customer wants to bet on a market he uses one of two words: "lagana" or "khana". If he thinks India will win, he phones up and says, "86 lagana India". If he thinks England will win he says, "86 khana India,"' Vinay says. 'Lagana' means back [to bet on a team to win] and 'khana' means to lay [to bet against an outcome]. It translates as 'to eat'.

'The lunch favourite is offered as a forward bet, or pre-match bet, so it is not available when the match is in play. It allows the customer to be betting on whichever side is favourite at the lunch break in a Test match or at the innings break in a one-day international.

'It doesn't matter who the team is, England or India. That is your team.

'The forward market we close just before the toss because of the weather and team news. They have big impact on our odds. So earlier today my friend who is at the stadium in Hyderabad called me and said: "It is overcast." So we have to adjust our prices because that favours the England bowlers. Team news is very important. If a player like Kevin Pietersen is not playing, that can have very huge impact on the odds. You see why bookmakers in India love to get their hands on information? They can make money from that.

'But for now the match odds are 86–89 India favourites. If a customer bets, say 15 lakh [£18,000] on India at 86, it means that our liabilities are 0.86 multiplied by 15 lakh.'

It is worth noting the difference between the Indian and the UK markets in terms of the format of the odds offered. The Indian market uses a decimal system, which is favoured because almost all customer accounts are credit accounts. The formula is: stake x decimal odds = payout. In the UK, bookmakers still use the traditional fractional odds and in this regard are rather stuck in their ways. Fractional odds go back centuries, as proved by Shakespeare, who wrote in *Henry IV*, 'If we wrought out life "twas ten to one."' Fractional odds quote the net total that will be paid out to the bettor should they win, relative to their stake. For example odds of 5–1 imply that the bettor stands to make £100 on a bet of £20. If the odds are 1–5 the bettor will make £4 from a £20 stake.

The match odds, lambi, brackets and lunch favourite are the only four markets that the structured Indian system operates. 'We don't take these fancy bets on which bowler will open the bowling, number of runs off an over, the toss,' Vinay says. 'There are some very small bookmakers who might, but the bets are restricted to 25,000 Indian rupees [£306]. Very small time, very small time.'

This explodes the first myth about the Indian system, which although vast and unregulated in terms of legality, does not tolerate chaos. The notion that one can approach an Indian bookmaker and ask to place a wager on a weird or wonderful event occurring during a match is farcical, according to Vinay. It is systematic and methodical, making a mockery of reports one might have read about the number of markets available. I asked whether any specific bets might be available: such as the outcome of the toss at the beginning of a match, the end from which the fielding captain elects to bowl, a set number of wides, players being placed in unfamiliar fielding positions, individual batsmen scoring fewer runs than their opposite numbers who batted first, batsmen being out at a specific point in their innings or the timing of a declaration.

'None of these,' Vinay says.

'What about the number of no-balls?' I ask.

'Ah, I see why you are asking,' Vinay says. 'The Pakistan spot-fixing trial in London. No. Nobody is making money on that. There is no such market. The match odds, brackets, lambi, lunch favourite – these are the only markets across India. Sometimes there is a market for there to be a completed match because of the weather. But we don't take all these fancy bets that people say.

'I don't know of this Majeed [Mazhar Majeed, the fixer convicted in the spot-fixing trial at Southwark],' he said. 'There are much smarter ways to manipulate betting. Look, I'll show you.'

He logs on to Betfair, the betting exchange. Set up in 2000, it is a person-to-person exchange that allows customers to choose their own odds, just like people on the stock market choose the price at which they want to buy and sell shares. Betfair matches all the bets. On average, Betfair attracts about £15 million for an England one-day international. The money comes from gamblers logging on from their laptops all over the world. Vinay opens up a new window to send via SMS the updated odds to bookmakers across the country after it is announced that India have won the toss and will bat first. He prices India at 85 (5–6 in traditional fractional odds).

Vinay is acting as the syndicate, who normally decide what the betting odds should be, and has been all morning, I notice. 'I thought you were a first-tier bookie?'

'Ya, but sometimes we set the odds. Sometimes we see that we are capable of managing the market. For example, if we are earning from last six months continually, we are getting a huge amount of money. We are the kings. Those bookmakers will follow us. It is all linked. Directly or indirectly, all bookies are linked.

'Now watch how I move the Betfair market,' he says. 'I have sent the odds to all the bookmakers and soon Betfair will have our odds showing. It is currently India 1.95 [20–21]. Watch how they become 1.85 [the

Betfair market includes the 1. because it requires a stake] in line with our odds ... wait, you'll see here how it works ... we want to get India short because it will be difficult to chase at Hyderabad ... there, you see, India 1.85 now on Betfair.

'Indian bookmakers move the Betfair market up and down as we get the odds. If there are only three-figure sums available on Betfair, the India market is not present. It is when you see four- or five-figure sums.'

Vinay is referring to the amount of money available to bet on the match odds market on Betfair. Gamblers are given the opportunity to back or lay the two teams (and a draw if it is a Test match) on the exchange and there is a limited sum of money available to do so on each set of odds. For example, one might want to back England at 2.00 (even money) on Betfair, but there is only £500 to do so. Vinay is suggesting that is not Indian money. Only when one sees greater sums, or liquidity as Betfair calls it, are the illegal bookies pumping in their cash.

With the match about to start, Vinay's two mobile phones are competing for attention.

'Bookies,' he says, as he ends one call and prepares to answer another. 'They want to know about any information my man in Hyderabad has.'

Vinay's speech is in rapid-fire mode, rattling off instructions and advice in Hindi, each conversation ending with a soothing 'theek-hai, theek-hai' (OK, OK) before he has to send more odds via SMS. One telephone call is from a gambler in New Zealand, who Vinay says is one of my followers on Twitter. He passes over the phone and we talk about England's prospects in the match and the series. Neither of us is able to give a ringing endorsement against the more experienced home team.

India have made a slow start in the game, however, and Vinay is watching the odds on Betfair carefully. At 17 for no wicket off three overs, their odds are beginning to drift, suggesting gamblers were expecting India to score runs more quickly. On the fifth ball of the fourth over, Parthiv Patel, the India opening batsman, is run out when he is guilty of backing up too far at the non-striker's end as the angular reach of England's fast bowler Steven Finn deflects the ball on to the stumps. India's odds lengthen further to 2.02, although, noticeably, there are only three-figure sums available to bet with. The Indian money is not present.

'We don't want that,' Vinay says. 'We want India shorter than that. Here,' he says, nudging the computer towards me, ' … send out the odds so we can get India's price shorter.' He instructs me where to type in the 'message' to send to bookmakers and prices India at 80. I press 'send'. A few seconds later, the 2.02 on India is no more and thousands are available to bet on the home team at … 1.80.

'We move the market,' Vinay reiterates. 'We cannot lose when we are able to change the odds to what we want them to be.'

How can they lose, indeed? Forget arbitary estimates about the number of bookmakers in India and the volumes of money they generate. This, in a hotel room in Bhopal, is the illegal market in all its powerful and unrelenting glory.

The ability to move a global betting market – and Betfair is exactly that, with customers from Palestine to Panama – is a trick of the gambling gods. At the click of their fingers or of a computer mouse, the Indian bookmaker dictates to the rest of the world. It is not a delicate alchemy, it would appear. It is not done with smoke and mirrors. It is sheer weight of money. A controlled landslide.

At the very least the tentacles, or 'arms' as Vinay describes them, manoeuvre odds in their favour so to allow them to 'hedge their bets'. Profit is guaranteed and can be generated almost at will. By playing the odds much like a trader might the stock market, the bookmaker renders the bets he has struck with his customers largely irrelevant. The broker will aim to buy low and sell high (or vice versa); the bookmaker will do the same. For example, a bookie may have accepted a wager from any Tom, Dick or Hari of £10 on England to win at even money. This has the potential to cost the bookie £10. However, when England's odds during the game drift to 6–4 (greater than even money) either by momentum siding with the opposition or Vinay sitting in a hotel room in Bhopal manipulating the market, the bookie can lay off or, to continue the stock market analogy, 'sell high'. The original bet struck risks him £10. By placing a wager on England at greater odds of 6–4 for £10 he wins £15; £15 minus £10 is guaranteed profit of £5. Now consider the potential when four or five figures are involved.

This talent to move markets is at its most interesting, and potent, in the context of spot-fixing, particularly the 'script' for the India versus Pakistan World Cup semi-final. In this example, bookies could have been able to manipulate the odds they were offering their customers and doing the same on the betting exchanges. While the bookies were betting with their eyes open, the rest were blindfolded.

A professional gambler will often pontificate about how, when it comes to betting on sport, timing is everything. To be a successful gambler, bets need to be placed before a match- or game-altering incident occurs: a break in serve in a Wimbledon semi-final, a sending-off in the local derby, a wicket in a World Cup semi-final. Mere mortals can only guess when such events will occur, events that guarantee a seismic shift in odds. The bookie or fixer knows. It is written down in front of him. The 'script' is, literally, a licence to print money.

When told of 'the script' for the India versus Pakistan World Cup semi-final, Vinay nods sagely and talks about the money that can be made from fluctuating odds. Frustratingly, however, he does not know the men behind the fix.

'Ya. We heard about that game. But I didn't know the details that you did. We just heard a lot of talk that India would win the game so we priced them very, very short in the odds. People bet on them, but because the game was close for periods we were able to use the Betfair to manage our positions. Not a problem for us.

'I hear about matches, though. A bookmaker friend phones me and says: "Don't sit in this game, it's fixed." So I phone 30 bookies and say this. My business partner refuses to sit in games with Pakistan because he doesn't trust them. He worries the fix is on. It is more punters who try to fix things now. They know the players and ask for favours. But this is the life. People say: "Legalise betting in India and fixing will stop." We are ready to pay tax. I'm tired of paying off the police. But it will not stop fixing. Never. Everyone wants to make money.'

This manipulation of odds may have led to the erroneous belief that Indian bookmakers offer a wealth of markets to bet on. If a fixer has approached a player to bowl a no-ball in a one-day international, it is assumed that he is doing so in order to place a bet on that event occurring at that particular time. But according to Vinay this is not possible. Instead, a no-ball in a limited-overs match, particularly a Twenty20 match where a free hit is an extra punishment – a reliable source of extra runs to a team's total – can be considered an event which moves the odds enough to generate profit. Indeed any of the 'phantom markets' about which I asked Vinay earlier – the outcome of the toss at the beginning of a match, players being placed in unfamiliar fielding positions, batsmen being out at a specific point in their innings and the timing of a declaration – would allow a bookmaker, punter or fixer with prior knowledge to manipulate the odds.

'You have it exactly right,' Vinay, triumphantly, says. 'You know, so much money could have been made from that India–Pakistan game by bookies moving their odds just before a wicket fell. What is that saying? Information is power? No. Information is money. All information we can make money out of.'

Vinay's phone rings again. It is his wife reminding him to pick up his son.

'Oh, I am sorry, I must go. My son, he is two, and he is always hiding my phone. He is very naughty. Come to lunch tomorrow at my home and we can talk more of this fixing. I'll send a car.'

CHAPTER 6

THE ANATOMY OF A FIX

Before leaving the hotel, the last thing Vinay said, through snorts and grunts of laughter, was: 'My driver … in English … his name means … "lamp".'

'Lamp' is on time, driving a beige and battered 1990s Mercedes with blacked-out windows. He is not much of a conversationalist, preferring to grin inanely in the rearview mirror every few miles and thrust a thumbs-up in my direction.

He proves most adept, however, at avoiding the cattle – omnipresent in India, of course – as we chug on gamely, passing endless farmland. Women, clad in pink, green and yellow saris work the fields, lighting small fires that shroud them and the occasional goat herder in an ephemeral mystery.

Our destination is on the outskirts of Bhopal. The streets are tight and buzz with the sound of scooters zipping past the people buying their daily goods from the fruit, food and spice stalls that line the road. We stop outside a mobile phone shop. A mottled youth wearing an ill-fitting cream shirt and 1960-style NHS spectacles taps on the car window and motions for me to get out. I have no idea who he is, but assume he has something to do with Vinay.

I follow him into the shop past bemused staff who gawp and whisper, to a back office where, sat in a large leather chair behind a desk and a small television showing CCTV images from the shop front, is Vinay. 'I'm not just a bookie, my friend,' he says exultantly with that now unmistakeable smile. 'I wanted you to see where else I do business. Not bad for someone who started off on 100 rupees a day, eh? That is barely a pound to you. Come, sit down.'

Vinay runs the mobile shop as part of a franchise deal. He also has a property development business. 'Bookies in India are never just bookies,' he says. 'They have lots of work.' He explains how he has just 'won' the right to build on a prime plot for a development just outside Bhopal. 'I know the man who makes all the planning decisions,' he says. 'He is a good friend of mine and he helps me out. Of course I have to pay, but this is how things work in India. You are nothing without money. They had a lottery to see who would get the best plot and we got it. I'm excited about that.

'In the real estate business we take the property and improve it, convert it and keep it. Then market rises and then we sell. Other business is construction. We do that also: build houses. We buy; we build. It's a good business. Huge profit. Again, we have to pay the right people. We have good contacts with the municipal corp. They tell us "this is the site that has proposed road construction" or about malls. Any mall being built increases the price of your land.

'Of course, we pay for this information. But nothing is free in this world. Nothing is free. Everyone wants to make more money, so it is all fine.'

I tell him that he is a man with many fingers in many pies but he has not heard of this analogy. I explain it.

'Ya, I've got to work in many pies like you say because I have two children and a wife to support, plus my parents. And my brother and his wife and child. I am head of the family because I'm the eldest. They all live with me. This is our culture. You can meet them later.'

The awkward, bespectacled fellow walks into the office. He produces three fat rolls of cash from his pockets and hands them to Vinay. 'This is Rahul, my assistant.'

'There must be about three or four lakh there?' I ask.

'Ya. More than that. Five lakh [£6,000]. This is hawala money from the match yesterday. We had a good day. We won around 18 lakh [£21,500]. If England would have won we'd have lost 30 lakh [£37,500] because we traded the game, you know, so that as the game got closer to its end we had more and more money on India.'

Vinay counts the cash and then hands it back to Rahul, who pockets it in his jeans and disappears.

'He is off to make sure it gets paid to the right people now,' Vinay says. 'All trustworthy; all fair. If I don't pay them the winnings then I don't have a business.

'Rahul is good for me. I have known him since he was very young. He is only 18. He works for me across all my businesses and ... ' Vinay trails off. He spots something from the CCTV images and calls through a male shop worker and barks what would appear to a rebuke in Hindi. The man wobbles his head from side to side vigorously.

'Are you telling him off?' I ask.

'Oh no. I just remind him that I want the weather forecast for the next few days because of the one-day internationals coming up. He will print them out for me. You remember how I told you that weather forecast is very important, yes?'

We return to our discussion of yesterday. Vinay insists that any piece of information, no matter how small, is key. 'If I had information on players then, wow, boom, you know?' he says. 'Not fixing them to do things in matches, but who is fit, who is batting well, bowling well, batting badly, bowling badly.

'This is difficult for me to get though, because I'm a bookie and players won't talk to me. They are scared, I think. It is colour of my skin, too. I'm brown. You are white. They would talk to you but not me because they would worry.'

I suspect that Vinay's 'nothing is for free' mantra might be soon applied to me. In this instance there is perhaps no such thing as a free lunch. He has shown me how the betting market works, so does he now want something in return?

'Hey, I tell you what. When I'm in Mumbai I'm staying at the same hotel as the players, so if I find out any information I will let you know, yes?'

'Ya. That would be very good for me,' he says.

I wobble my head from side to side vigorously. It is a peculiarity of spending a chunk of time in India that one picks up, without noticing, the habit of the Indian head wobble. It is generally accepted that the faster the wobble, the more readily someone understands. The slower wobble is a sign of friendship. Vinay is wobbling gently and smiling.

'Because England is a place where you can contact anyone you see,' he starts up again. 'From there you can contact anyone. From India you can't. All the world sees English people with a different view, Indian people are seen with a different view. It is a different mindset. Everyone knows that. If you contact someone they will respond to you, if I do it they won't. And you have the reputation; you are a journalist. As you are living in England, you might be able to have contact directly with players. It is not a tough job. By living in India it is tough. As soon as they know I'm Indian … '

I get the picture. Another vigorous head wobble is in order.

'Ya, ya, you understand,' he says. 'Come, we must go for the lunch. I have told my wife you are coming and she's very excited that an Englishman is coming. We eat well.'

Vinay fires up a Hero Honda motorbike and I sit gingerly on the back, clinging on so the blood drains from my knuckles as we negotiate the backstreet obstacles. We swerve past goats, bend round a cow, dodge pedestrians, duck a Sikh family of four on a scooter and veer past an elephant. Occasionally Vinay turns round to point out landmarks – 'this is my brother's electronics store' – but I ignore him, hoping he will concentrate on the road.

'You have not experienced India,' Vinay says when we reach his home, 'until you have been on a motorcycle.'

He is proud of his home – a three-storey terraced building which overlooks a thriving street below. 'Granite floors,' he says as he nods to his feet. Then he gets me a glass of water.

'We purify it ourselves,' he boasts. 'It's safe to drink.'

He points out fixtures and fittings, which he commissioned a carpenter to craft. And the hundreds of mobile phones charging in his dressing room, blinking in unison, which have helped to pay for it all through bookmaking.

'Ah, I almost forgot,' he says excitedly. 'I want to show you the software which allows us to record all the bets.'

He shows me into a sparse living room, with only a huge flatscreen television and two L-shaped leather sofas that hug the walls. On one of them, a dozy two-year-old boy stirs grumpily. 'This is my son,' Vinay says before rushing off and shouting back. 'I'll be back in a minute, I need to get the software.' His son eyes me warily with one eye, the other wrapped in sleep. I sip my water. Vinay rushes back.

'You'll like this,' he says. 'We record every bet we take from our customers, right across the syndicate. But we leave out the last two zeroes of every sum because we don't want the tax man to find out.' A spreadsheet showing row after row of names and numbers appears.

'There are also bookies recorded. They are betting with us. All the bookies pass their bets to other bookies, a percentage of their bets. If he keeps all his bets the amount will be too huge, profit and loss … too much for one person. Lalu, Suj, Ahmed, Cash … these are Jayanti Malad [the biggest bookmaker in Delhi]. His account is also managed by this software. So, you see, he has 12 lakh rupees [£14,400] in his account.

'If you want to see your position on a certain market [clicks on a new spreadsheet] … this is the bracket for the England game yesterday after 20 overs. The result is 78. So it shows that we will earn 50,000 and these are the bookies who we have been in partnership with, who we have taken percentage shares of their bets. We call it a party. Party. It's a good group.'

Vinay clicks on more options, showing the profits and losses for individual customers and bookies. There is even a spreadsheet that shows how much money the syndicate is making state by state. 'Here is Maharashtra, Uttar Pradesh, Madhya Pradesh … so, you see, we know what we are doing. This is business. We are not fools.'

Vinay shows me to the dining room where suddenly three women appear – Vinay's wife, mother and sister-in-law – carrying plate upon plate of food. They are shy, but each beams with a smile as they sashay out of the room, nodding deferentially and clasping their hands together in front of them. Pointing to a feast of rice, parathas, dal, sambhar and curd, Vinay says: 'I'm five foot six and 71kg. It is too heavy. This is why.'

During lunch conversation turns to fixing, as Vinay promised. I am keen to understand the anatomy of a fix. Although there has been much written about corruption in cricket, few have deciphered how a fix is set up and money is made. I suggest it is assumed that it is the bookmakers who are the chief corruptors, a charge that Vinay refutes vehemently.

'Fixing is not good for my business,' he says. 'Why would it? I want my customers to bet with confidence and I know that it can be difficult for them because of all this talk about fixing. I'm not saying bookies do not fix, but I would think that is the punters who do most of it.'

'So individuals are fixing matches rather than syndicates?'

'Yes, this is the way it is now.'

'The betting syndicates are not doing the majority of fixes?'

'Punters also fix the match. In the recent past bookies fixed the match, but nowadays punters fix the match.'

'In the past how did it work?'

'There were a few bookies. They were not capable of managing the market like we do with Betfair. If they post a price for India at 87–90 and anyone says "put my 15 lakh on India" and then another customer does the same, they get a huge liability on India, so how can they pay the total amount if India win? If India lose, everything is OK. But if India win, how can they pay? For that situation they used the fixing factor. It was the necessity of the betting syndicate to fix the match 'cos they don't have so much money in the past, they were not so rich and it was illegal – they had to pay the police, the parliament, the players.'

'How long ago was recent past?'

'In 1999–2000. Now only some punters who are in contact with the players in that "you are a cricket player and I am your friend". They ask the player, "Please do this for me, I pay for you."'

'How does that punter make money?'

'He makes about two crores [£240,000] for a single bracket.'

'Does he bet on it himself?'

'Yes.'

'Does he sell that information to other bookmakers?'

'No. He doesn't. He fixes the match with the players.'

'So he bets himself?'

'Yes.'

'How does he get his bets on if he is doing a fix? Why won't you as a bookie say: "I know this guy, he keeps winning"?'

'No, no. India market and England market there is a difference [in England bookmakers will close the account of a gambler who wins too often]. There are some bookies in India who don't do it like a business. The punter has a strategy. Because of that you can't close my account. If you close it, I will send another person in my place to open an account. He will not tell you I am behind the curtains.'

'So a punter who has a fix will place multiple bets with multiple bookies using multiple accounts?'

'Yes. This is how it works. He will have his friends placing the bets all over. There is a big connection. Some punters are connected like the bookmakers are connected. If a punter has 50 friends, he can get 50 bets.'

'So if I know a player and he has agreed to make sure no more than 35 are runs scored in the first ten overs of a Test innings, with that info I can come to you and as many bookies as I can and I bet on that?'

'That's how the punters earn money. Continually betting. One day he comes to us and after three matches he doesn't come to us. They mix it up. They are sharp enough. Different bookies. Different matches.'

'How can it be worthwhile for a punter to pay a player for a fixer? How much would they pay a player? 10–15 lakh [£12,000–18,000]? How much profit is he making from that?'

'Around 50 lakh [£60,000] or more. Up to 200 lakh [£240,000]. Depends on how many bookies he is betting with. There are so many bookies that 200 lakh is a small amount. It is not like England, when there is a paper trail. They can't see the money when it is spread over bookies. It is not like Ladbrokes. Here it is black money. In England it is from banks. But there are punters who fix the match for big sums. They pay big sums to the players. Assume in yesterday's match only the openers were fixed.'

'They only fix with openers because they set the tone for the lambi [the innings runs] and brackets?'

'Yes. Yes. They can fix English players also. I can bet that everyone from top level of ICC to lowest level of cricket-playing nations, everyone is directly or indirectly related with bookies. Indian or whoever. Every game, you know that.'

'How many games on television would you say are fixed, whether the result or a bracket?'

'I would say 50 per cent.'

'That's very high. Is it international matches, Indian Premier League matches?'

'Domestic matches are easy to fix. International matches are very hard because of the police, the anti-corruption unit. You have none of this with English county games. Three years ago a Delhi bookmaker called me up and said a county game was fixed. I forget the game 'cos it was long ago. He said he would tell me and I would have to pay three lakh [£3,600] for the information. I thought this was too much, too much of a sum to pay ... it could go wrong. So I said no. He said I could have the information for free. He was right. And he was right for the next three games in England, too. They were one-day matches, not Twenty20.'

'I have heard of the toss being fixed in Twenty20 matches. Is this right?'

'Outcome of the toss? It can be fixed. We don't bet on it. If one of bookies further down the chain is taking bets, we might take bets, too. You can't bet more than 25,000 rupees on this and you will only get 95 per cent of winnings because of commission. But you know how the fixes work, with the bookies able to move prices in their favour on Betfair or with the customer, ya? I showed you how this works yesterday. The toss is fixed so we can move the match odds in our favour, not so we can bet on it. If we know a result is happening before a game, we are going to make sure that the team we know will lose is going to be the most attractive to bet on. That goes the same for any market – lambi, brackets. The punter, who is doing the fixing, can also be on Betfair, don't forget that.'

'So how much would a player be paid to bowl a no-ball in a Twenty20 match?'

'A player would be paid three lakh [£3,600] for a single no-ball. His board [say, the England and Wales Cricket Board or Australian Cricket Board] is giving him five lakhs [£6,000]. The prices for lambi or brackets move a lot with a no-ball in a Twenty20 game because there is a free hit.'

'Is the punter going to make enough on that?'

'The bookies will understand in time that this punter is always winning on this. There are not enough bookies around to take the bet, so the life-cycle of that fix is small. The big market is the match odds. It is a risky one, too. The match can turn quickly. The rates come down and up, down and up in a close match, and every time I know that is the fixer coming into play. The IPL? Do you think those are fair? You know about the ICL matches four or five years ago? They were fixed. We had a strong connection at that time, so were able to make money from the fix.'

'How often do you hear of a fix?'

'Not very often. But the Sussex v. Kent match this season, it was fixed. I can bet on that. Kent won the match. A 40-over domestic game. That was a fixed match. One of our bookmakers called me in the match telling me to "leave it, don't bet on it, don't take bets". I ask if there was a problem with the police and he said it's a fixed match. Kent will surely win. I told all my friends and bookies to please leave this match. I called 30 big bookmakers in India.'

[Later I discover that an ECB anti-corruption unit investigated this match.]

'How bad is it in county cricket?'

'Very often. English county, ICL, IPL. These are all the same. Lots of games, lots of players. County cricketers do not earn a lot of money. They are easy for a punter to get their friends in the players. They need the money. It is very easy to fix a county match result, but very difficult to fix an international match result.'

'How do you fix a county game?'

'There are local guys who know the players personally. The bookies or punters contact them. Everything goes well. They have a go-between or fixer who works for the bookie or punter. The fixer is important because he makes the contact with the player. He will trust them. So the player will not even meet the punter or bookie, you know? He is just working with his friend.'

'How do the go-betweens, fixers, operate?'

'I do not know exactly know how they work. There is one in India who is known as a go-between. He works for a punter. Dheeraj Dixit. I think he works for a punter. He is not himself a punter 'cos he has not enough money. He is a go-between, fixer for punter and player. Dheeraj Dixit is in the media a lot in India. People are writing about him being into the fixing. They say he can do a lot of Bollywood actresses.'

'What do you mean "do"?'

'He can get them to meet the players. It helps make the players his friends.'

'Why are international games too hard to fix?'

'Too many players needed and it takes too much money to pay them. You need three or four. The county is the whole team.'

'How much is a county match worth in turnover?'

'Probably 300 crores [£3.6 million] turnover for the first- and second-tier on the Indian system. All the teams at county do it. All IPL teams, too. People say Australians are difficult to fix and they don't do it, but I don't believe it. Aussies are easy to fix. They fix the match, I'm damn sure.'

'What percentage of matches in the IPL?'

'I can't say, but there is big percentage. The owners are telling the players what to do.'

'Do you think owners are using their influence over teams and coaches to make money from betting?'

'Definitely. Definitely. If I own a team, you have all the information and we need information. You are in touch with all the other team owners. They are working for a single aim – to earn money. They can sell that information or they can back or lay on the basis of that information. If there is a match between Bangalore and Mumbai and they know that Chris Gayle [the West Indies batsman] will not play today, it'll cost. The value of Chris Gayle to a team is around 20 clicks to the price [so a team without Chris Gayle might drift in price from 2.00 to 2.20]. The value of Sachin Tendulkar is around 30 clicks. If Sachin and MS Dhoni are not playing, it will be around 50 clicks. This is big information. All the players pass this information on. "I'm not playing, the pitch is not good," or whatever information they have. What is the need of XXXX XXXX to tweet that the weather is OK? "The pitch is this". "I am tired." These types of tweets. These are not fair. XXXX XXXX is, I think, in contact with bookies. And XXXX XXXX, XXXX XXXX, XXXX XXXX. And XXXX XXXX, XXXX XXXX, XXXX XXXX. They are influenced by bookies. That's why I am telling you, if you have contact with players, you can make money. Make good contacts with players and people who know the weather. At some day or some point you will make money on this. If you give information to me, you will make money. You can make this your business also.'

'Is there any way you know a market or match is fixed?'

'Yeah, I know. They phone to tell me as a warning. Please don't sit in this game. Don't take bets. Our friends, bookies, well-wishers for me. They tell me, don't take the bets.'

'What was a recent game that was fixed?'

'England against Sri Lanka in Wales.'

'The first Test in Cardiff in May 2011?'

'I know of names in the Sri Lanka team. I know very well a bookie who is a good friend of players. We get information [as far back as] 2004. We get this type of news.'

'Were you warned about this game in Cardiff?'

'Ya. From Delhi. But I think the match-fixing guys are more from Delhi than Mumbai. All the world knows that Mumbai is the hub, but damn sure they do it Delhi.'

'How much prior warning?'

'It was four hours before the start of play on the last day. I called my friends in our syndicate that I got this news. We have to keep an eye on that. We don't do anything. Who has informed us? Who is in contact with him? And we won't take bets from those persons. We are sharp enough for that. It's a business. We adjusted our prices. As we got the information, we adjusted the prices. We can fluctuate the market as we want. We can fluctuate the market by putting a huge amount on a single thing.'

'Is it probable that if there was a England v. Sri Lanka fix, it was set up late, maybe the night before the last day?'

'Ya. It was prefaced there would be a result in this match. We knew there would be weather to come into the picture and every time weather comes into the picture it will not be a draw. Any game in the past when weather comes into the picture first or second day, it'll not be a draw. When we were given the information, we wanted people to bet on the draw, so we made the price better than it really was. What you have to remember is that lots and lots of money would have been bet on the draw by customers in the Indian market, so there was a lot of money to be lost by the syndicates. As soon as people here see rain in England, they think the match will be a draw, so they want to bet on that. Any result was better than a draw.'

England won the Test by an innings and 14 runs.

CHAPTER 7

BOOKIE V. PUNTER

As I head back to Bhopal, with Lamp once again behind the wheel, the smoke from the field fires has dispersed and the highway is soaked in a lucid, brilliant pink light from the setting sun. After two days with Vinay I now have a greater understanding of how money was made from fixing and who was making it: the bookmakers and the punter. The go-between, or fixer, apparently being used by both.

It is clear that fixing, whether the result or the lambi or brackets, is not an exact science insofar that there is more than one method and more than one protagonist. There are many layers to this type of corruption.

The assumption that it is largely bookmakers who fix matches would appear to be wrong. There would seem to be little doubt that the all-powerful syndicates, of which Vinay is a part, wield massive influence and would have the funds and organisational ability to fix elements of matches or the results themselves.

The bookies and the punter can be considered to be enemies in the mould of the old-fashioned pork-pie-hat-wearing oddsmaker and his traditional chancer customer. But with a difference. Instead of pitting their wallets against each other, with the bookie invariably coming out on top, this is a battle of inside information. Who knows more? The only guaranteed consistent loser is the workaday customer, who hopes he knows something, yet in reality is closeted and witless.

Of the two operators, the bookie strikes me as the sharper. His is a subtle fix employing tried and trusted methods. A fraud steeped in history. The punter is an altogether cruder beast. Whereas the punter takes a chance (the age-old status quo at least survives here), the bookie is calculated. Once the bookie has his fix organised, no doubt thanks to a fixer, he can employ two methods to rake in the lakhs.

Pity the poor customer who is tempted by the false odds repeated endlessly on the bhao line, cajoling him into parting with his hard-earned cash when the bookie knows the result beforehand. Vinay gave the example of how, armed with prior knowledge that the Test match between England and Sri Lanka in Cardiff would not end in a draw, the odds were set so that more people would bet on the stalemate. It is like the crafty sorts you meet selling postcards at India's tourist attractions. 'Five rupees for ten, sir ... lovely gift, sir.' What is the harm? you think. Only upon returning to the hotel and opening the pack do you spot that you have been sold blank cards sandwiched between two postcards.

Can the bookmakers' customers be so consistently naive? Of course, it is only a 'few rupees'. Remember the size and reach of the illegal Indian market with its 'tentacles'. 'All bookmakers are linked,' Vinay had said. This is a ruse that hundreds of thousands can fall prey to, without even a whiff of the hard evidence that a couple of tattered postcards provide.

Sharper still is the manipulation of markets on the betting exchanges, where the largest returns can be made, given the way Vinay is able to move the odds by sending out a solitary SMS to his network. That is almost a mathematical art form. The punter can do likewise, of course, and Vinay suggests that he does, but he comes across as a more simple operator. His original way of making money from fixes, which would have been used in the days of Hansie Cronje and before the betting exchanges were commonplace, is less sophisticated. It requires much poking and prodding of contacts up and down the country, hoping the minions will do the bidding correctly. It is a system that primarily takes advantage of the sheer size of the industry: a few lakh in Mumbai, a few more in Delhi, then a few more rupees somewhere else. Next week mix it all up again and hope you don't get found out. It is a role reversal of the big syndicates taking advantage of the customer. They might set fake odds, but the well-connected punter sends 'fake' customers.

In an effort to outmanoeuvre the punter who has inside informa-tion, the Indian bookmakers have been known to change the terms of the brackets. Instead of the usual ten-over spread, they might reduce it to, say, eight overs. This is what happened ahead of the third one-day international between England and Pakistan at the Oval in September

2010. The *Sun* newspaper reported they had evidence of anticipated scoring patterns. The ICC's ACSU rejected the story, saying there was no 'compelling evidence'.

If the methods of the bookies and the punters were now as easy to digest as Vinay's wife's memorable lunch, then some of his revelations about the England–Sri Lanka Test and county cricket were not.* The Cardiff Test allegation we will deal with in detail now. Whether you think it is more shocking than the claim about county cricket may well depend on your views of the Sri Lanka team, an often buccaneering and magical outfit who have made friends the world over for the way they have played the game: a snarl on the pitch, a smile away from it. What cannot be doubted, though, in this instance is that as well as being an unregulated, rampaging behemoth riding roughshod over its domestic and world betting markets, the Indian illegal system and its workers do not respect reputations – either of individuals or contests.

The Cardiff Test was a match that Betfair called the 'most stunning turnaround in cricket betting history'. Andrew Strauss, the England captain, said it was 'one of the most extraordinary cricket matches any of us have ever played'. Yet it would appear to have had all the ingredients for the perfect fix.

A draw looked a certainty when on the fifth and final day the players opened their hotel room curtains to be greeted by a grey slate of drizzle falling across Cardiff. Only one innings had been completed – Sri Lanka had been bowled out for 400 – and England had replied with 491 for five. Not surprisingly, with play not starting until 3pm and only 55 overs left in the match, England were available to back on Betfair at 999–1, the maximum odds, and the draw was 1–99 (bet £99, win £0.99), the smallest possible odds. Thousands were wagered on the stalemate at these odds.

England batted on for two overs, allowing Ian Bell to reach a century, before they declared. At this stage they could have been backed at 99–1. Just over an hour later, at the tea break, there were signs in the market that Indian money was influencing England's price. Despite the home

---

* The Sri Lanka Cricket Board, contacted on 26 July, did not reply when asked to comment about the Test match in Cardiff.

team needing another eight wickets in 39 overs and Sri Lanka trailing by only 63 runs, they were available to back at 17–1, when seasoned price watchers would have expected them to have been at least twice that.

In the first over of the last session, England were just shy of 11–1. When Sri Lanka slumped to 37 for four, England were 4–1 and the draw was 1–4. The collapse – of both the Sri Lanka batting and England's odds – continued, of course, and the touring team were bowled out for 82, beaten by an innings and 14 runs.

Whether one believes Vinay or not, there had been rumours surrounding the Sri Lanka team for some time. Hashan Tillakaratne, the former captain, said in April 2011 that match-fixing had been going on in the team since 1992. He played 83 Tests and 200 one-day internationals for Sri Lanka and was suspicious about the World Cup final against India in 2011. 'I am not saying that this match was fixed. But, anyway, match-fixing is something that has been in this country over a period of time. This has spread like a cancer today,' he said. 'Why were four players changed for this match? Those are questions that should be asked. We who have played cricket talk about this. We were playing an entirely different side.'

There is also an obscure fact about the Sri Lanka team that took the field in Cardiff that will ensure scandalous tongues wag at his conspiracy theory ... they had not been paid since the end of the World Cup in April. Not a single rupee in more than eight weeks.

The Sri Lanka Cricket Board had run up debts of 3.7 million Sri Lankan rupees since financing the building of three stadiums in Hambantota, Pallakele and Colombo to host 12 matches in the tournament. The sports minister had submitted a cabinet paper requesting one billion Sri Lanka rupees to bail out the Board, but the treasury said it could not release that amount. Even Board staff members could not be paid: the secretaries, the office assistants, the janitors.

It does not take a particularly cynical mind to come to the conclusion that a cricketer who has been treated with such little regard for his welfare and that of his family, might – just might – be tempted by the offer of payment to throw a Test match, particularly a Sri Lanka player who suffered the harrowing experience of being a target for terrorists in Pakistan in March 2009. Players are paid to play for their country, but it is often assumed they would do so only for the love of the national flag. When one has almost been killed in the line of doing his duty as an entertainer and then suffered the indignation of empty pay cheques, it is a stinging slap in the face.

This is supposition. What is not is the high regard in which some of Sri Lanka's players are held. Kumar Sangakkara and Mahela Jayawardene spring to mind. They are two of the most well respected players in the world game and it is unthinkable that two such characters could be involved in such a scam. Discussing their lofty character is not an attempt to criminalise them, merely an attempt to make sense of such claims. Their presence in the Sri Lanka team that day is a ready-made rebuttal to loose talk.

Sangakkara, eloquent, charming and a trained lawyer, remains revered for an almost statesman-like reputation in the game. He received a standing ovation after he delivered a redolent and moving Cowdrey Lecture at Lord's in July of that year, recalling the horror of the terrorist attack on the Sri Lanka cricket team in Lahore. In a speech lasting more than an hour in the Nursery Pavilion, Sangakkara spoke about how violence had reminded him of the sacrifices his countrymen had made when he was growing up during a time of bloody unrest in Sri Lanka. He revealed how he prayed for his life and how a bullet whizzed past his ear as terrorists raked the team bus that was taking them to the stadium. He also spoke about the need to rid cricket of the 'scourge of corruption'.

Jayawardene is equally esteemed. Away from the cricket field he is a fierce campaigner for a cancer charity, which aims to build a 750-bed specialist centre in a district of Colombo. He was sufficiently psychologically scarred by the death of his younger brother aged 16 from a brain tumour that he gave up cricket and had to be persuaded by his parents to rebuild his career.

Vinay's claims are easily dimissed. A judge, administrator, player or, perhaps, an ACSU officer, can wave them away with contempt. They are unreliable because his trade is illegal, they will say. The conundrum for cricket is obvious. Does it start listening to folk who, like it or not, are at the black heart of the matter when no one else appears to be willing to talk?

Vinay, to all intents and purposes, could probably be termed a gangster. He is an illegal bookmaker. He pays off the police. He pays building regulators for information. He has a driver and a car with tinted windows. But he does it with a disarming and unthreatening smile that makes one take him at face value.

What Vinay is trying to do is beat the system with, if you will pardon the pun, a straight bat. He is not malicious or threatening. But he knows how his country works. Tit for tat, information for information, favour for favour. He is a good man providing for his family from an illegal industry which, it would seem, cannot be tamed, nor is there an appetite to tame it.

Occasionally this means he comes across information, which could be right or wrong, which most cricket fans would find unedifying. Included in that was the World Cup semi-final between India and Pakistan. He did not receive the script that I did, but he knew there was 'chatter' about the match. He also knows of Parthiv's operation and how he is connected to one of the top syndicate men, Shobhan Mehta. 'We heard about this game,' Vinay said. 'But I don't think it was fixed.' The bookmaker grapevine was buzzing. So if there was a fix, then it perhaps came from the hand of a punter.

CHAPTER 8

PUNTER

'I'm getting the heebie-jeebies right now, you know that? He sees you … I don't know … fuck! "Who's this guy?" he'll say. "Man, all bets are off."'

It is unlike Murali Krishnan to be on edge. An intrepid investigative journalist for more than 20 years, Murali is used to meeting undesirables. A bear of a man, with a salt-and-pepper moustache, he is a former editor of the Indo-Asian News Service and when part of the investigative team at *Outlook India*, the country's leading news magazine, he was a specialist on cricket corruption. He was the first reporter to interview Mohammad Azharuddin after the 2000 fixing scandal broke and was gifted a signed pair of batting gloves by the disgraced player. Murali keeps them in his bedroom cupboard. They are surprisingly small for such a money-grabber.

But today Murali is ticking. 'Fuck on toast' – his favourite phrase – 'I don't know how this is gonna play out.' He has set up a meeting with Rattan Mehta, one of India's most prominent punters. He does not know I'm coming.

'He wouldn't agree to meet you,' Murali says. 'He might walk straight out. Or he might not, he knows I've got good info on him.'

Murali meets Mehta regularly to keep an ear close to cricket's gurgling underbelly.

'He's connected,' Murali says. 'Oh hell, he'll be swish and suave, smile, cut-glass accent but don't buy that.'

Mehta is not only notorious by word of mouth. It is in black and white, too. In a cast of hundreds in India's CBI match-fixing report of 2000, Mehta was a key character. In a statement by Pawan Puri, a well-known gambler, Mehta was portrayed as the archetypal punter who fixed matches (although Mehta strenuously denied this in his CBI interview). He hosted the Pakistan team at his restaurant, the Mini Mahal, in Delhi when they were on tour in 1999 and gave them 'small gifts'. He was also friends with Ajay Jadeja, the India player who was banned for fixing, in no small part for his relationship with Mehta, although that was later quashed by the Delhi High Court.

Puri told the CBI that he had known Mehta for ten years and that he used to bet four to five lakhs (£4,800–£6,000) on a single match. He said that Mehta would frequently ring up Jadeja on his mobile phone and was always 'secretive' when in conversation. Presumably after one such call, Puri was party to helping Mehta make sure he got his bet on. The CBI report reads: 'Mehta asked him to ring up Shobhan Mehta [the Mumbai bookmaker who is connected to Parthiv and Big G], a Bombay bookie and asked him to place a bet to the effect that the ongoing match between India–New Zealand at Ahmedabad [in 1999] would end in a draw. He was surprised as to how Rattan Mehta could anticipate this since New Zealand were in a precarious position and very few persons would have reckoned that the match would end in a draw. He dialled Shobhan's number and placed a bet to this effect. Even Shobhan Mehta was sceptical and … he advised him not to place this bet. However, he told Shobhan that he was placing bets on somebody else's behalf.

'On being asked as to why Rattan placed bets with Shobhan through him and not directly, he stated that Rattan does not have an account with Shobhan and hence he had to place this bet through him. [Rattan] Mehta, after getting drunk, boasted that he had exact information about the outcome of the Ahmedabad Test match and also placed bets with some other bookies, whose names he did not remember.'

The Ahmedabad Test did end in a draw. The 'precarious position' New Zealand were in was a first-innings score of 211 for six at the close of the third day, trailing India's mammoth 583. India included Jadeja in the team and were captained by Sachin Tendulkar who, after his side had bowled New Zealand out for 308 in first innings – a lead of 275 – did not enforce the follow-on. New Zealand were eventually set 424 to win and were able to bat out 94 overs, for the loss of just two wickets, to earn a stalemate.

Tendulkar was summoned to meet K Madhavan, a former CBI investigator who conducted the Board of Control for Cricket India (BCCI) inquiry into the 2000 match-fixing scandal, to answer questions about the match. He was exonerated and was allowed to have his wife present when quizzed. 'I did not suspect him at all,' Madhavan says today. Indeed, Tendulkar does not even warrant a mention in his report and has regularly spoken out against corruption during his glittering career.

Mud has stuck to dirty Mehta's reputation, however, despite his repeated denials of wrongdoing. Puri had more stories about his friend. He recalled how there had been talk among bookmakers that Jadeja, who was captain of the India B team for a Challenger Trophy Series in February 2000, had agreed to lose matches against India A at the 'behest' of Mehta. Puri claimed that when he met Jadeja on a flight from Mumbai to Delhi, the player spoke of how he had 'done' matches for Mehta in that series. Puri said that Mehta had earned around 20 lakhs (£24,000) betting on the matches, but Jadeja had told him that he had made only 'one or two lakhs and that he would teach Rattan a lesson'. According to Puri, there were rumours that whenever Jadeja fixed a match through Mehta, Mohammad Azharuddin and the former wicketkeeper Nayan Mongia were involved. Mongia was never charged and was exonerated. Another statement, this time from Tipu Kohli, a punter, alleged that Mehta had paid Pakistan to lose in a 1997 series in Sri Lanka.

Jadeja's statement was riddled with inconsistencies as far as his relationship with Mehta was concerned. He had known him for 'many years' and had remained in 'close contact', but did not know he was a punter. He refused to answer questions on why he fraternised with such a character. When asked about a call made from his mobile phone to Mehta's, he claimed he did not know him and had never made such a call.

Mehta was more savvy when the CBI came calling to his house in the Panscheel Enclave of Delhi. He admitted to being 'very friendly' with Jadeja, who had visited his restaurant, but said he had not fixed games with him or paid him any money and only asked for his 'judgement on matches sometimes'. Mehta said that he had no prior knowledge of the follow-on not being enforced in Ahmedabad and had merely asked Puri to get the odds from Shobhan Mehta, the bookmaker. As for Kohli, well, he was maligning him because they had fallen out over money.

After that Mehta went quiet. Not until 2004 did his name appear again in the headlines. It was a story in *Outlook* magazine, written by a certain Murali Krishnan, that Pakistan had thrown a 1999 World Cup match against India. If lightning had struck twice 12 years later, Mehta was a man who might know something.

It would appear that, although Mehta had given polished answers to the police back in 2000, he was rather too boastful about his relationship with the Pakistan team. He said he was 'very friendly' with a number of Pakistani players and named a number of individuals. The ears of the ICC's ACSU officers pricked up.

Mehta was under the scanner again. A Delhi businessman gave a statement to the ACSU that Mehta had told him before the match, which was played at Old Trafford, Manchester, that it was fixed. Lord Condon, then ACSU chief, wrote to the Pakistan Cricket Board and referred to the role of Mehta in 'arranging the underperformance' of Pakistan players.

The businessman told the ACSU that he had met Mehta by chance in Monty's Cigar and Wine Bar in Sloane Street in London and that he had been making telephone calls to players including Salim Malik, who achieved notoriety when becoming the first cricketer to be banned for match-fixing in 2000 (although this ban was later lifted by a local court in Lahore in 2008), and Azharuddin. 'I saw Mehta make and receive in excess of 20 calls on his mobile phone. He had two mobiles with him, one was Indian and one, I think, was British,' the statement read. 'In some of the calls, he was making bets or moving money, but others were obviously to cricketers. At various times, Mehta told me who he was speaking to. Mehta was making notes all the time.

'After the phone calls at Monty's, Mehta told me that the fix was on, with a number of Pakistani players "sorted" and that India were going to win the forthcoming World Cup match against Pakistan. According to Mehta, he had enough of the Pakistani players sorted for India to win.' The businessman added: 'Mehta told me I could bet on it with certainty and that he didn't mind if I advised my friends as well. After Monty's, we went to the Chinawhite nightclub. Again during the evening, Mehta informed me that India would definitely win the match against Pakistan.'

India did win. It could have been a blueprint for the return fixture in 2011. India batted first and posted a modest total, setting Pakistan 228 to win. Pakistan made a solid start before falling away. They were bowled out, barely raising a whimper of defiance, for 180 to lose by 47 runs.

The more surprising element, however, if you believe that the match was fixed, was that it was played against a backdrop of nationalistic fervour. The armies of the two countries were engaged in a stand-off over Kashmir, the disputed territory in the north-west of India, and there were concerns that rival supporters would have a war of their own. National pride being staked in sporting contests has become a tiresome and diluted cliché in the years since, but there can be no doubting that, to the workaday Indian or Pakistani on the street, that game meant everything, which is why it is so incredible that it has been tainted.

Murali says: 'He made big monies on that '99 World Cup game. He would say that he had the Pakistan team in his pocket.'

With Murali's help I have arranged to meet Rattan Mehta at Select City Walk, the most expensive mall in Delhi. It is six acres of consumer excess. The new India, if you will, with the old reservations – metal detectors must be negotiated airport-style and security guards frisk those who look like trouble. Murali and I wait for Mehta in the incongruously comical location of the TGI Friday's restaurant. Over-zealous waiters, weighed down by pin badges, greet us like family at Christmas time. We order two beers.

'If you ask if he still fixes matches he'll walk out,' Murali says. 'If you ask him if he is still a punter he'll walk out. If you ask him about '99, he'll walk out. He reckons he retired from the game years ago. I'm not so sure, though, you know? This guy has made a lot of money, a lot of money. You just don't give that up.'

Mehta has claimed he stopped being a punter in 1999 and said that he had been under suspicion for match-fixing because of nothing more than 'guilt by association'. Cricketers wanted to be with him because he was a 'social celebrity'. He has argued that it wasn't his fault he got invited to 'a lot of parties where cricketers land up'. Supercilious indeed.

'Tomorrow, if a photograph appears showing me with two players, does that mean they are into match-fixing? Can one impute motive?

Let's be realistic. I know lots of people as my status gives me the time to meet such people,' he once told Murali in an interview.

Murali's phone beeps. It is a text message from Mehta, who says he is going to be four hours late. 'I know what he's doing,' Murali says. 'There's a one-day series on.' [England are on tour in India.] 'He's sorting out his bets ... that's why he's so late.'

Murali and I drain our beers, twiddle our thumbs and amuse ourselves by tormenting the TGI staff by pretending it is my birthday. We get a free chocolate cake, although our ruse backfires when I am forced to stand on a chair and dance along to 'Happy Birthday'.

'If Mehta walks in now mate, you're screwed,' Murali laughs.

We leave Select City Walk for the Gymkhana, Murali's club, in an exclusive residential part of the city. 'This is where I get most of my stories,' he says as we walk through the lobby and towards the bar. As we swig beer and flick freshly roasted peanuts in our mouths, the discussion inevitably turns to how to deal with Mehta. 'Just be cool, don't say too much,' Murali says. 'I'll do the talking, make him feel at ease, you understand that?'

On our return, Mehta is waiting for us. He is sat in the corner, towards the back of the restaurant, away from the hullabaloo. The Bon Jovi song 'Living on a Prayer' is howling out of the stereo. He looks a picture of overindulgence. Everything about him is rotund, perhaps shaped by eating at his restaurant every day. His belly stretches the seams of a yellow Ralph Lauren polo shirt and I spot on his sockless feet a pair of Ferragamo loafers. His eyes narrow as his chubby cheeks squeeze them skywards when he welcomes Murali with a smile. But this is quickly devoured by a scowl when he sees me.

'Who's this?' he shoots back.

'This is Ed, good friend of mine, he's writing a book about match-fixing so it'll be good for you to talk.'

He doesn't walk. Is Mehta disarmed or disinterested? After some inane chit-chat I excuse myself, as previously agreed, so Murali can try to convince Mehta to stay. When I return he waves me to sit down, motions to the waiter for some beer and launches into a jokey tirade at Murali about the dull-witted police. 'You know, they pulled me in because they said Shobhan Mehta [the Mumbai bookmaker] was pictured at a player's wedding?' he scoffs. 'I said, "Guys, there's more than one Mehta in India. It doesn't work like that."'

'Yeah, Ed knows Shobhan,' Murali says. 'You're meeting him next week in Mumbai no?'

This is a curve ball. I do not know Shobhan Mehta, but I see where Murali is going with it.

'Sure,' I say casually as Mehta fixes me with a look of surprise.

'He's meeting you? He's a big bookie. One of the biggest. Why would he meet you?'

'I've been in touch with him for a couple of years, trying to get him to talk and hopefully I'll track him down next week.'

This is an off-the-cuff lie. But it works, as Mehta's next question proves.

'Tell me about your book?'

So I begin to unravel the story of the fixed World Cup semi-final between India and Pakistan to the man who, allegedly, fixed a previous tournament meeting between the sides. I tell him about the bookie, the contact in Dubai, the Twitter message, the time of its arrival, the minutiae of detail, the accuracy of the predicted fall of wickets. My astonishment that such a high-profile match could be tampered with.

'Why are you telling me this?' he says with a sneer. 'This isn't interesting. Every match is fixed.'

I wonder, briefly, whether a nerve has been touched. Is this boastful punter jealous that there is a rival of greater talent for conjuring results?

'Nothing surprises me at all,' he continues, whetting his whistle with a drink. 'This is a game, it is on television, there is a huge interest in bookmaking circles. There is a lot of money to be made. And they would have made a lot of money from that, by the sounds of it. With the way the odds would have fluctuated and they would know the fall of wickets.'

I ask him whether he would like to see the script.

'Why would I? This you have to understand. Bookmaking is a good business. But at every stage of life there is corruption. In any business, if you are a bureaucrat, law guy, media guy, politician, anything. I'm in the property business and when I want to build a property, at every stage I have to pay to get it done. So cricket is also a business.'

Mehta appears to enjoy being the lecturer. Playing to his immodest nature, a look of surprise, a shake of the head or a verbal expressing of disagreement prompts him to keep talking. He has more to prove. More to show off.

'The betting has become so big now. I see sometimes on Betfair millions of dollars. There are people who are manipulating the odds. They are accurate. If they tell you they will score 60 runs in 15 overs, it'll be 60.' Mehta laughs. 'They score 53 or 54 in 12 overs – how can they stop at 60?

'They are professional. They control the game. You are writing your book. Every page is under your control. Likewise, every ball is under their control ... what they want to do. They start bowling wides, no-balls ... When we are watching the match, we don't know how the captain is setting the field or which bowler is. That is the worst play. Look at the cut shot. You just move that player four steps aside, just four steps, and give that slight room and ask the bowler to bowl on the off stump ... he'll do it ... the runs will start flowing.'

Mehta looks pleased with himself. He starts to chuckle away and the laughter rises to a crescendo through his next story. 'Everything is fixed, my friend, I'm telling you now, ten overs, 15 overs, 20 and then the middle overs. The big betting is the outcome of the match and the betting for runs every ten overs. Outcome of the match is big money. The higher the odds, the better it is. Suppose India get out for 200, England will be favourites. If they are 60 for no loss and then they lose the match, from there that's big money. You know what I'm saying? Or India score 300 and they [England] chase and they get close, that's big money. The odds [moving his hands to denote prices varying]. When you play odds, you multiply the odds.'

A bit more doubt for good measure. If it is so prevalent, why do more stories not come out?

'Why do think it never comes out about Aussies?' he says. 'Because they keep it together in house. They don't talk. The Pakistanis ... the captain will take the big slice, maybe 200k, and feeds that through to the players. The less important the player, the less they get. So when you have a situation when it is not equal, it is easier for people to talk, you know?

'With this no-ball thing [the Southwark spot-fixing trial involving the three Pakistan players and their agent] also that has no monetary value … it is just convincing the guy that "I know the players". No monetary value. "The third ball a no-ball" … it's just that "OK boss, I'll show you that man is mine". "How will you show me?" … "He'll do a no-ball on the third ball."

'In Pakistan they can't even afford to live properly back home. Once you get into it, you can't get out. In India the cricketers are basically middle class. Sportsmen are from middle-class backgrounds. The British and their royalty started the game, in India only the princes played the game. But now it's middle class …'

Mehta then mentions a name which causes such shock that I drop my bottle of beer, which smashes on the floor. This causes Mehta to look under the table … at the broken glass, at the yellowy liquid lapping at his expensive loafers, but not, mercifully, at the tape recorder I have, unbeknown to both my companions, in the palm of my hand, outstretched under the table so as to get it as close to Mehta as possible. I fear my anxiety, each time a TGI waiter returns with a mop, is palpable.

'There is more and more money involved in this game. So much. Anyone will get into it. XXXX XXXX also can't come out of it; he has connections. He's just … he's a big name. He can't do it in the open. He can't get out of it. Once you're into that … '

The dropping of this name is a bomb blast to the thought process. A hundred questions splinter and fragment, all rushing for the vacuum. Mehta, perhaps sensing he has said too much and spotting the fire of sensation in the eyes of the two journalists sat in front of him, meanders down a less interesting path about how there was potential to make reasonable sums back in the 1990s by betting on a batsman to be out hit wicket. Offshore gambling sites would offer odds of up to 80–1 about a batsman being out in such a way. 'These kind of bets, they get exposed,' Mehta says.

It is not until Mehta begins to discuss another betting market – 'You can bet on players' runs. Big betting in Punjab for this' – that I can once again ask about XXXX XXXX: 'Is that what he does then?'

But Mehta does not rise to the bait.

'His value would be 40-odd runs,' he says. 'You bet more than 40 or less than 40. But suppose you say [bet] he makes less than 40 for 10,000 rupees per run. He scores 20, 10,000 rupees he'll score less than 40, so he scores 20 so you win 20 runs – 20 runs at 10,000 rupees per run. It can multiply like that [20 x 10,000 rupees = winnings].'

Mehta appears to be describing spread betting, in the English gambling industry's sense of the word. In India spread betting is the term often used for a fixed-odds bet and fixed-odds stake when a market is over or under. For example, one might bet £10 at fractional odds of 5–6 that over or under 50 runs are scored in the first ten overs of a one-day international. If you lose, you are £10 poorer. It is, however, the first time I have heard that spread betting of the sort an English gambler might be more familiar with is available in India.

A spread-betting website in the UK explains the medium thus: 'If someone asked you to guess their age you might say "somewhere between 35 and 40". In the same way, a spread bookmaker makes a prediction by offering a range of 35–40. If you wanted to bet you would either "sell" at 35 or "buy" at 40, depending on whether you thought the person was younger or older. For every year you are right or wrong, you win or lose your stake. So if the person is 40 and I have staked £1 on a sell at 35, I lose £5.'

In the example of XXXX XXXX, if he scores 20 and I have sold for £1 at 40, I win 20. If he scores 60, I lose £20. Notice how the amounts you win or lose are not fixed like they are with traditional odds bets.

Before I can ask Mehta another question he is up and off his seat and making his excuses. He shakes Murali's hand, and then mine, which has been warmed by the recorder I've been gripping for the past 20 minutes. I ask for his contact details, but he bluntly says: 'Murali has them.' Then he is off. Not quite waddling, but his stride is one that would shake less sturdy foundations than Select City.

'When you went to the loo he said: "Who the fuck have you brought?"' Murali laughed. 'You know, the first thing he will do now is call Shobhan Mehta. His face when you said you were meeting him. Fuck on toast!'

CHAPTER 9

'FIXER'

It is easy to find Dheeraj Dixit. Helpfully (although not for his wife, who has become exasperated at journalists seeking interviews), the Indian media plastered his address across sport and news sections for much of September 2011. The cricket photographer, who travelled the world following the India team, had been accused of match-fixing. The claims were made by Veena Malik, a Bollywood actress of Pakistani origin who added the titillation to the story that had everything: the Pakistan spot-fixing scandal.

Veena was a former girlfriend of Mohammad Asif, the Pakistan bowler who was found guilty of producing no-balls to order. She had been on Indian television to expose Dixit as a fixer, a go-between. She claimed that Dixit and Asif had met in Bangkok to discuss fixing and she provided the ICC's ACSU with phone records in an attempt to prove it.

Veena, speaking on television, said of Dixit's claims: 'Come up with the proof. That's the easiest thing to do … the character assassination of a woman. I knew it already that Mr Dheeraj will make this stupid kind of statement.'

Dixit, who admits to being 'very, very good friends with Asif', did not keep his silence either and an old-fashioned war of words erupted between the two. The Indian tabloid newspapers were in rapture. Dixit said that it was Veena who was the go-between for Mazhar Majeed, the players' agent jailed at the Southwark trial of Asif, Salman Butt and Mohammad Amir.* Dixit has alleged that Veena had approached him

---

* Veena Malik was given the opportunity to respond to Dixit's claims. Her spokeswoman, Nisha Sahdev, said: 'I have spoken with my client and we wish not to comment on something we find is baseless allegations from a third party.'

to put her in contact with Indian cricketers. Dixit is 'known of' by the ACSU, whilst Veena has been 'spoken with'.

Regardless of who was speaking the truth, Veena appeared to get one thing right: Dixit knows a lot of Indian celebrities. This much is evident as I sit on the sofa of his apartment in the wholesome north-Delhi neighbourhood of Pitampura. There is a picture of him, his wife and two children with Sachin Tendulkar hanging on the wall behind me. But that is not all.

'Look, I show you,' he says, beginning to scroll through pictures on his iPhone with various past and present international cricket personalities, interrupted by other stars and the odd tourist snap: Waqar Younis, Danish Kaneria ('in New Zealand'), the House of Commons, the mayor of Bromley ('receiving award for good pictures'), Benazir Bhutto ('she has died'), MS Dhoni, VVS Laxman, Puja Bedhi, a Bollywood actress, MS Dhoni again ('me and Dhoni in his hotel room'), Preity Zinta, another Bollywood actress, 'Pakistan winning the Twenty20 World Cup … here I am carrying the trophy at Lord's … I am carrying the trophy here too …,' Sachin Tendulkar, Simon Taufel the umpire, Dhoni again, this time at Lord's, Tendulkar ('at the Lord's again, he is a very good man'). Get the picture?

Dixit began a career in photography in 1984, starting out as a wedding photographer and then progressing to photographing Indian celebrities like Shahrukh Khan for Bollywood films. He opened two studios in Delhi and became a cricket photographer in 1994. He calls it a 'new innings' and followed India on tour. He can't remember in how many countries he has watched India play.

'My way of taking the pictures was different,' he says. 'All the photographers, they sit together. I always sat far away because I know if they click, the picture angle would be the same. So I wanted to take the pictures separately, a different angle. The cricketers like it, they start liking my pictures. They want a copy. I give free copies to all players. I never ask for money. Tendulkar has definitely, definitely got some. The players were glad to meet me.'

Since Veena made her allegations, however, Dixit has not worked. The BCCI has revoked his press accreditation. Hanging on another wall opposite the family shot with Tendulkar is a BCCI calendar. The month October. The year 2009. Scattered on the coffee table beneath it are the computer science textbooks of his 17-year-old son, who told me as I waited for his father to arrive for our meeting: 'I'm hoping to go to university ... he will decide which one I go to.'

Dixit is an odd character. He has an earnestness when speaking, particularly about his photography, which is charming, but when quizzed about Veena's allegations this proves to be fleeting. He is not as sure of himself and he becomes jokey, almost too keen to be friendly, like when I arrived he made what was at first an amusing joke about his wife being his girlfriend. But he made the joke twice more. It was terribly awkward after the third telling. Whether serious or slippery, he rarely holds my gaze, looking away quickly.

'I am innocent,' he says. 'I lost my faith to everybody. No one is coming out to help me out because whatever I have done ... I am suffering.' Out comes the iPhone again.

'This is [Virender] Sehwag's number, Viru. You want to see Sachin? I got the Sachin. Sachin Tendulkar. I show you the message from Sachin. I wrote to him, and he gave me a Diwali message last year.' It reads: 'thanks a lot, wish you and your family v happy diwali. Cheers'. 'Sachin help me always. He knows me. I show you this one message.'

'Dear sachin, i would like to draw your attention to my carrier [career] in cricket photography which is breathing on last stage due to bcci non co-op towards me. I really need your help to sort out the matter of the past controversy. Bcci have rejected press accred for uk tour. I want to tell the truth to enable to start work again. If poss plse allow me to call you.'

'He said, "Wait for few months, wait for the right time and you will do your work again." I am waiting for that. I don't know when it will be.'

It could be quite some time. Veena has damaged Dixit professionally to the point that his 'reputation' precedes him. Vinay was sure that he was a link man between players and corruptors. The BCCI and the players who Dixit thought were his friends have cast him into the wilderness.

'You ask anyone in the game and they will tell you I am a good man. I have good contacts with Sachin, MS Dhoni, Sri Lanka players, Pakistan players, West Indies players, English and New Zealand.'

'Which English people?'

Dixit names one former and two current English players.

'I see the faces, I know what the players demand, they are also a human being. I am friends and I can get them things, extra things. If they need some, like, special food, like dal makhani, chicken curry or Nandos, I bring it. Sometimes I cook myself with the potato bread. They like it. I cook so many times for them. Sometimes 30 or 40 breads for all players. I put the symbol on the bread, this is for Tendulkar, this is for MS [Dhoni], this is for [Gautam] Gambhir.'

It was this kind of apparent access to players – although Dixit's desire for self-promotion makes one doubt if he can really call any player a 'friend' – that attracted Veena to Dixit. Dixit claims she called his home three times 'after 12am' when he was on tour with India in Bangladesh in January 2010, his wife answering each time. I suggest his wife must have thought he had another woman, which made his earlier jokes seem all the more inappropriate.

'Yeah. Veena Malik was just telling her, "I like him, I love him, he's a very good guy." My wife says, "If you love him, do you know he is a married man, I am his wife." She said, "OK, is it possible to give his mobile number in Bangladesh?" She gave it. Veena Malik called me three days running. She told me, "I am Hindu, people in Pakistan are not safe." She was trying to get emotional intimacy. She was trying to make me feel sorry for her. She wants to get closer to players. She wanted to meet Indian players. She also took the name of a few players, who she met, but I don't want to disclose the names because it is sensitivity.'

'She met India players?'

'Yeah.'

The reason why Veena was keen to meet players is a twist to the Pakistan spot-fixing saga, according to Dixit. Veena, he says, worked for Majeed and Asif.

'Majeed's a very cunning man. I don't know him, I've never met him. What was his secret? He just wants to get all players to fix the matches.'

Dixit explains that Majeed was beginning to lose his grip on the Pakistan players, fearing that they were being bought off by rival match-fixers and that he needed new players to attempt to corrupt. Pakistan players were breaking promises made to Majeed on fixes, instead selling their service to the highest bidder and making sure there was 'extra money' paid for 'swapping sides'.

'Majeed's scared of all Pakistan players. If Majeed promise to give $100,000 to Asif to fix the match, then that is Majeed's risk. They agree on it. But Majeed risks someone coming to pay more. That is a big loss for Majeed. So that is why Majeed was scared. He might have lost that money. He was not happy with the Pakistan players. Sometimes Veena Malik told me that they had ditched Majeed. That is why he was looking for Indian players. They demand four times bigger money. She told me. That is why she approached me. She thought it would get her close to India players. I was the only man who would get around them. Asif told her only one man can do it and "that Dheeraj". I was close with Asif. My friend. Yes, we were in Thailand [on holiday], but there was nothing shady. I helped him with many things when he came to Delhi to play in IPL, that's where I first met him. Now, as soon as I heard he was in match-fixing I don't know him.

'She offered me big sums. She wants me to be go-between. I said "no". I didn't take a single penny. It is not my culture. She told me, "Come to London, Pakistan matches are fixed in London." The last tour. I said: "How can you say that?" and she replied: "This year's matches are already fixed."'

If Dixit is to be believed, then the timing of this information pre-dates Pakistan's tour of England. Recalling that he said Veena contacted him on 13 January 2010, that is around seven months before the first Test at Nottingham. 'I think she wanted to show … I think she wanted to give me money to attract Indian players. She said "I can give you 15 lakh rupees [£18,000]." That a lot of money. "If you fulfil your requirements."'

I ask Dixit whether it would have been so bad to take the money from Veena to introduce his friends in the India team. 'I can't do it 'cos my culture never allows me. I earn money through my hand. Not through dodgy things. This is the cheating. You are playing with the emotions of the cricket lovers. Once she offered me, I was scared she was not the lady I can rely.'

'But everyone is at it, Dheeraj?' I say.

'Not me.'

In fact, Dixit, who insists he only met Veena once but spoke 'many times' on the phone, says that he attempted to play whistle-blower by recording Veena's offers. He says he went to a newspaper reporter whom he regarded as a friend. 'I called a senior reporter in India that some girl from Pakistan is offering me money to fix matches. She had also told me to look for big businessman in India and if you find him I'll oblige you with handsome money. Give me some money, give me some business-man, give me bookies. Everything she said I told the reporter. I don't want to take his name. He told me how to record her voice. But I didn't know how to operate the voice recording when someone is calling you. I don't know how to record incoming calls. She called me and asked: "What did you think about? I've already met the Indian player." I can't say who. I will be in trouble.'

I mention the names of two players I have heard a lot of talk about. 'It's them isn't it?'

'You can do the permutation, but I will not take the name.'

I press Dixit again for the names of the two players.

Dixit shakes his head and wags his finger. 'I will not take the name!' Then he is off again, smearing his nemesis. 'Veena told me, "If you want to see my quality of work, how to operate the players, how to fix the match, come to London and I'll show you." I asked through my news channels [contacts in journalism]: "Something is happening. If you help me do a sting operation, if you want to work with me, come with me to London." They told me to leave it, it won't work. So I did leave it.'

At that moment Dixit's wife interrupts us with offerings of chai and barfi, an Indian dessert. The barfi is sweet, sickly almost. Dixit does not pause. He goes on to declare that it is possible that a team can be 'split down the middle', one side working for one bookmaker or punter and others operating for another 'Both groups are involved with the fixings,' he says.

'Suppose this group is earning so much in fixing, they try to demolish the plan of the other group. [The players can be] working for another bookie. So in one team you have two groups, one trying to win the game and the other trying to lose it.'

Pakistan's record at the time was poor. In 2010 they lost 67 per cent of matches they played in Test, one-day or Twenty20 cricket. Dixit repeats the widely reported allegation – mentioned in the Southwark trial – that the Sydney Test against Australia in 2010, which Pakistan lost, was fixed. Recordings of Majeed boasting to the *News of the World* that 'Let me tell you the last Test we did. It was the second Test against Australia in Sydney ...' were played to the court.

When I challenge him about why he is so sure of this information, suggesting that his plea of innocence seems a contradiction, he is quick with his catchphrase, 'Veena Malik told me.' These four words now accompany every nugget of information, including the job description of the fixer, and the tricks they use to get close to players. When pressed for these details, Dixit retreats into his shady shell once again. I try to ensure he holds my gaze.

'OK, OK, I tell you. Suppose Pakistan team playing with England, OK? Pakistan staying in Marriott [hotel], OK? But the fixers know where they are staying two, three months before. They book the hotel. They know. They very professional. They know people in the cricket board. Veena Malik told me. They are paying the selectors money.

'The first transaction is paying the people in the cricket board to find out where they [the team] are staying. Suppose they are staying on the seventh floor. That is the ICC code of conduct. No one can go, without asking anybody else, on the seventh floor. But they pay the board money, to the hotelier, they stay on the same floor. The ICC ACSU put the cameras there as well, but if they book the room no one can stop them.'

'So they get the board to book them in as if they are in the team?'

'Yes. It is not possible to keep an eye on everything all the time. They are paying guests like everyone else. So the ACSU cameras are not useful. The fixers talk to the players on their hotel phones to agree to meet and then they go out in small groups and then they fix things. The ICC ACSU warned the Pakistan tour manager that there are people looking suspicious, "Please don't allow these people on the seventh floor," but they didn't stop it. That is why the match got fixed. The no-balls. The

ICC warned them because he [Mazhar Majeed] was caught on camera. He was always familiar with Salman Butt, Kamran Akmal and two more players. The ICC warned them he is looking suspicious. "Keep a watch on that. Make a suspension. Don't allow him to go to the same floor as the players." Why is he there? But they didn't care.

'Also, some selectors pick players on who will be good to take the money. They pick a player because he will be good to fix a match. This is, you know, how do I know? 'Cos Veena Malik told me. She never told me how much they pay. The Veena never comes in front of the players. She works behind the camera. Behind the players. Like Asif is the main guy of her. She is just like a puppet [master] telling him to "do it, do it".

'Money is the main factor. If you give them [the player] £10,000, you say, "Just go, take it, just go." This is for pub, girls, shopping, whatever. Purchase it. "Go. Go [thrusting his hand out in front of him with his palm flat and fingers pointing to the sky]." This what they tell the players. When it comes match day they say: "Do you want more money?" "Yes." "Then do one more thing, I want some work, yeah? If you do it I'll give you five times more money than I gave you yesterday." Once the money has been taken, it's a bug. They can't come out.

'That small thing would be something in a cricket match. Like, don't score more than 20. This is a test. But not a no-ball. You can't bet on that.'

I ask Dixit what happens when a player says he doesn't want any more money after taking an initial payment of £10,000. 'I've never seen a player do that,' he says, looking me in the eye and holding my gaze for the first time. 'Everybody likes money. I also love it, but I love a different kind of money. If you are a stranger to me and give me money, "Why is he doing this?" I think. Nobody gives a glass of water free of cost in this world.'

'Hold on,' I say. 'You said "I've never seen a player" turn down more money?'

'Veena Malik told me.'

One wants to believe Dixit. Yet his weight of knowledge about the fixing game is great. He has no hesitation in questioning the India versus Pakistan World Cup semi-final, too. 'Ah yes, Mohali, Mohali. I heard the same thing. But I am not interested to listen to these things. I got a text message as well to my friend's mobile and he showed me the same certain amount of runs. Wickets in quick succession. This is the style to make big money.

'A name like Deepak is a guy in Dubai. He is Indian and, I think, was involved in the fixing of that.'

Why did he not go to the ICC with such information? As well as the World Cup semi-final, Dixit claimed he had been told the results of matches that Pakistan were playing before they had taken place. A call to the ICC would have rid him of the apparent pestilence of Veena Malik and almost certainly saved his job. The BCCI would not have revoked his credentials had he been an informer for the ACSU.

Nor did he get in touch when, according to Indian media, a Mumbai bookie who had been linked with Chhota Rajan's gang telephoned him. 'He called me once. He wanted to meet some India players from me. I said, "Why do you want to meet? If you have some prospects, some assignment, some endorsement, then tell me first 'cos sometimes I do the PR for players, approach companies for them to do endorsement business."'

Why did this man, whose life has apparently been ruined, not go to the ACSU for help when he was taking calls from the associates of crime lords and possible match-fixers? 'I was afraid. After the match-fixing allegation against me by Veena Malik I was facing threatening calls, particularly from Pakistan, +92 numbers. They said, "You ruined our life, I'll ruin your life."'

Dixit does, at least, not blame Veena for the death threats, but I indulge him his storytelling. 'How did the death threats make you feel?'

'I'm OK, still alive. I am worried, but I'm a habitual worrier [laughs]. Do you want to see the bullets?'

'Oh, there has been an actual attempt on your life? The stage is yours, Dheeraj. Tell me.'

'From start to finish?'

'Yes.'

'I show you the pictures on my phone. They didn't find the bullet. It went through the glass. Then they hit me with sticks. Pieces of glass cut my face. These are pools of blood. This happened on 10 September [2011]. This is the police. That's the blood.

'I was going to meet my friend for coffee. He is a restaurant owner – lots of policemen here, look, trying to find bullet – they chase me for five kilometres, the guy who shot at me. I realised someone was following me. There were three people sitting in the car. I was at the traffic light. They were looking at me. Staring. Wouldn't stop. This was unusual. So I thought I would drive off quickly.

'It was a bit of a car chase. If I slowed down, they slowed down. "Something is dangerous," I thought. Then I started very fast. I didn't stop. Fast, fast. Suddenly after two kilometres, one of the guys from the window seat was swinging the leather bag. "Come, I'll kill you now. How can you run fast, I'll kill you now." One-handed. Left hand on the car wheel, right outside the window. This means "come, I'll kill you". I didn't know why. I was scared. Why he threatening me? I moved so fast. Then they fired one bullet, it went like this "schoom". From behind the driver's window. I was in the extreme right; they were on the extreme left. He doesn't want to come closer to me 'cos I had a big car and they were in a small car. They were trying to hit from the third lane, so they shoot. "Crack!" Missed. I was totally scared. Then I drive mercilessly. Quick, ya? I didn't care who was in my way. They fired one more, but that also missed. Then I tried to block the way. They are also driving very fast. They came on the first lane; I came on the third lane. I didn't want this 'cos it would be very easy to hit me. They shot from across straight at me and it broke the glass. I was a bit more scared now. Boom-boom-boom my heart beating. Sweat.

'I didn't know what was happening, my family's faces coming in my mind. I was driving fast, about 120 kilometres an hour. Suddenly I saw a big traffic jam ahead at the bridge so I changed direction, there was also a traffic jam there. I thought, "I will be gone now." But they had no bullet. They come with the stick. Hitting, hitting me. But the police were there and they saw them, I ran back to the car and drove the wrong way down the motorway to get away.'

Dixit blames the henchmen of Dawood Ibrahim of D-Company fame. It is the first time that the infamous gangster's name has been mentioned since I arrived in India on this journey. Dixit is adamant when pressed.

'This guy is bad news, Dheeraj,' I say. 'Even I've heard of him.' He is not one for casting nervous glances over his shoulder, however, instead puffing out of his chest, turning up his chin and declaring: 'My water and food is written in my destiny, no? No one can snatch it. If it is written I will be killed.'

Having left Dheeraj helping his son with his homework at the kitchen table, I am reminded of how an ACSU officer described the men whose job it is to 'get their hooks in' to players: 'They are really engaging characters, they have the gift of the gab and you end up liking them when you really shouldn't. That's their skill.'

Dheeraj, eventually, is difficult not to like, despite his troubling knowledge of corruption in cricket and the methods to which players can fall prey.

CHAPTER 10

THE MAIDAN

The Maidan Oval, Mumbai, four in the afternoon. An oppressive sun, its heat dissipating as it dips west into the Arabian sea, casts shadows across the golf-course rough of the grass, providing welcome respite to the hundreds of amateur cricketers absorbed in their matches.

To spend time at the Maidan is to understand India's obsession with the sport and the purpose of this brief sketch is to attest that the humdrum cliché that 'Indians love their cricket' is true. This is a yearning, a cultural compulsion which cosies up to a neurosis. To watch the countless games during any minute, hour or day is to behold a very public love affair. A fatal attraction that punters, bookmakers and gangsters are able to exploit.

Like any relationship, it is far from plain sailing. To sit and watch for an hour or so is to mostly observe tiffs and tantrums. The air surrounding this much-needed green lung in the smoggy, southern business district is punctuated by the cries of the indignant and ill-treated. Matches come to a standstill as rows rumble over whether the fat kid, chest heaving as he argues his case, was short of his ground on a run-out; bats are flung after leg-before decisions; umpires are rushed by wide-eyed and open-mouthed players, aghast at injustices. There is gesturing and hands on hips and much uttering of India's favourite insult 'gaand mao saale' (go fuck your arse). Then the game restarts.

To draw a wholly unruly picture of the Maidan would be unfair, however. It is a retreat from the push and shove of the city. That much is clear when you enter its gates and read the signs displaying its rules: 'No commercialisation through advertisements/posters/banners or in any other manner is permitted on the fence or in the Maidan; no cooking; no cattle, no horses, stray dogs; no hawkers and peddlers are allowed; cricket pitch lessees can sub-lease/rent their pitches only for the purpose of cricket; in general, except cricket, no other organised activity is permitted.'

The reverent hum of this place is such that the rules are adhered to, even by the rascally stray dogs and hawkers who ordinarily have no respect for such things. It is a sacred place. The Maidan was rescued from developers in the 1990s. The city had been encroaching for years and it was once part of a vast open space known as the esplanade which lay beyond the old Mumbai fort ramparts. Oval stands for Organisation for Verdant Ambience and Land.

At the vast boundary edge, men sleeping off the exertion of their morning's work lie among the shredded skin of the palm trees, oblivious to the threat of balls fizzing and ricocheting into the foliage and railings that surround them. Through the Maidan's heart is the pathway that links east to west or the university library to the 1930s art-deco apartment blocks. White-shirted office workers hurry through, a tight grip on tiffin boxes, furtively casting eyes left and right for the stray ball that could spoil their spruceness. At one point, a woman clad resplendently in a green sari and carrying a box of boiled sweets, no doubt for Diwali celebrations, was so unnerved by the potential damage of a cricket ball ripping the air as it travelled towards her ankles, that she dropped her sweets, scattering them across the path. The street kids playing nearby helped her pick them up, with one hand returning a fistful of the goodies, the other stealing two or three for their pocket. A watchful eye is a necessity in the Maidan.

It has six 'marked-out' cricket pitches, which are leased by the owners for a small fee. These overlap to the extent that a fielder standing at long off will be precariously placed at third slip in the game taking place behind him. Not that this is an inconvenience. Often enthusiasm for one game is matched for the one next door; players chasing and pouncing on balls from far afield matches, whose players get their attention by imploring them to 'catch!'

These are mostly inter-school matches. From the boundary, the batting side lounge under canopies, keeping score on blackboards with distressed metal number plates. When a batsman is out he swaps batting pads and gloves as he passes the youth taking his place. When he returns to his teammates they pat him on the back and offer commiserations. The rest kick their heels through the dust as they suck ice water from plastic bags or chew on channa.

Alongside these six games are the scores of knockabout matches in the style of the back-garden game one might have played with a sibling when young. The bat might be a piece of wood and the stumps bark found in the undergrowth around the edge. A rock at the other end denotes the full 22 yards. A bowler, lithe and graceful, charges in with the promise of a memorable action only to deliver a blatant chuck. It is curious how few bowl with legal actions. No one complains. The glory of 'bowling' fast is equal to that of the batsman who swings through the line of the ball with abandon, sending it whence it came with greater speed.

Hanif is one such chucker. He is lucent in a gold-trim kaftan which flashes as he bounds in with all his might, the dust from the scorched red clay soil fogging his feet. Every day he comes here to play with his friends from a nearby Muslim college. They all take turns to bat or keep wicket, a most important job, as their tennis ball has a tendency to fly through the railings and onto the road. It can be ten minutes before they get it back, if at all.

'Yes! Yes! You English person!' Hanif, who must be about 15, shouts to me. 'Come be umpire please, please?'

I agree … to much excitement and laughter. In turn each of Hanif's friends comes up to shake my hand. Hanif gives me his mobile phone and sunglasses to hold as he returns to his run-up, whipping up the dust once more and delivering a blatant 'throw' … It is fast – of course it is – too fast for the batsman, who hits the ball straight up into the air to be caught by the wicketkeeper listening to his iPod. There is much celebration. But I have my arm outstretched to denote a no-ball.

'No-ball? No, no, you are wrong!' Hanif laughs as everyone bar the batsman looks at me aghast.

'You are throwing it,' I say. 'Bowl properly.'

'Yes, you right. I am very sorry. I do it properly,' Hanif replies, shaking my hand. 'You are very fair to me.'

An Englishman can be in demand at the Maidan for umpiring duties in impromptu games or for bored cricketers wanting someone new to talk to while they wait their turn to bat or to avoid fielding duty. Kamran joins me on a bench and asks the usual questions of a tourist: 'Where are you from?' 'Are you on holiday or business' and 'Do you like cricket?'

He is wearing an India one-day shirt and is appearing in a tournament for his hotel against other establishments across the city who play in the colours of Sri Lanka, England, South Africa and Pakistan.

'Yes, we love cricket,' he says. 'We play tournament every Diwali. I am hotel worker, a cleaner and we all look forward to this moment.'

I ask him about the team colours as South Africa take on Sri Lanka in front of us. 'It makes it more special for me. We get them from Colaba Causeway market [a tourist trap near the Gateway to India] for very good price. Do you want? I get you very, very good price …

'As you can see, I am India. We play England in this afternoon and we very much hope we beat you. But most of all we want to beat Pakistan! They are bloody terrorists and very stupid match-fixers!' he laughs. 'It is OK, I can say this because I am Muslim. We are all Muslim. It is our tournament.'

My discussion with Kamran is interrupted by a small boy tapping me on the shoulder. He has been sent by a group of four or five older boys to ask me to play. His name is Abhi and I have seen him before. He works on one of the sugarcane juice stalls, passing the cane through the grinder over and over again for hours on end and then selling a full glass for ten rupees. At night he sleeps on a bed of sugarcane resting on the roof of the stall.

'Come, come,' he says and I follow. Every three strides he turns round and beckons me to keep following. His friends are excitable, unable to contain their glee at the Englishman who has joined their game and agreed to bat. They leap and jump and dance and rush over to shake hands, mimicking the shot I should play: a leg side heave for six. I face six balls, all thrown, of course, and do enough to restore the reputation of England's batsmen – England are losing heavily in the one-day international series. After my over the novelty has worn off and the boys want to get on with their game. 'You wicketkeeper now,' says one boy, who appears to be in charge, wearing a Mumbai Indians, the IPL franchise, T-shirt.

So I keep wicket. The tennis ball stings the hands as it leaps from the rock-hard surface, propelled by more illegal deliveries. Abhi comes to join me, asking questions in Hindi and giggling when I cannot answer. His hands caper when he talks. His bare feet dance. The 'stumps' come up to his neck. He shows me his bat, a Gray Nicholls Scoop which has seen better days. In blue biro he has scrawled 'INDIA' on its face and drawn a World Cup trophy. 'Favourite player?' I ask him, 'Tendulkar?' He shakes his head, and leaps up to brandish his bat, which looks unwieldy in his grasp, playing an expansive cover drive. 'Raina!' he shouts.

Pandemonium breaks out once more when an Irishwoman watching from the path approaches the head boy and asks to have a bat. Abhi is off, tugging at her sleeve, jabbering away. Others skip in from fielding positions to give her advice. Three times she swings and misses in that taut-armed, repressed manner of the non-cricketer. From the fourth ball she manages contact, the ball looping directly towards to Abhi who steadies himself for his moment of glory. The head boy, though, wants to be the hero and with Abhi unaware, approaches from behind, stretches out his arms and takes the catch above Abhi's head. He sets off on a victory lap, others following. Abhi trails behind, scowling and shouting at the dishonour. In the distance, the floodlights of the Wankhede Stadium, venue of India's World Cup final triumph, angle in such a way that they strain their necks, as if trying to glimpse future talent.

CHAPTER 11

THE TAJ

It was on the morning of 26 November 2008 that the Taj Palace Hotel was attacked. Gunmen raked guests with bullets and blasted more with bombs. When they were sated they moved on to other targets in Mumbai.

From my room I can see where the boats carrying the terrorists, who were trained in Pakistan, disembarked; the Gateway to India is a monument to the country's independence, as it was the entrance and exit point for forces of Empire rule. Before even the first trigger had been squeezed, the terrorists had pinched the nerve of a fiercely nationalistic country.

The consequences of that bloody day were terrible and tragic. If it had occurred in any other country apart from India, to discuss its impact on cricket – a trifling sport everywhere else – would be churlish in the extreme. Yet it is appropriate for this story. Regardless of the true tapestry of that Mohali semi-final afternoon, Pakistan's cricketers were cast into the wilderness in the aftermath of the Mumbai terror attacks. They were banned from India and its cash cow, the IPL, opening up a gulf in earning potential between themselves and the rest of the international fraternity. Pakistan instantly became the bottom feeders.

Consigned to the cricket wilderness, it is easy to imagine a bookie or punter offering large sums to a Pakistan player to manipulate a match, convincing the target that a few extra quid would come in handy, particularly when their peers were buying houses, fast cars, yachts. From such a lowly platform Mazhar Majeed's spot-fixing scam was built.

In the marbled opulence of the Taj's lobby is a memorial entitled 'In Loving Memory' featuring the names of the dead and bearing the epitaph 'For now and forever you will always inspire us'. Looking at it, one gets a hint of the panic and sense of injustice that would have risen up in India had Pakistan made it to the World Cup final in 2011 … at the expense of the victim. Back to open old wounds. Thank goodness it did not happen.

Today at the Taj the security is tight and fierce. There are four armour-plated vehicles with military print blocking the road that runs along the seafront and intersects the hotel and the Gateway to India. Special forces soldiers, dressed all in black, brandish sub-machine guns. Their thick-bristled moustaches on immovable upper lips have menace. They do not flicker when the whooping and hollering begins as the India and England cricketers disembark from their respective team buses.

England look a weary lot. Dead-eyed, they have seen this welcome before ... the fourth time on this trip ... the 24th time in the last six months. Some muster a smile; others look down, lost in the music that fills their ears from oversized headphones. The rest have that self-important, middle-distance stare which says to the autograph hunters and picture pushers 'not now, busy'. It is a demeanour honed by the experienced players, the veterans. Yet Kevin Pietersen, an expert, does not quite pull it off, his eye distracted by a burly Australian moving in from his flank with an oversized Pentax. The Aussie manages to get close enough to Pietersen, who keeps walking, to steal an image for posterity with the granite-mugged batsman. 'Not very sociable, was he?' he says to his friend as they admire their work in the viewfinder.

The trudge and drag in England's collective gait is that of a beaten side – they are 3–0 down in the five-match one-day series. India's play-ers, feted as heroes even when they take out the trash at home, take the bonhomie in their stride. MS Dhoni holds aloft the series trophy for a giddy public, hands are shaken, backs are patted. The Indians still listen to their music, and have the vainglorious stare, but shoulders are back and noses try to sniff the ceiling.

The posturing and preening all looks rather foolish, though, as the players converge on the lobby lifts at the same time. There is a deliciously awkward moment as the rivals are forced to acknowledge each other's presence. Embarrassed glances, looking at watches, humming the elevator song. Two or three players are disconcerted enough to step back towards to the throng and risk a photoshoot and autographer's cramp.

As evening draws in, and the crowds have dispersed, the players quite happily stroll about the hotel. Andy Flower, the England coach, holds a press conference by the pool for a dozen or so journalists holding Dictaphones in their outstretched hands, hoping to be fed juicy morsels. Tim Abraham, the Sky Sports reporter, rows with hotel staff about filming permission.

Abraham gets his shot with Flower, somewhere among the foliage of the pool so as not to give away the Taj's secrets. They are a sensitive bunch for good reason. As Flower wheels away with his mini suitcase, there is another uncomfortable moment. Duncan Fletcher, Flower's adversary, is coming in the opposite direction, and the two exchange inelegant nods before hurrying off.

In the main restaurant, England's inexperienced squad members dine in one corner. Ravi Bopara, Jonny Bairstow, Scott Borthwick and Jade Dernbach giggle between mouthfuls of fine food. In another corner Gautam Gambhir, the India batsman, chats with friends. Kevin Pietersen has a mooch around the shopping arcade. The fast bowler Steve Finn heads to the gym. A clique of journalists make themselves comfortable at the bar. This is the downtime of the international cricket tourist and it is at times like these – in lobbies, restaurants and bars – that the ACSU fears players will be exposed to approaches from corruptors. Somewhere among the patrons, one might suppose, are the ACSU's spotters, lurking behind grandiose furniture, hiding behind pillars, peering over the top of newspapers, primed to leap out at any moment when an undesirable comes into view.

The reality may be less *Tinker Tailor Soldier Spy*. Holed up in a stuffy room in the bowels of the complex, the ACSU's spotter may be watching CCTV pictures of the entrance and exit, scanning grainy images for the faces of punters and bookmakers known to the unit. There are cameras, too, on every hallway on whatever floor the players are staying on, metal detectors as soon as one leaves the lift and a security guard slumped, slack-backed in those awfully uncomfortable-looking gold-painted conference-style hard chairs. Does this really reassure players or is it more to satisfy the ICC and the ACSU that they are doing something? It has to be the latter. No punter or bookie known to the ACSU would waltz into the team hotel. Any meeting would be clandestine, away from the glare and attention of this transitory circus, in restaurants or private homes.

Of course, if the face of an agent of illegal fortune is not known to the ACSU, then once they have passed under the steely gaze of the special forces, negotiated the metal detectors, been handed back their mobile phone and wallet by the muscular-buttocked women police officers in tight khaki trousers, they too can stroll the lobby, eat at the restaurants, drink at the bar, peruse the shopping arcade.

Parthiv is not a wanted man, he tells me. So he will come for dinner tomorrow.

'I want to meet some players,' he says. 'Are they there yet?'

I inform him of the star-spotting I've indulged in.

'This is great,' he replies. 'Would be great to speak to players. Very beneficial to us.'

CHAPTER 12

GROOMED

Parthiv fits in at the Taj. He looks at one with the Mumbai jet-set: flash trainers, designer jeans and shirt, iPhone, Gucci sunglasses perched above chunky dark eyebrows which kiss in the middle of the brow, giving a permanent look of seriousness.

'You don't look like your picture on Twitter,' he says. 'I almost don't recognise you.'

He is 25. He has been working for Big G since he was 20. It is his job to manage Big G's profits and losses with the five partners dotted around the city. Sometimes he will work as the bhao line operator or record customer bets. He says he earns two lakh (£2,400) a month.

'I like this work. It can be busy, you know, like now when we have one-day series and very busy for the IPL too when games are two a day. Other times are quiet. Lots of free time.'

Tomorrow, he says, he will have the day off.

'I bought us tickets for the game [the fourth one-day international at the Wankhede stadium] – you will be my guest. I have never been to a cricket match with an Englishman before.'

Attempting not to sound ungrateful, I tell Parthiv I had hoped to watch the match with him when he was working, so to see first-hand how the bhao line works and how bets are recorded.

'This is not possible for you,' he says. 'Big G cannot allow it. Yes, I have asked for you, of course. He is your friend, of course. But this is a big secret for us. We don't know where the betting will happen yet. This we don't know until the day of the game because of the police. It will be outside of Mumbai for sure. Never in the city. It is the police. They are trying to catch us.'

As Parthiv talks, his head is on a swivel. He is looking out for players. Anyone who walks behind him, he has to turn around to check out.

'The players are staying here?'

'Yes, I told you the players I saw.'

Most international teams stay at the Taj. It is the grandest hotel in the city, an enclave of excess, a haven from the gripes and groans of the traffic, the pinching and pulling at your elbow from the beggars and the pilferers. It is not to Parthiv's taste, however. He balks at the price of a chicken burger and is open-mouthed when I tell him how much it costs for a guest to log on to the internet in a room. It is Parthiv's first visit to the Taj, surprising considering the potential access to international and IPL players.

'No, some IPL teams stay at the Trident,' he says. 'West Indies stay there also. I can't come here. It is too risky. If I am seen trying to talk to players I could get in trouble. Not now. I am talking to you. You are English, so it is OK. We would be able to talk to them together without worry.'

'Any information is good for us. I told Big G that I was coming. We can make money on team news and the pitch information. Really good for us. It all makes a change to the odds.' Parthiv's head twists and turns. 'Arrgggh! Where are the players! If we see one, you ask about the pitch. This is most important.'

No player is in sight, which is a relief, for I am not keen on getting embroiled in Parthiv's scheme. His eyes, darting, give him away. He is a man constantly searching for the next money-making opportunity. I tell him that the players are probably in bed, tucked up for an early night ahead of tomorrow's game. It is an opportunity for him to talk about his second favourite subject – our 'biz partnership' – about which he has sent emails on an almost weekly basis. His eyebrows jump and fall, breaking the slightly sinister, straightened monotony of his brow. His eyes are still.

The plan is for me to attract 'big punters' through my Twitter account with the guarantee that they will not be restricted on stake. But they will not know they are betting with an Indian bookie. I will be a 'front'. A ghost bookmaker.

'You say you are their private bookie, yes?'

Parthiv has correctly identified the potential for profit. Professional gamblers in the UK find it a struggle to get their bets accepted for the stake they want by traditional high-street bookmakers. Joe Bloggs will phone up Ladbrokes to place a £500 wager on India to beat England in the fourth one-day international, but he will be told he can only have £100. Most bookmakers also operate a policy of closing down the accounts of gamblers who win too often. This is why professionals need to explore other routes for their money and so an illegal bookmaker would be attractive.

But there is a flaw in Parthiv's proposal. Where one aspect of the UK industry helps him, another hinders. An illegal Indian bookie, who must rely on his customers to pay their debts because of the credit system in operation, would not be confident that foreign customers, used to betting without credit, would be trustworthy. If they are to be trusted, winnings and losses could not be paid via bank transfer. The hawala system would need to be used, crossing continents.

'This is where you are at your best,' Parhiv says. 'You would find the punters to trust. You trust them, we trust them. We give you a big sum with hawala money at the start and you pay them out of your bank and you collect into your bank. Thirty per cent of profit to you, no risk.'

'I know four or five pro punters who would be really keen,' I lie. It is what Parthiv wants to hear and he sits back in his chair, his eyes flitting again. A favour for a favour. So we move on to my favourite subject: the World Cup semi-final in Mohali. Parthiv is noticeably anxious. 'You know I can't tell you about this. Very high level. I do not know much other than the script I gave you.'

'Yes, but you must know where you got it from and if you made money.'

'Ya, this is true. I have a contact in Dubai. It was all coming from there. All the fixes I spoke of. A lot of people made money, but I don't know who fixed the match. I think it was a government agreement. There has been much talk among the bookies in India about that game. Bookies didn't fix it, I think. It was some punters.'

I ask him whether his contact goes by the name of Deepak, who was mentioned by Dheeraj Dixit, and whether he can find out more details. 'No, that's not him ... Hmm, this was a long time ago. It is difficult for me because you can't ask questions. It is trouble for me. If I ask people questions they say, "Why you want to know? What's in it for you?" I think some bookies are worried that it was someone like D-Company involved. For sure it is why I don't want to talk of this. We all have to be careful of him in this business.

'He is at high level. You know he is very dangerous? Some bookies are even talking of some idea that India and Pakistan government had decided that Pakistan could not win the game because it was not good for them to come to Mumbai to play in the final after the attacks.'

I suspect Parthiv regrets sending me the script. He looks nervous when he speaks of it and reduces his voice to almost a whisper. As well he might if Dawood Ibrahim is involved. There is also the notion that talking of a fixed match that favoured India in their effort to win the World Cup is a profanity. Ruffled as Parthiv is, I drop the subject, reckoning that we have plenty more time to speak of the Mohali match.

Parthiv, reluctantly, leaves the Taj at around 11.30pm after I convince him that the players are unlikely to be making an appearance in the bar or restaurant at such a late hour on the eve of a game. 'Get up early and meet them for breakfast,' is his parting instruction. Before I have put my card into the lock on my room, my phone beeps with a text from Parthiv, reminding me to scavenge for team and pitch information. Before I have taken off my socks another text arrives, this time from Vinay, 'Please ask players about team choice and state of wicket.'

Barely have I sat down for breakfast when Parthiv and Vinay send their first messages of the day. 'What teams?' Parthiv says. Vinay wants to know whether Ian Bell, the England batsman, will play, because he will 'make a difference to the match odds'. Also in the restaurant are Alastair Cook, the England captain, and Andy Flower. Between eating pieces of fruit they are in deep discussion, no doubt cogitating tactics to halt the team's slide toward a whitewash. Duncan Fletcher, wearing the hangdog expression for which he is known, does not look approachable as he scrutinises the *Times of India*. MS Dhoni, wearing flip-flops, nonchalantly advances on the buffet counter.

I do not doubt that any attempt to engage these protagonists would be met with anything other than sincerity. 'Here is a cricket tourist making polite conversation,' they might think. They would not imagine

I was asking on behalf of a bookmaker. Never. All because of the colour of my skin, I suspect. But I resolve to try to do so. My rationale is to get information for Parthiv so he will agree to speak more openly about the Mohali script. A favour for a favour. India's ancient rule. Parthiv will not bat back my questions if I can uncover something he will find useful.

In the corner of the room sits Trevor Penney, the India fielding coach. He is detached from the herd, a limping gazelle grazing alone. A soft target. Be casual. It's a perfectly honest question.

'Morning, Trevor, will it be four–nil after today?' A soft soap of a starter for ten.

'Hope so.'

'What's the pitch like?'

'Not sure, mate,' Penney says. 'Haven't had the chance to get a good look at it.'

With that Penney's eyes drop to his breakfast. The exchange is over. More texts arrive from Parthiv and Vinay. I can guess what they say. Identifying those who have become separated from the pack, the loner, the disaffected tourist, is perhaps how the fixers work. It is a strategy worth continuing, I decide.

With breakfast digesting, England's players congregate around the pool: Craig Kieswetter, Scott Borthwick, Steven Finn, Graham Onions, Ian Bell, Alex Hales, Jonny Bairstow. I take a sun lounger nearby, attempting to eavesdrop on conversations. Jonathan Trott and Samit Patel make an appearance before leaving in the direction of the gym. Bell, Bairstow and Onions take to the pool for lengths with the fitness coach, a barrel of a chap, monitoring the session. When the drill is over, I splash in. Onions is taking time out at one end, Bell the other.

Onions is guarded. He is not going to be playing, but this is not news. The Durham fast bowler was merely an afterthought, called up as injury cover. He 'thinks' England will play the same team that was beaten in the last game in Mohali. 'Thinks' is not likely to cut it with Parthiv or Vinay. Onions does reveal that the pitch is 'very flat' and that 'dew won't be an issue', referring to the trouble bowlers have of gripping a wet ball in the second innings of day–night matches.

I take a few lengths of the pool before approaching Bell, who is supporting his weight on his arms, which rest on the ledge of the pool, head tilted back and soaking up the rays.

'I'm hoping I'll be watching you bat later, Ian,' I say, truthfully. He is widely regarded as a certain addition to the England team by both India and English media, a remedy for a spluttering batting line-up so far.

'No such chance,' he says.

'Really? I thought you were a certainty to play.'

'Well, unless there's going to be a last-minute change of heart ...'

Bell is an affable sort. He chats away quite contentedly, telling me that England are going to make two bowling changes, one of them likely to be a debut for Stuart Meaker, the Surrey fast bowler, but there will be an inspection of the wicket before that is confirmed. He asks me whether I'm in Mumbai as a cricket tourist.

'No, I'm here to research a book actually ... been travelling around a few spots, Delhi and Bhopal.'

'Oh yeah? Great. What's the book about?'

'It's about match-fixing, how the bookies in India work and how the whole industry works, that sort of thing.'

'Right. So what's the main thing you've found out, then?'

'Well, oddly, given the reputation for being dark and unpleasant, the industry cannot work without trust ... and also that this idea that they are hellbent on violence and intimidation to get what they want just doesn't fit, in my experience.'

'Interesting.'

'Yeah, that and there seems to be quite a bit of fixing going on.'

'To be honest, I stay away from all that sort of thing.'

'Well, you're quite right to.'

Bell wishes me the 'best of luck with the book' and returns to his lengths. I dry off and go back to my room, sharing a lift with Trevor Penney. He says the wicket should spin. I text Parthiv and Vinay: 'Bell not playing. Two changes to Eng bowling, but waiting for final look at pitch. Meaker has good chance. Pitch is v flat. Eng say no dew.'

A few quid in a brown envelope slid under a hotel room door, perhaps an iPad left at reception or a drink bought at the bar would be all it would take for Onions, Bell and Penney, in the eyes of the ACSU, to be guilty of corruption. It is as easy as that. In its simplicity, the difficulty facing the sport is clear. These are the types of conversations players have over and over again when they encounter supporters: in hotel lobbies, outside the ground signing autographs, walking to the nets, in restaurants, in shops. They would almost certainly consider them banal and harmless. Ninety-nine times out of 100 they would be right.

Today was a one per cent day. They were banal conversations. But they were not harmless. Markets could have been manipulated off the back of that information, garnered from unwitting sources and passed on to bookmakers. In the eyes of the ACSU, I do not doubt I am the one guilty of corruption. I have not been given any cash or an iPad but I will, hopefully, receive more information regarding fixing in the future. A payment of sorts in an effort to uncover a greater injustice. A favour for a favour, I mutter to myself hoping that I have not just been 'groomed'.

Parthiv and Vinay are grateful for the team and pitch information. It has not stopped them asking for more. 'Will it be better to bat first?' 'What about the India team news?' Eventually they give up and Parthiv's communiqués move on to discussing where to meet: Churchgate station, just across the road from the Maidan.

I wait for Parthiv by the railings, away from the black mouth of the station, and watch the India supporters, clad in the distinctive light blue colours of their team, flow into the sunlight kicking or treading on the rats that scurry with them. Parthiv, too, is wearing an India shirt and a Nike baseball cap.

'As a bookie I lose money when India win,' he says. 'But today I wear the shirt as it is my day off. Come on, India!' Parthiv laughs, slaps me on the shoulder and we begin the walk to the stadium.

It is another Mumbai swelterer. The sun saps its pound of sweat, taking it drop by drop with every stride. The only breeze comes from wafting away pushers selling flags, counterfeit India shirts and face paints. At the gates to the ground, hundreds swelter and sway, jostle and push to take their seats as quickly as possible. It is not a queue. It is a scrum. The security staff, intent on reducing the mass before it becomes a seething one, give cursory glances at tickets.

We have missed the start of the game. England are already two wickets – Alastair Cook and Craig Kieswetter – down. Parthiv high-fives his countrymen as we take our seats up in the gods. He immediately shouts to the pizza seller, 'Dominos! Dominos!' waving 100 rupees in the air.

When the India cricket supporter is not ordering pizza, or cola, or crisps, or cake, or ice cream, he is, according to the aficionados of this sport, the most revered. It is easy to see why. To watch an Indian crowd is to be reminded of a Shakespeare play. They act out the comedy – the 'Happy Diwali England' sign held upside down; the tragedy – the hand-wringing of a billion fans if their team stumbles could be responsible for many an unseasonal warm front in the west; the romance – the close to orgasmic joy that erupts when their team has even the most minor of successes.

Indians are in love with their cricket team. And only one thing can turn their heads from their betrothed: a television camera. If the Indian cricket team causes lovesick histrionics, then the TV crew that suddenly turns up in the stand sparks a transitory, illicit lusting while their partner's back is turned. Anything goes to get the attention of the cameraman: waving, dancing, taking off one's shirt (then waving and dancing, sometimes explicitly), hugging the stranger next to you, waving a misspelt sign upside down. They come from miles around, it seems, running between the aisles, hurdling the seats, tripping over empty pizza boxes, just to get a look.

For me they are a welcome distraction from the action on the field. This is not because England are losing. To attempt to sniff around corruption in the sport is to put a nostril to milk on the turn: you recoil, crinkling the nose and gurning in distaste. I find myself questioning the authenticity of every delivery. Why was no boundary scored during the ten overs of mandatory powerplay? Isn't that one of the bracket fixes that Vinay said was popular? Why is the batsman changing his gloves? Isn't that a sign that a fix is 'on'?

This could be the cold, bony fingers of paranoia gripping the neck and disturbing the flow of messages from the brain, a symptom of investigating the impure, which passes with time. Or it could be naivety. Take Parthiv. He has no aversion to attempting to corrupt, as he proved at the Taj with his keenness to seek out players. Yet here he is, wearing his

India shirt, cheering Indian batsmen, blissfully aware of both contest and corruption. His patriotism, pride and participation in the spectacle are at odds with his daily reality and his work. Has he flicked a switch in his head?

'I don't understand,' I say to him. 'You know of corruption in the game, yet you cheer on your team who you know was given a bye to the final of the World Cup. Come on, man, what about that semi-final?'

'We can't speak of that,' he says, irritated. 'Big problems for me and Dubai contact if that gets out. Man, you gotta remember, this is India's occasion, these matches. I forget my work and I am an ordinary supporter. Come on India! This is our fun, time out, you know? You gotta enjoy.'

Could it be, then, that cricket in India is not a religion after all? For if it was sacrosanct, holy and pure, then no misdemeanours would be tolerated. Certainly the congregation would not consume its preaching with such gusto. Instead, is it India's 'time out', their entertainment?

It is a theme which has been repeated in Delhi, Bhopal and now Mumbai when discussing corruption. Most Indians I have spoken to will admit to being suspicious about whether the match they are watching is a genuine contest instead of something staged like, Lord forbid, American wrestling. Like the retired major at a Delhi bar who pitied my inexperience, rubbing my shoulder condescendingly as if to say 'poor sap, he knows little' when I told him that this book was being researched.

'This is not a story, young man. You think it matters? You think a player throws his wicket or a match and he worries? He is paid. He still gets his sponsorship. He still gets picked. He is still worshipped.'

In the hotel lobbies, cafés, airport lounges, plane seats and taxis much the same sentiment has been expressed, although in a less patronising way. Sal, a businessman who travels frequently to the US, compared cricket to the Hollywood boom during the Great Depression. 'People need to forget about their struggles. Yes, we have Bollywood, but cricket is the real escape. I don't think people really care whether things are fixed or not.'

Parthiv, who has remained stiff-tongued, certainly does not. With India closing in on victory and the stadium reverberating to chants of

'Ind-ya, In-di-ya' mimicking the heartbeat of a nation, the man who told me the biggest game of all time on Indian soil, involving players on the field in front of us, was fixed has left his seat with his mobile phone to record a 40-something man, dressed for the office, dancing on his seat. He thrusts his hips and throws his arms in the air, orchestrating and cajoling those around him, careening left and right, shouting, 'Come on, India!' with every turn. If his limbs were on string, the puppetmaster's movements would be quick and short. To a weary, Western eye he is making a fool of himself. But perhaps the joke is on us.

15. Delhi's finest

CBI report into match-fixing, 2000

K Madhavan report into match-fixing for BCCI, 2000

The solitude of sin, *Outlook*, 27 November 2000

The democracy tax is rising, *Economist*, 11 December 2008

16. The fix that wasn't

Mike Atherton meets Mohammad Amir, thetimes.co.uk, 20 March 2012

Majeed spun web of lies as his empire fell into ruin, *Daily Telegraph*, 3 November 2011

Agent claims Butt was driving force behind Pakistan fixing scam, *Daily Telegraph*, 3 November 2011

Australians are biggest fixers, agent claims, *Daily Telegraph*, 11 October 2011

17. What does the ACSU do?

ICC needed *News of the World* to supply bullets, *Daily Telegraph*, 2 November 2011

ICC failed to follow tip-off due to lack of resources, *Daily Telegraph*, 3 November 2011

Corruption unit to try new tactics in the endless war, *Sunday Telegraph*, 6 November 2011

18. Afternoon tea with the commissioner

Controversies that have rocked the IPL so far, thatscricket.com, 4 April 2012

I was threatened by underworld for not fixing matches, Modi, *Times of India*, 2 November 2011

The IPL and Lalit Modi, Cricinfo, 28 August 2011

Lalit Modi profile, Cricinfo

The IPL's legal battles, Cricinfo, 8 April 2011

Concerns over details of Kochi ownership details, Cricinfo, 12 April 2010

Rise and fall of Lalit Modi, *Forbes* magazine, 25 May 2010

Modi involved in betting, murky deals, *Times of India*, 19 April 2010

Lalit Modi: India's maverick impresario, BBC, 26 April 2010

19. The English disease

Danish Kaneria talked Mervyn Westfield into spot-fixing, court told, *Guardian*, 17 February 2012

Pakistan spinner Danish Kaneria named by Mervyn Westfield as alleged corruptor in spot-fixing case, *Daily Telegraph*, 17 February 2012

20. The fix that was?

Ryan Tandy found guilty of match-fixing, *Sydney Telegraph*, 6 October 2011

Younis offers to quit as captain, Cricinfo, 13 October 2009

Never met, don't know Majeed: Harbhajan, Yuvraj, *Times of India*, 11 October 2011

The Qayyum Report, 2000

CHAPTER 13

THE ROAD TO NIMBAHERA

Nimbahera, Rajasthan, is a six-hour drive north of Bhopal. It is a typical bustling, small-town-India scene. The mosque imposes itself over the smallholders. The cars blast the bicycles. The bikes send shrill warnings to pedestrians. The pedestrians threaten the stray dogs by feigning to pick up rocks. Set back from the road, away from the jostle and dust, is a terrace of shops: the sweet seller reading the newspaper, the shoemaker shining and the sim-card outlet with a queue spilling onto the street. In the corner is an open doorway leading to fading yellow steps. Up we go. Swallowed into the gloom, leaving behind a timid February breeze.

Vinay's holler reverberates off the marble floor and walls. 'Sumer! … Sumer!' No response. Somewhere in the murk a child cries. More steps. A crouching woman clatters tin pots. She does not look round. 'Sumer! … Sumer!' We find an empty bedroom and sit on the mattress. Vinay makes a call on his mobile. 'He is coming now.'

Five minutes later Sumer arrives. He is a tall man with thinning, black, neatly parted hair, fierce eyes and an inscrutable face. There is barely a flicker of recognition when he shakes my hand. Sumer is one of Vinay's four partners in the bookmaking business. When Vinay plays the role of the syndicate or is tending to his property business or shop, it is often Sumer who does the work. Elsewhere today, mostly in Bhopal he says, three more of Vinay's 'offices' will be operating.

Sumer unhooks his laptop bag from his shoulder and sits down. He and Vinay talk in Hindi. I lounge on the mattress, drumming fingers on my knee. Vinay and Sumer are supposed to be taking bets on the Twenty20 international between Australia and India in Melbourne. But there is a problem. The match is minutes away from starting and Vinay and Sumer seem distracted from impending work.

'We are hiding,' Vinay finally breaks off. 'He says it is not safe here. The police have not been paid off.' Why? 'They could give no guarantees so why should we pay?' The local minister responsible for the area has declared that all betting should cease. 'We wait,' Vinay says. 'Then we go to another place, 20 kilometres from here.'

The prospect of at least another 40 minutes in a car is not a gleeful one. On the journey to Nimbahera there were regular reminders of why India's roads are the graves of 130,000 people a year. The country has the dubious honour of having the worst road-traffic accident rate in the world. Overtaking on the inside on a dirt track? De rigeur. Cars travelling in the wrong direction on a dual carriageway? That is what the horn is for.

Vinay, of course, dozed throughout. We were unable to talk betting because his driver does not know he is a bookie. When I forgot this rule, Vinay unsubtly waved his finger in front of his lips and conversation for the duration was cancelled. I sat tense-legged, tense-backed, sweating, swallowing hard after each near miss.

So as well as cars, we will now dodge the cops. The sweet seller has fallen asleep, the shoemaker has moved on to polishing and the sim-card queue now snakes around the corner. Vinay is in high spirits, although Sumer remains deadpan as we take our seats for another hair-raising ride. Sumer speaks in a whisper to his partner, as if he is concerned about me hearing. But I can't understand him. He speaks no English.

'He is talking about the police,' Vinay says. 'It is best to get out of here. We don't want to be arrested.' Neither of them has been arrested before. 'We pay normally, you see.'

It is not the confiscation of bookmaking paraphernalia, like mobiles and laptops, which worry Vinay and Sumer. Nor is it the humiliation, fine or possible jail term. It is the beating meted out by police. 'They are very harsh,' Vinay says. 'Very harsh. If we are caught today at this place they will just come in and start hitting, hitting, hitting. They don't care who I am, who you are. They will bruise us badly. Some bookies we know have been badly beaten.'

The police may have trouble finding us. Ten minutes from the main road is a small enclave of four-storey buildings, distressed and disintegrating into one another. They are tightly packed, creating a labyrinthine network of alleys and passageways around them. We duck down one and move quickly into one of the buildings, walking straight into a first-floor flat and into a bedroom. 'This is how we do the betting,' Vinay announces.

On the bed a man with a bouffant of black hair and dressed as if it is 1979, sits cross-legged. He rests an elbow on a cushion in front of him. With the other hand he holds a red mobile phone to his ear. He is the bhao line operator, the man who will shout continuously the odds to customers who will telephone numerous mobile lines to hear his voice. Sumer takes a seat next to the man, who until now has been communicating the odds and recording the bets on A4 lined paper. Sumer takes responsibility for recording the wagers and opens his laptop to begin inputting the data into the same software program which Vinay showed me on my previous visit.

In front of them are two heavy black suitcases, opened at right angles. The vertical half of each case holds 30 mobile phones, 15 in one, 15 in the other. They are wired to a speaker system in the horizontal half of the cases. This is the portable nerve centre of the illegal Indian bookmaker. The numbers of these mobile phones have been given to customers and they are calling in their droves. Customers use a mobile that is known as a dabba, cellphones with modified sim-cards that do not receive calls and only make calls out to one pre-programmed number: the bhao line. They are hired by customers for around 780 rupees a month (£9). In the suitcase, each phone lights up as they are connected to hear the odds being spoken by the bhao. When customers decide to have a bet, their voices are amplified by the speakers so that Sumer and his right-hand man can hear.

Behind the cases is a homemade socket board which can house 30 plugs. This is the only hint of permanence in the windowless room. The white walls are bare. There is no furniture apart from the bed and two plastic garden chairs. The analogue-style television, which is showing the match, is perched precariously on crates, its wires being fed up the wall and through a hole above the door. Slung in the corner is a pair of flared jeans – probably belonging to the bhao – and a towel.

'This will be a difficult match for us. We have been unable to trade our wagers on the Betfair because it has been down [crashed],' Vinay whispers, trying not to disturb the bhao, who barely takes a breath as he continually calls the odds between balls. 'You recall how I showed you this when we were in the hotel that first time?' Australia are 88 for four after 12.2 overs. India are priced at 87–90. The innings runs are quoted at 155–156 – fewer than 155 or more than 156.

'Eighty-seven ninety … Eighty-seven ninety … Eighty-seven ninety … BOWLER CHALU! … khali [single] … Eighty-seven ninety … Eighty-seven ninety …'

Bets continue to come in, most of them for India. When a customer says 'chocolate' it means he wants a four-lakh (£4,800) wager.

'That's a big bet,' I say to Vinay.

'It's normal,' he says

'In England the average bet is probably around £20 or £30,' I say.

Vinay laughs and tells Sumer who, without looking up from his laptop, mumbles something back. Vinay giggles again. 'He says that is because in India we have bigger balls than you English!'

Australia's fifth wicket falls. David Hussey, the Australia number four, is bamboozled by a slower ball from Ravindra Jadeja, offering a simple caught-and-bowled chance.

'India sixty-six sixty-eight … sixty-six sixty-eight … sixty-six sixty-eight … sixty-six sixty-eight,' says the bhao. India's price is shortening as their chance of winning increases. The suitcase is glowing green with customers calling in to place their bets.

'Everyone is backing India,' Vinay says. 'The book is very bad. We are suffering a loss.'

India continue to dominate. As the wickets fall, so does India's price, down to 56-58 as the sixth batsmen departs, 45–47 for the seventh, 37–39 for the eight. Australia are restricted to 131.

'Everyone has been backing India,' Vinay says at the innings break. 'We are losing four lakh on India and winning very little on Australia.'

Sumer tells Vinay that 300 bets have been placed, the biggest being a 'pandrah' – a 15-lakh (£18,000) stake.

The bhao line operator, for the first time, removes the red phone from an equally red ear. He disappears for a moment and returns with Thums Up cola and biscuits for all.

'The red phone is the line to the syndicate, yes Vinay?'

'Ya,' he says. 'They are telling him the odds and he is then telling our customers.'

This scene is being repeated in thousands of bedrooms, outhouses, offices and back-shop rooms across India. To see it in action is clarification that the illegal Indian market works much like a franchise arrangement. The bookies, in this case Sumer and Vinay, are the franchisees, agreeing a 'licence' to use the syndicate's product, which are the odds.

Unlike a traditional franchise arrangement, however, where the supplier of the product is consistent, Indian bookmakers have to agree to 'licences' with other syndicates too, because they do not all provide the same type of odds.

In fact there are four syndicates in India, which have a monopoly on first-, second- and third-tier bookmakers. The live match betting odds are provided by Shobhan Mehta, the Mumbai-based bookie, to whom Parthiv and Big G are connected. Jayanti Malad, Vinay's friend and the syndicate he sometimes sets the odds for, offers the pre-match betting odds. A third syndicate, known as the Shibu, offers just session betting (the brackets – runs in the first ten overs). Labu Delhi is the Shibu's lead bookmaker. A fourth, and a 'rival' to Mehta's live odds, are the Nagpur syndicate, organised by a bookie called Jeetu Nagpur. Between them, the syndicates control the match odds, innings runs, brackets and lunch favourite market, the only betting markets available on the Indian system.

Two factors bind the first three syndicates and their bookmakers, one more important than the other. Trade secrets, like the sharing of information regarding match-fixing, either by the punter or syndicate, give each group confidence and mean that bookies rarely strike out on their own in terms of offering odds. Perhaps bizarrely, what is wholly relied upon to ensure that the system is fair, trustworthy and remains uniform is religion. According to Vinay (and we must take such an arbitrary number with a pinch of salt), 80 per cent of bookmakers in India are Jains. Shobhan Mehta and Jayanti Malad, at the top of the chain, are Jains. So is Vinay.

The religion has been described thus: 'Jainism prescribes a path of non-violence towards all living beings. Its philosophy and practice emphasise the necessity of self-effort to move the soul towards divine consciousness and liberation.'

Jains 'stick to their own'. Whereas they also adhere to the prevalent culture in India of 'you scratch my back, I'll scratch yours', they first look to do business with a Jain. The Jain community is extremely close-knit. For example, if a Jain is in financial difficulty and is being threatened with violence by a money lender, the community will rally round to pay his debt. A sort of 'community chest' fund exists. Likewise, if a Jain says to one of his brethren who he has not met before, 'I am in trouble, help me,' his complaint is indulged with no questions asked.

The illegal bookmaking system thrives because of this. A desire to keep the status quo and a fear of what will happen to anyone who steps outside the circle of trust also keeps it strong. Those who disparage or bring shame on the community are outcasts and whatever their business – bookie, retailer, advocate – the Jains make sure that they are ruined.

'Ya, we work together because we want to remain strong,' Vinay says. 'The saying is safety in numbers. I do my business with Jains … bookies, property and everything. It makes sense for me.'

India are 36–37 as they begin their chase of the target. The low price has not put off customers, who continue to want to back them. The bracket for the number of runs scored in the first ten overs is set at 74–75 – India to score fewer than 74 or more than 75. I keep a note of how India's match odds and the bracket odds change after Vinay spots something untoward.

On the third ball of the fourth over, Virender Sehwag, the India opening batsmen, hits a boundary four. Excitedly, Vinay tells me that before the ball had been bowled, the bracket odds changed for no reason.

'This is a hint of a fix,' he says. 'Did you hear [pointing to the bhao] how the syndicate moved the bracket just before that ball was bowled?'* I confess I did not. 'Ya, it moved from 66–67 to 68–69 for no reason. So they have moved the bracket up. I've seen this many times. When the odds are not correct like this, something is not right for sure. I think India will score under 74 in this ten overs. The bracket was opened at 74 and the odds are being manipulated. Most of our bets taken on the bracket are right at the start on the 74–75 price with customers saying "lagana" [backing more than] 75.'

From after the fifth over, the India score, match odds and bracket odds are the following:

29 runs for no wicket, five overs: India match odds 24–25, bracket 64–65

42 for none, six overs: India 14–15, bracket 70–71

43 for one (Sehwag out), 6.3 overs: India 30–32, bracket 63–64

47 for one, seven overs: India 26–28, bracket 64–65

54 for one, eight overs: India 16–17, bracket 66–67

66 for one, nine overs: India 6–7, bracket 72–73

71 for one, ten overs: India 4–5

As soon as the final ball of the tenth over was bowled, Vinay declares: 'I was right, you see, 71.' With the majority of bracket bets being taken at the start, Vinay confidently predicts that few Indian bookies have lost money on the bracket betting. The syndicate has done its job. 'The market was 74 to 75 at the start. Punters wanted more than 75. You understand this now.'

'So a fix, you think?'

'I think it is very likely, yes. I have been doing this since I was 21. I know the odds and I know when the odds are manipulated. This is my business.'

As impressive as Vinay's predictions are, I am not convinced. A study of the odds in those five overs does not suggest foul play. If the

---

* The BCCI were informed of the information about the Twenty20 match and were asked to comment. They declined to do so.

syndicate was aware of a fix with the India team to score a certain number of runs, then surely there would have been more obvious manipulation? The Australians could be exonerated, also.

For example, in each of the first four overs of Indian customers wanting to back India to score more than 75, they would have won money. After the fifth they could have backed them to score 65 or more, after the sixth, 71 or more and after the seventh and eighth overs backers would have won with wagers for more than 65 or 67 runs respectively. Only after the ninth over, with six balls remaining, would backers have lost money, expecting 73 or more runs to be scored.

Nor is there is anything to suggest a suspect betting pattern in terms of how the runs quotes reacted to runs being scored. Between the fifth and six overs, 13 runs were scored, resulting in the quote being moved up by six points. The following over saw Sehwag dismissed and, quite understandably, the quote was reduced by six points, given the batsman's reputation as one of the most destructive in the world game.

Such movement in odds is considered perfectly normal for a Twenty20 match, a view which would be corroborated by most oddsmakers working for well-known British bookmakers. One such oddsmaker once told me: 'You have to factor in "soft" factors, such as who is bowling/batting at the time of the price – certain bowlers coming on to bowl can add or subtract one–two runs/ticks from prices. The modus operandi for bracket fixes tend to be a super-aggressive start, followed by the brakes being applied rapidly – something we have frequently seen, particularly in Twenty20.'

Certainly there was not a 'super-aggressive' start. India's run rates from the first over to the tenth read: 6 runs per over – 5.5–6–6.5–5.8–7–6.5–6.7–7.3–7.1. This was steady.

The syndicate with inside knowledge, one would have thought, would have pulled more strings. For example, after the dismissal of Sehwag, the reduction in the bracket to 63–64 needn't have been so severe. Indeed, if it had been reduced to 67–68, granted backers would still have won, but it could have fooled customers into betting India to score 67 or less, largely due to the fact that Sehwag was no longer at the crease.

'Ya,' Vinay says. 'You may be right. But this is a subtle art a lot of the time. We can move Betfair markets to hedge our bets and everyone can see, but it is hush, hush for a fix, I would say. I say bets are most taken at the start. You haven't asked me about our book ... We lost on the match [India won by eight wickets], but won seven lakh [£8,400] on the bracket.'

CHAPTER 14

'WICKET GAYA!'

Just before I left Sumer in the crumbling, concrete-manufacturing town of Nimbahera, his stony face cracked. With Vinay translating, he asked if I would speak with his wife and daughter on his mobile phone. 'They speak good English,' Vinay said. He was right. They spoke cut-glass, flawless English, asking me how long I had been in India, whether I liked it, if I was married and what I did for a living. 'Better than most English people,' I told Sumer. He was overjoyed at this report, showing off a set of brilliant white teeth, shaking my hand enthusiastically.

Having been preoccupied by the car journey back to Bhopal, it is not until the morning that I wonder about Sumer's reaction. Woken by the sun rising above Bhopal's staccato skyline, I lie in bed and think whether there is a greater significance to it than just pride in his family's education. My thought process is interrupted by Vinay's son. He does not burst into the room like most two-and-a-half-year-olds. That is not mischievous enough. Instead he opens the door silently, creating a gap wide enough to poke his head through and then grins wickedly. Once he has your attention, he swings back and forth on the door handle, shouting instructions. He has woken me like this on each morning of my three-day stay. Today he is telling me: 'Breakfast is ready but I'm going to eat yours.' On most days his command has been: 'Give me your mobile phone, I'll beat you up.'

This is all in Hindi. He will not start learning English for another two years, Vinay tells me as we tuck into toasted vegetable sandwiches, followed by biscuits and chai. 'Sumer's wife and daughter spoke very well,' I tell him. 'Why was he so pleased about my comments on their English?'

'Ah yes, he is a proud man and he wants very much his family to be successful. Learning English is the way for us, you know? My son will learn English, and my daughter. I don't want them growing up in India, a part of all this corruption. I want to educate them in foreign universities. It's only going to get worse here. That's why he was so happy.'

Vinay spots the puzzled look on my face. He heads my next question off, that as an illegal bookmaker who pays off the police and greases the palms of planning councillors, he is part of the problem he describes. So too are his friends: Sumer the bookie, not to mention the forger and the money-lender we dined with on my first night in town. As we walked into a restaurant it felt like India's version of *The Sopranos.*

'I know you are thinking "what about Vinay, he is a bookie, he is illegal" and you are right. But I have to provide for my family. I want a better life for them so they don't have to do what I do. This is not good. I have already told you about the difficulty I had with my father when he found out. Let me tell you, some friends don't know what I do ... like the driver yesterday, yes? Definitely, definitely things will be bad in India when my children are grown up. If they are growing up in this India then it will be difficult for them.'

This is the perfect opportunity to ask Vinay about the power of Dawood Ibrahim, the gangster who has stalked this story from the beginning. He is India's most wanted criminal, having been accused of masterminding the Mumbai bombings of 1993, which killed 257 and wounded 713. According to *Forbes,* which annually produces a chart of despots and dictators, he is the world's third most wanted man, the death of Osama bin Laden earning Ibrahim a promotion. *Forbes* describes Ibrahim like this: 'Ibrahim has for years led a 5,000-member criminal syndicate known as D-Company. The organised crime group has engaged in everything from narcotics to contract killing, working mostly in Pakistan, India and the United Arab Emirates. Ibrahim shares smuggling routes with al-Qaeda, the US government says, and has collaborated with both al-Qaeda and its South Asian affiliate, Lashkar-e-Taiba, which pulled off the November 2008 Mumbai attacks, possibly with Ibrahim's help. Ibrahim is suspected of having organised the 1993 Bombay bombings. Though the Pakistani government denies it, Ibrahim is probably in Pakistan, where he has important ties to the powerful intelligence service.'

Ibrahim, whose daughter is married to the son of the former Pakistan batsman and coach Javed Miandad, has a bit more than 'ties' to the illegal

Indian market. Some say he runs it or, to be more precise, the syndicates. Men like Shobhan Mehta, the Mumbai bookmaker who distributes the live match odds across the country, and Jayanti Malad, who does likewise for the pre-match odds, are believed to take their instructions from Ibrahim via his brother Anees Ibrahim. Just as the thousands of bookmakers pay a cut to the syndicates for providing the odds, they in turn pay D-Company.

When in Mumbai, I spent an afternoon with Hussain Zaidi, a legendary investigative reporter, who confirmed the machinations of the operation. 'I interviewed one major bookie, Shobhan Mehta, for *Mumbai Mirror* and he said that "we go by instructions. We are told by the higher people". He refused to identify them, but said, "We are told to go out and fix the match or to accept betting on a particularly situation in the match." They don't decide. The don decides what to do and what not to do. The don is probably Anees.'

If this is correct, it puts Vinay uncomfortably close to the most feared organised crime unit in India, given his association with Jayanti Malad, the head of the syndicate of which he is a part.

'D-Company?' Vinay says. 'There is much talk of this. I think it works as you say. This is India. It is corrupt and there is someone behind the curtain always. Someone at the top always is being paid.'

It is this chain that gave Ibrahim the power to manipulate matches, starting in Sharjah in the early 1990s. And later his influence appeared to sway Mohammad Azharuddin, who, of course, had been banned for life for fixing three one-day matches. 'We have established his connections with the D-Company,' a tax official was quoted by Tehelka.com in August 2000. Since then the finger of blame is pointed at D-Company whenever a match is rumoured to be a fix.

'It is not like that, my friend,' Vinay says. 'I could fix a match. I have not done so, but I could. Small bookmakers fix the matches. It is very easy to do. All you need is to get to know a player and you can fix something. Maybe in the past it was only D-Company. But now anyone can do it ... punters with good friendships with players can.

'Those people are not D-Company. I mean to say, they do not act like D-Company. They don't attack; make violence. D-Company has given bookmakers a bad name. I ask you of me: am I a threat? Sumer? Jayanti Malad? No, we are the fair people. It is wrong to say that bookmakers make the threats.'

I remind Vinay of when we first met in Bhopal in October and how perturbed I was about the reputation of bookmakers, for the first time telling him about the warning from Murali Krishnan that he could try to drug me. He finds it hilarious.

'Me?' he guffaws. 'This is too much amusement for me. I hope you know me now, ya? But perhaps I understand why you were like this. Bookmakers in India are supposed to be all bad. No. We are trying to make our living in a corrupt country and we do this by taking any opportunity we can.'

Bookmakers like Vinay are opportunists. Vinay readily admits that if he had the time to meet players and get to know them, he would ask for a 'favour' on the pitch. Vinay does not seek them out, as he has other businesses to run and his bookmaking earns him 'some comfortable monies'. 'Maybe in time I will have this chance and I will take it,' he says. 'I think all bookmakers think like this for sure. Some try very hard to get to know the players and this happens. They become friends and most fixes are done because of friendship. There is not one person doing all the fixing of the brackets, lambi, that is too much hard work for a punter or bookie.'

I ask Vinay whether only someone as powerful as D-Company could have fixed the World Cup semi-final in Mohali. 'No,' he says. 'There are many people with the money for this and influence. D-Company is strong. They could have done it. It would take someone like this. It is not the sort of game a bookie like me or a small punter could have done. But you ask too much of this game, it is troublesome for you. I don't ask about this. Maybe it is D-Company. Maybe it is someone else.'

Vinay, just like Parthiv, won't ask associates about this game. There is an implied threat there. Granted, the majority of bookmakers or punters in India may well be as harmless as them both, but there is a line that they know they cannot cross. That line has been drawn by D-Company and, despite the information and hospitality they have afforded me, particularly Vinay and his charming family, it is one they dare not step over.

Vinay is sniggering again. 'What is it?' I ask.

'I'm laughing that you thought I poison you. Quick! Quick! Spit out your tea!'

Today is an early start. A new start? Vinay is showing me his commentary line business. It is legitimate. Well, almost. For India's matches, home or away, Vinay employs someone to travel to each ground and provide live ball-by-ball commentary. If India are playing abroad, as they are today against Australia at the Melbourne Cricket Ground in a one-day international, his man will sit in the stand with a mobile phone at his ear for every ball, every over, every run, every wicket, relaying the information to Vinay who, in the style of the bhao line operator, will shout into mobile phones to tell his subscribers what has happened seconds before it appears on their television screen. It is all about the transmission delay, buying bookmakers precious time to adjust odds. His customers are mostly the top syndicate men, the first-tier bookmakers who feel confident enough to set odds, and the odd punter.

No doubt cricket boards around the world would take a dim view of Vinay's man essentially broadcasting without a licence, but in a crowd of thousands he is difficult to spot, particularly, as Vinay tells me, he will often use an earpiece. 'Sometimes he has problems because people shout "shut up!" but this is fine. Matches at Lord's are difficult in the past because they don't like mobile phones there. Very strict.

'But it's a good business. I can't get in trouble for this. I don't want to tell how much people pay to subscribe to this because it will not be good for me, but I need to make money, good money for it. Today it will cost me probably £150 of British money to pay for the person at the MCG. I pay all his expenses, hotel, food.'

Rahul, Vinay's assistant of NHS-style spectacle fame, arrives with a television under his arm and multitudinous mobile telephone chargers sprouting from his pocket. He looks as though he has plugged himself into the set and he transmits a wired smile before disappearing into Vinay's dressing room. Vinay is taking calls on his two mobile phones. He is liaising with bookies and punters, talking team news, odds and sharing views about the weather. Vinay's son is swinging on the door handle once more, demanding to speak to his father's associates. He slams the door behind him after a stiff rebuke.

Rahul, having crashed around in the dressing room, appears once more. 'Come,' he says and I take my seat on a stool in the ten-foot by six-foot room. The television is in one corner, blocking the door to the loo, next to a laptop; Rahul is in the other, standing awkwardly. The ever-present mobile phones are plugged in and pouched. About 20 of them. A two-seater bench is reserved for Vinay, who takes his position in tracksuit trousers and a white vest, and his mobile phones. He is already speaking to his man at the MCG.

'There is rain in Melbourne today so we will get a lot of custom. We know everything about the weather,' Vinay says.

He logs on to a weather radar site for the state of Victoria, which shows how bands of rain are expected to move over the ground for the next hour. 'With this we can give a very good service. We know when it will rain, when it will stop. My employee at the ground confirms when it is raining and when it has stopped. The bookies need this information because there is sometimes a market for a completed match. It can be a very popular market with Indian customers, but it is often only for countries where there is rain, like your England. Because of us the syndicate knows when it is going to rain before the customers.'

'Barrish chalu! ('rain is falling') … Barrish chalu! … Barrish chalu!' Vinay shouts at the mobile phones, his words echoing around the cell. Rahul, robotically, checks the connections continuously and 'answers' any phone that rings, connecting the subscriber to the commentary.

'All the big bookies come to us for the weather,' Vinay says. 'Nagpur is calling me, you see [showing me the phone with the name of Jeetu Nagpur, head of the Nagpur syndicate]. They have no other option because they can't send their own person to the ground.'

In the next half hour the rain stops, the covers come off, the rain starts again and the covers come back on. Each time Vinay excitedly passes on the information. The broadcaster for the match, a Commonwealth Bank Series 50-over one-day international, is showing highlights of a VB Series match between Australia and England in 2002. Cricinfo, the revered cricket website, has a commentary service, but it is not focusing on the weather, instead indulging in chit-chat with readers. Vinay is providing minute-by-minute updates on the weather. He allows me to listen to his man at the MCG, a ghost-like voice barely decipherable against the background noise.

'If there are no futher delays, the match will start in ten minutes,' Vinay says. 'It's a 44-over match. Everyone else is tweeting 46, but our man on the ground says 44. You should tweet this also, it is good for your followers.'

Australia are put into bat after India win the toss. The home side start in circumspect fashion, scoring 11 runs after the first four overs. Vinay's animation is unaffected by the monotonous start. He rocks back and forth in his seat, rubbing his hands on the front of his upper legs, exclaiming to his listeners 'Bowler Chalu!' as the bowler begins his run-up. As soon as he hears what the outcome of that delivery is, he looks set to combust, almost leaping from his seat as if it helps him to force out the words more quickly.

'KHALI! KHALI! KHALI!' he shouts to denote a dot ball. And as he slumps back in his chair, we turn to the television to watch what Vinay has just described. There is a five- to six-second delay on the transmission. Vinay is up and down.

'DOUBLE! DOUBLE! DOUBLE!' he shouts as two runs are scored. 'TEEN! TEEN! TEEN!' for three and 'CHOCOLATE! CHOCOLATE! CHOCOLATE!' for a four. For the first ball of the sixth over, however, I cannot make his garbled, eager cry so I have to wait to see what has happened by watching the television. David Warner, the Australia opening batsmen, is out, bowled by Vinay Kumar, the fast bowler.

'What did you say for a wicket?' I ask Vinay.

'Wicket gaya,' he says. 'It means: "it's a wicket".'

Vinay is engrossed in his weather radar and five minutes before the rain starts falling at the MCG, he has warned India's bookmakers that there will be an interruption. Australia are 35 for two as the players leave the field. The break is a welcome relief from the hum of laptops, crackle of mobile phones, boom and bounce of Vinay's voice. I take my leave for a few minutes, only returning when I can once more hear Vinay's unmistakeable tones. The smell of sweat as I perch on my stool again is unpleasant, invading the nostrils and stinging the eyes. Vinay's shoulders have a sheen. Rahul, whose glasses have surprisingly not steamed up, leans, arms folded, against the wall in the corner. Still grinning childishly, his smile is topped by a sliver of condensation.

The conditions seem bearable, though, when Vinay chirps: 'Australia will win this game.'

'Why do you think that?'

'I know they will win. After the fourth over some punters called me. Friends for me. They told me Australia will win. I was damn sure they would call to tell me. Lots of ups and downs, but Australia win.'*

I have no evidence that this information was passed on to Vinay, only his word. As a man who follows cricket closely, it is not impossible for him to make an educated guess that India will lose the game. After all, his 'prediction' is hardly outlandish. It is a 50-50 call.

The match has been resumed 28 minutes. I tweet Vinay's information hurriedly, misspelling 'lots'. 'Lotts of ups and downs expected #ausvind. Hosts to win, though.' The tweet is timed at 7.46am GMT, 6.46pm in Melbourne. Vinay spots that I have passed on the details.

'Ha! Your followers will think you have all the information, but not too good at the spelling.'

As Australia's innings progresses, I watch Betfair for signs of the illegal India market involvement, remembering how Vinay said that when there are four- or five-figure sums available, it is bookie money. At 165 for five, nine runs after the wicket of Michael Hussey, India are available to back at 2.56 (8–5 in fractional odds) for a measly $98. Australia are 1.57 for a massive $53,903. The discrepancy in available funds is unmissable. It represents an odd betting pattern, unlike the Twenty20 international we watched in Nimbahera, but this does not seem at all subtle

'This is Indian money on Australia?'

'Ya. Of course,' Vinay says.

---

* The BCCI were told of the information about the Australia v. India ODI and were asked to comment. They declined to do so.

'But if Indian bookies know Australia are going to win, why are they making this money available?'

'They are hedging their bets, of course,' Vinay replies, irritated. 'I thought you would know this. Bookies have taken loads of bets on India, most of their money ... maybe 80 per cent ... so they have to be clever and get some money on Australia. What if India win? What if things go wrong? Later on the odds on India will be wrong. India will be too big. You will see.'

It is speculation, of course, but Vinay's analysis would appear to have value, given that the flood of cash on Australia has arrived just after they have lost a wicket. It is a rudimentary fact that when a team loses a wicket its odds go up and the bowling team's odds go down. In other words, the Indian market has waited until what it believes to be the most opportune time to hedge its bets, offering large sums of money at the highest possible odds. Indeed, if Australia do not get any bigger in terms of their price from this point forward, the Indian market would have made a shrewd move.

Australia do not lose another wicket in their innings and they post a total of 216. They scored at a run rate of 8.85 for the last 20 overs and did not get any bigger than 1.57.

As India's chase begins, Vinay is right about the move on India's price. The Betfair market cannot push out India quick enough as they lose wickets. When Sachin Tendulkar is first out for two with the score on nine, India drift from 2.74 to 3.70. When the second wicket is taken – Gautam Gambhir off the bowling of Mitchell Stark – India go from 4.30 to 7.20.

'You see, India price is now too big and Australia odds are too short. I know this. The odds are wrong. As I told you, I have been doing this for years and I know when things are not right.'

As India settle at 8.00 and Australia 1.13, I take to Twitter, with Vinay continuing to work the oracle. Here are nuggets of information (most recent last) that I tweeted:

Lots of ups and downs expected #ausvind. Hosts to win, though

Innings break #ausvind. Check out my tweet from an hour ago
about match result

a period of consolidation for india. 5 wicketless overs of calm
#ausvind

Next wicket coming at around 45 runs. India currently 32-2
#ausvind

Last over of that 5-over spell of calm we spoke about. Let's see
what happens. Ind 45-2 8.3

Not quite. lot of playing and missing. edge thru slips

Well, weren't far off with that prediction. Eight balls after the end
of the 5-over spell of calm and a wkt falls #ausvind

In response to those tweets, followers are fulsome in praise of my apparent skill for prediction. 'You're on fire,' says one, 'What's next?' another and 'Spot on with the predictions'. If only they knew I was being fed the information by an illegal Indian bookmaker.

'I am right again,' Vinay laughs. 'You are looking very smart on the Twitter, I said so. I told you to tweet these things.'

When Ravindra Jadeja becomes the sixth wicket to fall, with India on 114, Vinay has seen enough. He hands over duties to Rahul and we leave the stifling, sweaty 'commentary box'. We sit on Vinay's bed and he shouts to his wife to bring food. We can hear Rahul next door, shouting 'WICKET GAYA! ... WICKET GAYA! ... WICKET GAYA!' his voice breaking on the 'ay'.

'I'm not sure he has the voice for this work, I don't like to use him,' Vinay says.

'Oh, leave him be, he's doing a good job,' I say. Vinay, smiling, gently wobbles his head from side to side.

We munch on more toasted vegetable sandwiches, followed by chai and biscuits. Vinay's son appears at the door in his familiar pose. He comes in to take the biscuit I offer him and then runs off. We talk more about Vinay's hopes and fears for his family and the culture in London, where he hopes to live one day. He expresses surprise that one cannot leave one's door unlocked and muggings are commonplace. 'But the police will investigate, no?' he asks. I laugh. He looks surprised but moves on to fire questions at me about obtaining a passport.

'Perhaps you can help with this … maybe you can sponsor this for me.' Always a quid pro quo. 'And I need good Catholic schools for my children. Can you put me in touch with them?' My mother is Catholic, I tell him. He is most pleased and shouts at his wife to bring more chai.

CHAPTER 15

DELHI'S FINEST

The buildings of the New Delhi government watch over a city in the hazy afterburn of the lunchtime sun. Their red and pale sandstone compositions add to the feeling of dozy, half-eyed contentment. Immediately below, countless games of cricket take place, just like Mumbai's Maidan, atop one another on the lawns that surround India Gate, a monument to India's war dead.

It is a peaceful scene. One might argue complacent. With the spot-fixing scandal of 2010 invading the consciousness of cricket, and the doubts that surround the World Cup tournament the year after, it is fair to question what India's seat of power is doing about an illegal bookmaking industry that fuels corruption in the sport.

The answer lies in one of those wistful buildings. The Ministry of Home Affairs. Security guards half-heartedly frisk visitors, a powder-blue piece of paper gives free rein to wander red-carpeted walkways where lackeys snooze outside the offices of officials whose names are stamped in bronze letters on heavy oak doors.

One of them is MA Ganapathy. His name still shakes the spines of Mohammad Azharuddin, Ajay Jadeja and Ajay Sharma, the Indian cricketers banned for match-fixing in 2000. It was Ganapathy who, with a reputation as an enforcer with India's CBI, conducted the interrogations. He was also the author of the infamous CBI report, which laid bare the extent of corruption in the game.

The report was published in 2000 and was the result of nine months of investigation. It had three aims: to identify the betting syndicates operating in India and examine their activities; to unravel the links of cricket players or their intermediaries with these syndicates and their roles in the alleged malpractices; to examine the role and functions of the BCCI so as to evaluate whether it could have prevented the alleged malpractices.

It certainly delivered. Azharuddin, the India captain, was its most high-profile victim. The 'analysis of evidence' section in the CBI report, states he admitted to fixing a Titan Cup one-day international match in 1996 at Rajkot and 'some' matches in the 1997 Pepsi Asia Cup in Sri Lanka for MK Gupta, the bookmaker. Azharuddin was given a life ban although it was overturned in 2012. Sharma, a batsman, was given a life ban. Ajay Jadeja, an all-rounder, was banned for five years, although his ban was quashed by the Delhi High Court in 2003.

After contacting the police departments in Mumbai, Delhi and Kolkata for lists of bookmakers arrested, names and telephone numbers were put into a database. Then, on a random basis, Ganapathy and his team started checking to see which of them had connections with players or their friends or family. Bookies were put under surveillance. Ganapathy knew what time they got up, what they had for breakfast. A cliché, but true. It took six months.

'We had everything ... people said we had nothing,' Ganapathy says.

Then in true 'good cop, bad cop' Hollywood style, Ganaptahy turned the psychological screw. Bookmakers, including MK Gupta, were secretly taped confessing to having fixed matches. 'MK Gupta was the biggest,' he says. 'He was found to be in touch with Azharuddin. Over a period of time he was also friendly with a number of other players, like Manoj Prabhakar [Prabhakar was eventually suspended from all forms of cricket for five years by the BCCI]. We found he was in touch with other players. And other bookies were in touch with other players; Ajay Jadeja was in touch with Rattan Metha. Quite a lot of that kind of a nexus.

'It's human tendency to co-operate. For example, if I tell you that your sister lives in this place and she has two children, it psychologically affects you. And then you confront them with details that "you met such and such a player on such and such a date at this hotel. And here are the details from the hotel because we have spoken to them, too. Look, your name is booked in". They soon started singing, they had so many weak-nesses, we had so much information. They broke down when we did this, especially Azharuddin.

'In those days it was not actual match-fixing, although we called it that. More a case of spot-fixing ... specific parts of the game. Like what's happening right now. If I was to do the case again, I wouldn't call it match-fixing, I'd call it spot-fixing. Very rarely was a whole match done at any point of time.

'There were a few Azhar fixed, but that was more like you are on the verge of losing so you make fools of these bookies by playing along. This is the general sort of scenarios in those days. Fixing personal performances, not game fixing as such so, in spite of what the media says or the general impression, matches are very rarely fixed from my experience.

'We also named some foreign players. [Brian] Lara and [Alec] Stewart … most of the names came up in the testimony of MK Gupta. He was the biggest bookie at that stage. Most of the foreign players were named in his testimony.'

The CBI report stated that during an England tour of India in 1993, MK Gupta 'requested Manoj Prabhakar to introduce him to Alec Stewart. He paid a sum of £5,000 to Alec Stewart who agreed to give MK information about weather, wicket, team composition, etc, whenever the English team played. Stewart refused to fix any matches for him'. Stewart, who strenuously denied the charge, had to wait a considerable time before the ICC and the ECB cleared him of any wrongdoing.

Lara was more co-operative, however. 'Towards the end of 1994, West Indies came to India and MK met Brian Lara again. Brian Lara offered to underperform in two one-day matches and his information proved correct and MK made some money by betting on those matches. MK stated that he gave a sum of around $40,000 to Brian Lara for his information.'

Lara, it should be made clear, has never been charged with any offence by any cricketing body or police force. The batsman was investigated by Elliott Mottley, a Barbadian attorney, on behalf of the WICB in 2002 and was exonerated. A statement read that allegations against Lara were 'unfounded and not supported by any evidence'. Ganapathy suggested the evidence against Lara and Stewart was not strong. 'We had no legal recourse to bring them in, so we relied on one testimony, but we didn't really cover a detailed investigation. That should have been done by respective boards.'

At first glance Ganapathy does not strike one as the shrewd 'Cracker' type of cop. His manner is laconic, speaking slowly and deliberately, making sure each word is perfectly formed, and as he does so he lowers his eyelids to the extent that he looks as though he is sending himself to sleep. Occasionally he is interrupted by a telephone call. Then his tone, when he decides to speak instead of umming and aahing, is hushed. A lackey, offering coffee or chai, is waved away with the waft of a wrist. When asked about his memories of the investigation that could be considered his finest hour and will go down in the annals of cricket history, there is no sign of hubris.

'You must remember the background to how we became involved,' he says, drumming his fingers to a rubato beat on a huge desk. 'There were the tapes that were released for the Hansie Cronje scandal. They were not very convincing, but at the same time they indicated that something was wrong. Just after Cronje broke, it was said that it was time for CBI to launch its own investigation. At that point we didn't have anything. Nothing concrete. We didn't know who the players were, just suspicion. Everybody from [Sunil] Gavaskar ... that's how it works in India. Everyone is a suspect until proven innocent. There was a hue and cry from the media. If you cry something is wrong, then an investigation has to be done.'

There has not been similar clamour since. Despite the revelations and claims from the London spot-fixing trial in November 2011, India could barely raise a whimper. When Mazhar Majeed, the crooked agent who manipulated the three Pakistan players, said, in a recorded conversation played to the court, that he knew the India players Yuvraj Singh and Harbhajan Singh, the story merited barely 300 words in the *Hindustan Times*, the second most read English-language newspaper in the country. The BCCI said Majeed had made 'wild claims'.

Today Ganapathy's 'speak softly, carry a big stick' approach is being used to counter India's struggle against Maoist terrorism in West Bengal. In May 2010, more than 145 people were killed when a train crashed in the Junglemahal region after Maoist rebels sabotaged the rails. A government offensive against the rebels began in late 2009. Ganapathy could be a human metaphor for the story of India and its gambling problem. They have both moved on.

'Betting is a minor problem in this country compared to other issues,' Ganapathy says. 'Bookmaking, match-fixing and spot-fixing come a long way down the list. Match-fixing is not even a crime in this country. You cannot be prosecuted. It is an income-tax issue.

'So once the report came out we lost members of the team, people lost interest. We realised we couldn't prosecute because the laws were inadequate. For a police officer the end result is to prosecute. That is why you do the job, so after six months and you can't prosecute, then what do you do? If there was another inquiry tomorrow there would be no prosecutions and people would lose interest. It's not frustrating for me, it doesn't bother me any more.'

Yet there is a hint of dissatisfaction in Ganapathy's voice, as if the needle on the record player had jumped. Even more so when he is asked about the ICC's ACSU, which was set up in the wake of his report. His boss, Ravi Sawani, and many who worked beneath him, were asked to join the ACSU. He did not get the call. YP Singh, a former CBI joint director of anti-corruption, took over from Sawani as head of the unit in June 2011. It is understood Singh earns close to 80 lakhs (£96,000) a year. A CBI officer of Singh's previous rank may earn a third of that.

'I did not market myself well enough,' Ganapathy says. 'The others did. I would have gone if they'd have asked me, but would it have been frustrating? The ACSU have no powers. If you really want to get to the bottom of fixing you need certain legal powers: the power to search, intercept telephone calls, interrogate. They don't have these. They are not police officers. At best it's a psychological ploy, they come and sit in the dressing room and the players see them and they have second thoughts.

'How can they get such powers? They can't. How will they get power in England, for example? They become toothless. Maybe they are short on expertise. They should start with the database. Who are the bookies, who are the fixers, who are the runners? Who are they talking to? They could outsource it to a security company. It's a psychological body. It's more for the cricket public, I think. If the ICC were to be discredited by a betting scandal, they can say, "We have an in-house system." If it fails, well, they can still say they had a system. If they don't have that, it makes it worse. That is its purpose.'

Ganapathy is adamant that fixing will never be defeated, arguing that it is impossible to prove and that the Southwark spot-fixing trial merely strengthened that view. 'That was not about betting anyway and no-balls are so specific that it was easy to work out the chances of it happening. Fixing is nothing like that in terms of identification.

'How do you get the evidence that a player has deliberately bowled four wides or a batsman has got out? It is impossible unless you have prior information. And the money which they get for fixing, obviously that will be in cash. What happens is that when you get it in cash it is immediately transferred into a solid asset ... someone fixes a game tomorrow, gets paid the day after and after a week that cash disappears. Those calculations are very difficult. At most, players will say they received it from my advertising sources, haven't declared it and it becomes a tax issue, not a fixing issue. It's very difficult to prove because the transaction between the player and the bookie doesn't exist in "paper" terms. It's not cheques or drafts – it's cash. That cash can be made into a permanent asset.'

Police in India have only rare successes at prosecuting bookmakers. So rare is it that when some are arrested, it makes the newspapers. A few days before I met with Ganapathy, the Panchkula force in Chandigarh apprehended four. The *Tribune* reported that 'they were caught red-handed while laying bets for their clients on the second one-day international match between India and England that was played at Firozshah Kotla Stadium in Delhi'. Police said they recovered three suitcases, a television set, a laptop and 13 mobile phones, through which they used to contact their clients and their counterparts in Mumbai, New Delhi, Nagpur and Punjab.

'Someone forgot to pay off the cops,' laughs Ganapathy. 'Police raids are not common. I don't think it's a lack of appetite, though. It's as I said, there are bigger issues: drugs and prostitution. For the police there are two main reasons why it is allowed to continue. Number one they are getting paid [it is estimated that between 25 and 30 per cent of CBI officers are dishonest]. How much having to pay off police? Volumes I won't be able to say. But I think it's pretty decent. I don't think even the police have an idea of volumes. Whatever the bookies give they take. It's easy money and not an area of priority, but I've said that already.

'What does worry me, though, is the organised crime element, D-Company et cetera. Someone has to look into it now. Betting in this case can't happen without the blessings of the mafia. You need protection. The mafia got into the betting business directly because of the volumes, hundreds of crores per game [100 lakh = one crore]. Sometimes people refuse to pay and that's how the underworld figures get involved. The enforcement of the contract. The parties who approached them say a bettor has not paid an amount and they are instructed to go and get it.

'There was a layer of smaller bookies paying bigger bookies, and then bigger again. Like a food chain. There are bookies paying each other. Oral contracts have to be honoured, otherwise the whole system would break down so the underworld enforces them. Subsequently the underworld directly got involved.

'Maybe if we had one more year to do it [the report] … there was too much pressure. "Come out, come out with something," they said. Time pressure to come up with something. Maybe in six more months we could have dug up something. Maybe explored the underworld nexus more systematically.'

Cricket's only hope would appear to be the legalisation of betting in India. But in a country where gambling has become an accepted, open secret, it would need a groundswell in public opinion to make it happen. A 'hue and cry' on the level of 2000. Ganapathy will not be holding his breath. 'I don't think India players do it any more and I suppose that is why there is not a lot of interest. Now they are into big bucks, the kind of money even the bookies can't offer. Most of the big players are regular in IPL, the money they get there is easy, legit and the temptation to get this kind of money is much less. Except for Pakistan – it is a sort of game for them. The board is very loose; the players are constantly bickering. It's a game for them. Spot-fixing can always happen.

'If betting is legalised, at least some money could be channelled back through taxes. This has to be done, I think. This may reduce the fixing. Legalise betting. Make it mainstream and legalise. Get a licence for gambling, show your books. It will make corruption difficult but, sadly, not impossible.'

Delhi can be a cantankerous old city, shuffling its feet to the bleat of the yellow-topped and green-bellied tuk-tuks. On three-lane highways six lines of vehicles will jostle for superiority and when they slow to a crawl, scowling mothers who cradle comatose kids tap-tap-tap on the windows and ask for a handout.

It is particularly grumpy on the morning I leave for Saket, a middle-class surburb in the south of the city. A 20-minute journey takes almost an hour. My driver Bhupinder, although he insists on me calling him 'Bhupi', is phlegmatic about the jam. He passes the time by asking his favourite question, a reliable old poser to get him through the awkward silence when a beggar with a horribly twisted right leg peers, pleading and pained, through the driver-side window. 'How many beers you have today, sir?' None, I tell him. I always say none. 'I've had two!' he responds triumphantly. He always says two. It's 9am. 'Bhupi', despite his penchant for booze, gets me to Saket safely. It is not long before it is clear that the journey, to hear a man of some renown, was worthwhile.

'There is one distinguishing feature between Indians and the west. Twenty-five years ago an Indian was fully satisfied with what he had. He never wanted things he couldn't afford. If a person could only afford a bicycle he would not commit a crime to get a motorcycle. Now that has changed. Greed. Materialism drives the whole thing. A person with only a bicycle wants a motorcycle, a motorcycle man wants a car, a car man wants a saloon, a saloon man wants a Mercedes, a Mercedes man wants a Rolls-Royce. It keeps mounting as you go higher in life. If you can contain that at proper levels you are honest, but if you can't, you are prone to dishonesty.'

It is as succinct an explanation as one could wish for of India's apparent obsession with money. And it comes from the mouth of a man who should know a thing or two about the culture of a country that has a reputation for not examining the colour of one's character but of one's cash.

K Madhavan was for 30 years a CBI officer, rising to become joint director of India's premier investigative agency. He worked on government and bank fraud cases, often being seconded to Scotland Yard and the FBI, earning a reputation as a man with a voracious appetite for the truth and the long hours required to uncover it. In 2000 he was appointed by the BCCI to conduct an inquiry into the match-fixing report authored by MA Ganapathy.

'The whole country was watching my inquiry. I think it had a lot of good effect. I had retired from the CBI a couple of years before, being known as a very good investigating officer. People felt that if Madhavan says so, it must be correct. I look back with pride? I think I did a good service,' he says.

'But,' and he stops for a moment, allowing himself a smile, 'I think they chose me because I am a fast worker. For the past 40 years I am a very fast worker. No one needs to tell me. Even in CBI I was supposed to be the fastest. I don't allow things to keep pending. In fact, today I have no work from yesterday pending. My desk is clear. I find it very comfortable, you can relax and enjoy instead of work piling up … you would be constantly thinking about it. I start at 3.30 in the morning and go to bed at 8.30 at night. I have been like that from childhood. I get enough sleep.'

Now in his 60s, and working as a lawyer from a small, stuffy, annexed home office, Madhavan makes for a fascinating, if not challenging interview. Before answering each question he will pause, look gravely at a desk cluttered with files, a Mickey Mouse Sellotape dispenser and a peach tree gathering dust, and lick his lips several times before speaking for minutes at a time. The only problem comes with the distractions and interruptions. His assistant is back and forth through a ratchety sliding door, collecting files. Through the other equally squeaky door, which leads to the rest of the house, keeps appearing his wife, complaining about the internet connection. We both lose our thread. 'Corruption' in cricket and in the country he 'adores' gets us back on the straight and narrow.

An unusually long pause follows a question about whether the BCCI have adhered to one of the chief recommendations following his inquiry – that they must be responsible for enforcing discipline on players who are vulnerable prey to gamblers and bookmakers. 'I don't know. We don't hear much about match-fixing by Indian teams. Either they are doing it in total secrecy or we are unable to catch them. Or maybe the fact that Azharuddin was banned for life has stopped it. I think the players still remember that. Some of these people started their lives at that time. So in the dressing room there must be gossip. "Don't do such things." But the cricket boards around the world would not want such things to come out. They don't want it to come out. That is human nature. If I have defects in my household I would not like my neighbour to know about it. Things are swept under the carpet, I feel.

'The people of India probably think the same as me about their sport. I will still watch a match on television. My work on the inquiry didn't make me think "why has that happened?" when watching a game. That is a blessing because I do love cricket. I was a spin bowler, a leg spinner, you know? Not much of a batsman. I wouldn't be in for very long. I shifted to tennis at 21 and when I joined the CBI at 26 I had to stop everything because of so much work ...'

The door rattles and his wife shouts a question about downloads.

'What were we saying? Oh, yes ... You can't live your life that way. I was handling bad people in the police. If I allowed that to interfere with my thinking of every human being I meet, that would not be the correct way of conducting oneself in the world. Not everyone is a crook. A cynical mind is required when dealing with crooks, but once you leave the office and mix in the world, you must get rid of it and start believing people 'til they are proved to be ... bad. That has been my attitude to life. I believe in you when you come to talk, I believe in your sincerity. I don't suspect you.'

Madhavan has a mournful look when I remind him of some statistics gathered by Transparency International, the global civil society organisation that claims to lead the fight against world corruption. Its 2010 Corruption Perception Index ranked India a lowly 87th out of 178 countries. The UK was 20th and the US 22nd. It also claimed that more than 55 per cent of Indians had first-hand experience of paying bribes or influence peddling to get jobs done successfully in public offices. A November 2010 report from the Washington-based Global Financial Integrity estimated that India lost at least US$462 billion in 'illicit financial flows', another term for black money, from 1948 through 2008.

'And you wonder why cricket has a problem?' he says. 'It is an increase across all facets of life because of all bad activities of all human beings in past 50 years. Drugs have increased, alcohol has increased, prostitution, swindling, political corruption. People who never used to commit crimes in the past have become corrupt. Judges and politicians. These things were unknown 50 years back. It was crooks who committed offences. Not well-placed persons. Now well-placed persons also commit offences. And those who have no need with a livelihood, they are also committing offences because of greed. They want more and more.

'This is not unique to India, but India is worse than a lot of countries, yes. All over the world it is happening, particularly the USA also. The lobbies in Washington. They do nothing but corruption. You can call it by a glorified name, lobbying, and all that, but at the moment you have to lobby a political side to get work done ... things are not done for now, they are done for money. The so-called legalised lobbying going on in the USA is corruption, in fact. If the work has to be done for the people, you don't have to lobby for that. The NHS in the UK ... no one has to ask for it to be done. The government does it. Lobbying is when commercial interests are involved. And then you get corruption.

'I personally feel the level of honesty in New Zealand, Australia, and to some extent England is of a higher level than in India, Pakistan and Sri Lanka, maybe 20 to 30 per cent. Traditionally, because of poverty in India, it has been a very poor country, the level of poverty is very high. The middle class has become better off. There has been a constant struggle to live. At any means. That psyche exists today. Unfortunately, that exists even in people who don't need that psyche, who are well off and that exists more in Asian countries.

'But today I read that some prime minister from a small country [Ukraine] has been sentenced for seven years for corruption. These things are not normal. Fifty years back you would never think of a prime minister of a democratic country being sentenced for corruption. Ninety per cent of politicians had good intentions, now no good man joins politics in India ... he keeps far away. Only crooks join Indian parliament. So if you go to Indian parliament, 90 per cent are crooks now. Not bad people, but outright crooks. They are willing to commit any offence to get things done, including murder, corruption, cheating, fraud. And I think such denigration has happened all over the world.'

Madhavan may be guilty of quoting arbitrary figures, but he is not far off being accurate. From December 2008, 120 of India's 522 members of parliament were facing criminal charges. So it will perhaps come as no surprise that India's electorate and political system tolerates a man who abused his position of power so grossly that he was able to hold to ransom the sport that unites a nation. Madhavan, in his 2000 BCCI inquiry, called him 'despicable'. Effigies were burnt on the streets of Mumbai. Mohammad Azharuddin, India captain, banned for life for match-fixing, is now member of parliament for Moradabad in Uttar Pradesh.

'I am not surprised to see him where he is now, no,' Madhavan says. 'Honesty is not a necessary ingredient in India to becoming an MP. But, please, I have changed my view of him after these years. Of course, what he did was despicable. Please remember that all these persons are very immature when they became famous. Not like Bill Gates at the age of 50, when he became rich and big. These people [cricketers] become big by the time they are 22 or 23. Considering the wisdom that comes at age of 35 to 40 by making mistakes, at the age of 22 even I feel I was quite immature in my thinking and values, so I don't know whether he was crooked or it was his age.'

Azharuddin was three hours late for his appointment with Madhavan at the Ramada Manohar Hotel on 16 November 2000. 'He was deeply worried,' Madhavan recalls. 'He was ashamed he was caught. When initially I called him, he refused to come. Then through a messenger I showed him my purpose was not a witch hunt, my purpose was a fair inquiry and to only fault people who had committed some crime or some irregularities.' Having put Azharuddin at ease, Madhavan's first question was 'Aur tum desh ko kab se bechne mein lage huay ho?' ('Since when have you been selling the country?'). Azharuddin buried his face in his hands.

Despite his show of emotion and anxiety, Azharuddin stonewalled. He defended himself. Having admitted in Ganapathy's report that he had 'done' three matches, he denied he had done anything wrong to Madhavan. 'Most of the people who are caught in India,' Madhavan says, 'they keep denying until the end. Even after the Supreme Court says they are guilty, they deny. But there is one redeeming feature of the west that 50 per cent of the people confess. Clinton finally confessed he had an affair with Monica [Lewinsky]. In the past 50 years no India politician has confessed. No one confesses. Even a crossing a red light they will deny, which is a very minor violation. No chance in India. I have been noticing for the past 25 to 30 years in my specialisation as an investigating officer, the tendency to confess and seek pardon is more in the west than in India.'

PART THREE

ANALYSIS

CHAPTER 16

THE FIX THAT WASN'T

The story of Pakistan's tour of England in the summer of 2010 would have made good reading as a thriller. Intrigue, infamy, cash in suitcases, back-stabbing, even a bit of sex, thanks to Veena Malik, the buxom former girlfriend of Mohammad Asif having her say, and, finally, court-room drama. Salman Butt, the Pakistan captain, Asif and Mohammad Amir, the two fast bowlers, and Mazhar Majeed, the fixer, were each sentenced to prison for their part in bowling no-balls to order in the fourth Test at Lord's in August of that year. The four men, who all blamed one another for the crime, had been charged with conspiracy to accept corrupt payments and conspiracy to cheat at gambling.

It was considered a disastrous day for cricket. Aftab Jafferjee, QC for the prosecution, said: 'This case reveals a depressing tale of rampant corruption at the heart of international cricket.' He added that the extent of fraud made it hard for spectators to watch matches 'without a sense of disquiet'. It was, however, considered a great day for investigative journalism. The Pakistan cricketers and Majeed, who claimed to be their agent, had been exposed by a *News of the World* reporter. Hidden cameras showed Majeed talking to an undercover journalist called Mazher Mahmood, perhaps best known as the 'Fake Sheikh', who had a habit of embarrassing public figures, including the former England football manager Sven-Goran Eriksson, in sting operations.

Majeed was seen to propose three no-balls during the Lord's Test, two to be bowled by Amir and one by Asif. For this information he was paid £150,000. The video shows Majeed taking bundles of cash from a suit-case and counting it, riffling the £50 notes through his fingers. Majeed said that Butt would do his bidding. Amir, just 18 at the time, bowled two no-balls, one by nine inches and the other by 12 inches. These were huge and conspicuous, betraying his inexperience – and possibly his fear.

Asif, a veteran of Test cricket since 2005 and with a bowling action as smooth as honey falling from a spoon, stepped over the line by a fraction.

When it became clear that the *News of the World* had their men by the throat, Colin Myler, the newspaper's editor, summoned the cricket correspondent Sam Peters, and Richie Benaud, a columnist of almost 54 years, to the Wapping offices. 'Tomorrow, gentlemen,' Myler said. 'The *News of the World* is going to break the biggest story in its history.'

'Caught!' screamed the headline under a 'world exclusive' banner. 'Match-fixer pockets £150k as he rigs the England Test at Lord's'. And also 'We expose betting scandal that will rock cricket'.

Indeed, cricket was unsteady on its feet for many months afterwards and it is arguable that it had still not righted itself when jail terms were handed down to the four fixers. Butt received two years and six months, Asif one year, Amir six months and Majeed two years and eight months. Myler was right. The story that had everything was a bestseller.

But did it really have everything? The answer is, unquestionably, no. In the backstreets of every Indian city from Nimbahera to Mumbai, in outbuildings or bedrooms of crumbling apartments, from Vinay to Parthiv, never above the jabber of the bhao line operator and the echo of punters placing bets, did a bookmaker cry 'souda fok!' – all bets are off, it's a fix – when Amir or Asif bowled those no-balls. When they overstepped the line at Lord's to spark the crisis that the ICC called the biggest scandal to hit the sport since the Hansie Cronje affair, there was no meltdown by India's bookmakers. There was no panic on the streets of Lucknow. In other words, there was no betting scam. There was no spot-fix.

It is the great irony of this tale. A story purported to be the latest in a litany of match-fixing scandals in the sport, to be placed on a par with the Cronje crime and, for the first time, see cricketers convicted in a court of law, was far from removed from the illegal Indian market where the 'fix' supposedly had its roots.

'Maybe the monies had gone elsewhere,' Parthiv said. 'But having read the *News of the World* report, it seemed clear to me they had been scammed.'

Recordings by the newspaper showing Mazhar Majeed, a Croydon-based businessman, predicting when the no-balls would be bowled would appear proof of match-fixing or spot-fixing to the layman. But to anyone with a semblance of betting knowledge it was anything but. The *News of the World* spent £150,000 and failed to get a bet on. The money paid was for Majeed to prove that he could control the Pakistan players.

Amid the media storm, not once was the question asked: if the newspaper had wanted to make money betting on the Indian market on those no-balls, could it have done so? We know the answer to this. Parthiv, Vinay and Rattan Mehta, the Delhi punter of renowned infamy, have each confirmed that it is not possible to bet on the timing of a no-ball. Dheeraj Dixit, our 'fixer' friend from the suburbs of Delhi, and MA Ganapathy, the author of the CBI report on match-fixing published in 2000, did the same.

Yet it was convenient for the media to ignore this point. It would have spoiled the story otherwise. Today, if you type 'Pakistan Lord's Betting Scam' into the internet search engine Google, 1,840,000 results are returned, including stories from the BBC, *Daily Telegraph,* Sky – organisations one might consider bastions of accurate, diligent journalism. Instead, it was preferable to portray Indian bookmakers as crafty, money-grabbing crime lords who would not raise so much as an eyebrow if someone attempted to place a bet on a no-ball. The contradiction is glaring. The fallacy laughable.

The illegal Indian market is a monster. It is vast. It is unregulated. But it is structured and it is certainly not complacent. Remember that there are only four main markets available to gamblers in India and all bookmakers sign up for those odds provided by the syndicates.

'Do you think we're fools?' Vinay said to me. 'If someone says they want this no-ball bet for big monies and I'm Ladbrokes in London, I tell them to go away. No bookmaker in the world takes this bet.'

One does not need to be connected to Indian bookmakers to understand this. It is common sense. If you, the reader, were to walk into any betting shop on the high street and ask for £1,000 on an outcome as specific as a no-ball in a Test match, the cashier would say 'wait a minute, please' and disappear to make a telephone call to head office. Upon his return she would tell you that they could not accept the wager. 'It's not our policy,' would be the bluff. The real reason would be that they suspected you had inside information. It is no different in India.

But let us suspend reality for a moment and consider a fantasy world where there had been a betting market for the *News of the World* journalist to exploit, to get his bet on and ensure that his story truly was a betting scam. How hard would it have been? The phrase 'needle in a haystack' is apt.

The *News of the World* would have to have found a multitude of Indian bookmakers operating outside of the syndicate system. These are the small-time bookies Vinay spoke of. The ones who accept wagers of no more than 25,000 rupees (£306) on the regular match odds, brackets, innings runs and lunchtime favourite markets but also occasionally on 'who will win the toss', how many runs Tendulkar will score. Not, however, no-balls to be bowled at a specific time.

They are a discordant bunch. They are not structured. They are not connected to one another. And, most importantly, they do not have the safety net of the syndicate if their losses get too great. They are far less likely than the high-street bookmaker to take 'requested' wagers.

With that in mind, for the *News of the World* to break even from their £150,000 outlay, the minimum a fixer would expect, they would have had to seek out hundreds of these small-timers, who sometimes operate from the shop floor of factories, paying commission to the owner for a pitch to tout their wares.

To be precise, 490 separate wagers would have been needed to be placed at the maximum bet of 25,000 rupees. And that was if the bookmaker would offer odds of even money – unlikely, given that they were being approached by gamblers they had not previously met, and certainly did not trust, on a market they would never have chalked up. Frankly, it would have been nigh on impossible for anyone on the Indian system to have made money out of those no-balls being bowled at Lord's.

In this example, the notion that one is able to fix weird and wonderful elements of cricket matches is once again exposed. Substitute the no-ball 'spot-fix' for a wide, a boundary being hit, a fielder being placed in a peculiar position, a bowler to open at a particular end. It is unfeasible, just as Vinay said. The minutiae of inside information is used to manipulate markets in the favour of the syndicate, bookmaker or punter, not to win specific bets.

A no-ball in a Twenty20 match adds to the batting team's total and offers the batsman a free hit. One cannot bet on that no-ball occurring, but the syndicate, bookmaker or punter can manipulate the odds in his favour for, say, a bracket because he knows that runs will be scored. It is a potentially game-changing event as there is a maximum of 120 legal balls in a Twenty20 innings. Its importance in terms of inside information is significant. A no-ball in a Test match does not have the same impact, or even close. In one day of play in a Test match there are at least 540 legal balls. The runs quote for a bracket would not move the market sufficiently to be worth manipulating. It is not a game-changing event. A run has been scored. So what?

One could argue that in the case of the Pakistan 'spot-fixing', it is irrelevant that one would not have been able to bet on a no-ball being bowled. Pakistan were shown to be guilty of corrupt practices. They were cheating the game, their teammates and the spectators. And one would be absolutely right, but only if the court they were being tried in and the judge that would sentence them was aware that a no-ball is not a betting opportunity in India. The court was not aware. The judge was not aware. This much is clear from the erroneous sentencing remarks by Mr Justice Cooke: 'Bets could be placed on these no-balls in unlawful markets, mostly abroad, based on inside advance knowledge of what was going to happen … Individuals in India were making £40,000–£50,000 on each identified no-ball. On three no-balls, therefore, the bookmakers stood to lose £150,000 on each bet by a cheating punter.'

Mr Justice Cooke was apparently convinced that there was an opportunity to wager by evidence given by the prosecution's first witness, Ravi Sawani, the former general manager of the ACSU. He told the court it is possible to bet on a no-ball. However, and to widespread astonishment, he also admitted he did not know what a bracket was.

Butt, Asif, Amir and Majeed went to prison for charges that included 'conspiracy to cheat at gambling'. If there was no bet placed, if there was no opportunity to even place that bet and therefore no one was defrauded, can anyone really be guilty of such a charge?

The Gambling Act of 2005 defines 'conspiracy to cheat at gambling' as the following:

1. A person commits an offence if he:
   (a) cheats at gambling, or
   (b) does anything for the purpose of enabling or assisting another person to cheat at gambling.
2. For the purposes of subsection 1 it is immaterial whether a person who cheats:
   (a) improves his chances of winning anything, or
   (b) wins anything.
3. Without prejudice to the generality of subsection 1 cheating at gambling may, in particular, consist of actual or attempted deception or interference in connection with:
   (a) the process by which gambling is conducted, or
   (b) a real or virtual game, race or other event or process to which gambling relates.

It would be difficult to consider the conviction of the four men under this charge as robust simply because of the absence of an opportunity to bet on a no-ball, the earthquake that no one heard or felt. Butt, Asif, Amir or Majeed could not have been 'cheats at gambling' or done 'anything for the purpose of enabling or assisting another person to cheat at gambling' if there was no method to do either. That they could have been considered aware that they were 'enabling or assisting' is a moot point perhaps. In the case of Amir, he has since claimed he was unaware that he was asked to bowl no-balls for betting purposes, instead blaming Majeed and Butt for tricking him into thinking his career would be under threat if he did not do as his captain told him.

So what the *News of the World* sting revealed was not spot-fixing, but corrupt practices within the Pakistan team. That was the justification for the scoop, although there has since been a lingering level of discomfort among journalists about the way it was conducted. Clearly it was a set-up, a classic *agent provocateur* – a person associated with individuals suspected of wrongdoing with the purpose of inciting them to commit acts that will make them liable to punishment. It is interesting to note that the Press Complaints Commission upheld a complaint by Yasir Hameed, the Pakistan batsman, on a similar 'sting' operation by the *News of the World* in relation to the spot-fixing scandal. Hameed argued that his privacy was breached by hidden cameras and recording equipment when he was speaking to the 'Fake Sheikh' about corruption in the Pakistan team.

Mr Justice Cook said the *News of the World* had 'got what they bargained for'. He could have said that the *News of the World* were the corruptors – and to all intents and purposes that is exactly what they were. Without their money, those no balls would not have been bowled.

Nor would the no-balls have been bowled if Mazhar Majeed was the fixing 'kingpin' as he was portrayed. The 'sting' would surely have been drawn from the *News of the World* if Majeed was indeed the experienced fixer that he claimed to be. In 'sales' chatter to impress the undercover journalist, Majeed boasted of his knowledge and expertise in the field: 'It's been happening for centuries. It's been happening for years. Wasim [Akram], Waqar [Younis, who was the coach of the Pakistan team during that series against England], Ijaz Ahmed, Moin Khan – they all did it.

'I've been doing this with the Pakistani team now for about two-and-a-half years, and we've made masses and masses of money. You can make absolute millions.

'We are working towards next month. It is going to be big. I will give you an exact script of how it is going to happen. We've got one result already planned and that is coming up in the next three-and-a-half weeks. Pakistan will lose.'

Majeed said that it would cost between £50,000 and £80,000 for information for a bracket, £400,000 to fix a result of a Twenty20 match, £450,000 for a one-day international and £1 million to fix a Test match. There was no mention of how much a no-ball would cost because Majeed, correctly, did not believe one could bet on such an outcome. Yet when the *News of the World* reporter was talking about placing bets on no-balls, Majeed, instead of hearing alarm bells ringing in his head, heard the shrill ringing of the cash register. Had money not been on his mind, he might have recognised he was being scammed.

Instead, he was focused on providing the no-balls that had been demanded, believing that if he could prove that Pakistan players were under his control, there would be more money to come. When Majeed met the journalist at the Copthorne Tara Hotel on 25 August, the evening before the Lord's Test match, it was, in fact, the fifth time they had convened. Majeed was sure that Butt, Amir and Asif would do as he said. He was unequivocal, where in the past he had been sketchy about details discussed from a previous Test at the Oval. 'I'm going to give you three no-balls, OK? … right? … to prove to you firstly that this is what is happening. No-balls are the easiest and they're the clearest. There's no signal, nothing. These three are definitely happening.'

Majeed was true to his word. Amir bowled a no-ball the next day from the third ball of the third over and Asif overstepped on the sixth ball of the tenth over. The third was not delivered because the poor weather, which had delayed the start until 1.40pm, also cut play short with only 12.3 overs possible.

Keen to reassure his 'sponsor' that a third no-ball would still be delivered, Majeed rang the journalist that evening. He told him that Amir would bowl a no-ball off the third ball of his third full over as he still had three balls to bowl the next morning following the disruption. Majeed confirmed this with Amir via text message.

However, for an unknown reason, Majeed attempted to get the 'fix' called off. He phoned the journalist, telling him that there 'was no point doing the third now'. It is this volte-face that is crucial in exposing Majeed's inexperience. Alarmed at the prospect of his scoop losing some lustre, the journalist thinks quickly and tells Majeed that he must go through with the third no-ball because his 'syndicate' has already placed the bets. This is important. The 'syndicate' is claiming to have placed wagers on the timing of no-balls before the match had started. 'So you can place money on the no-balls then?' Majeed asks. The journalist says yes. 'What sort of monies?' says a surprised Majeed. This is the partially sighted leading the blind.

There can be no doubt that an experienced fixer would know that it is not possible to bet on a no-ball. If Majeed had been the shrewd, shady operator that he claimed to be, and the *News of the World* had been only too willing to enhance this 'reputation', then he would have immediately recognised that the journalist was lying.

Indeed, Majeed's ignorance is stupefying. For a start he should have known that it was not possible for the 'syndicate' to place these 'bets' on a market that did not exist. Secondly, a fixer well-connected to the Indian industry would have known that even if such a market did exist, it would have been out of the question to have already placed such a wager before the Test match had started, as the reporter said his 'punters' had done. Someone asking for odds for a no-ball from a bowler's third ball off his third full over on the second day would have been laughed at by any bookmaker in India or anywhere else on the planet. All odds pre-match are run by the Jayanti Malad syndicate and they only offer match odds, team innings runs and lunch favourite. For someone to try to bet on a no-ball before a match had started would be unthinkable.

So why did Majeed not realise that his game was up? The most likely explanation is that he was desperate for the money. His Bluesky firm, which had contracts with local councils to renovate derelict houses, was shown at the time of the trial by Companies House to have five County Court judgements against it. It also had unpaid bills of more than £74,000. Two more of Majeed's companies were the subject of applications to strike off, a third was in liquidation, a fourth was in receivership and a fifth, also in liquidation, owed £596,000. The court was also told that, at the time of his arrest, police had found Majeed held 30 bank accounts showing total arrears of £704,000. These are not the trappings of a man who boasted about making 'masses and masses of money'.

It is possible that Majeed was an aspirant fixer, which would go some way to explain the child-like delight that Amir described when he arrived in his hotel room at the Marriott in Swiss Cottage 'looking like he had hit the jackpot, he was so happy' to give the young bowler £1,500. 'He said. "You are my younger brother" and he was buzzing with excitement.' One would have thought a veteran fixer would have recognised this as 'business as usual'.

There are other clues to suggest that Majeed was an unproven operator in the field. For a start, there was the failed fix in the Oval Test that summer. Majeed had met with the *News of the World* reporter for the first time on 16 August at the Park Lane Hotel, two days before the start of that match. The two parties were feeling each other out, establishing one another's authenticity. Perhaps they were fooling each other.

It was not until their second meeting two days later that the discussion turned to fixing. They met at the Bombay Brasserie in London on the Gloucester Road. The journalist wanted no-balls to be bowled 'so that our boys have got an indication this is on. Then they'll invest big'. Majeed agreed and, ever the showman, added 'I'll give you two if you want.' When the pair met for a third time, on this occasion at a restaurant on the Edgware Road, Majeed confirmed a fix was on after he was paid £10,000: 'All right, just to show you that it's real, I'm going to show you two no-balls tomorrow … I'll call you on another number, yeah, and I'll call you about 8.30 in the morning and I'll give you the two balls they're going to do it on.'

Of course, it was not on. Majeed failed to give any details of when the no-balls would be bowled and by whom, suggesting that he was not as capable of influencing players as he said he was. Majeed started to stall for more time. He said the no-balls would not be bowled at the Oval on the third day because Waqar Younis, the coach, had warned the team about the number of no-balls on the opening day of the Test. Waqar, giving testimony to the ICC tribunal about the case, denied he gave such a team talk. Majeed then said there could not be a no-ball the next day either because Saeed Ajmal, the spin bowler, was bowling and he was not under his influence.

In an attempt to appease the journalist, Majeed told him that he had agreed with Butt that the captain would play out a maiden in the first over on 21 August with the captain tapping with his bat the middle of the wicket after the second ball he had faced to confirm. Butt did not tap the pitch and there was no maiden.

Could it have been that Majeed was frantically trying to buy time to get players onside? Butt, whom Majeed had described as a 'million per cent' trustworthy, most likely was close to the businessman – he had made personal appearances to promote his faltering property firm and during the Oval Test was scheduled to open an ice-cream parlour in

Tooting in which Majeed had a stake – but it would appear doubtful he could trust anyone else in the Pakistan side.

At this stage the *News of the World* must have thought they had a dud. 'He [Butt] didn't do it [the maiden],' the journalist told Majeed. 'What if we give you £150,000 and he doesn't do it and then we put the big money on and it's all over?'

And then, pertinently: 'They don't listen to you; they don't take your orders.'

Majeed replied: 'OK, boss. Just remember you're telling me that they don't listen to me, right? I've been in this game a long time and, remember, you're the one who contacted me.'

Wounded by this criticism and worried he was about to be found out by the 'syndicate' for being a fraud (oh, the irony), a probably desperate Majeed hit upon a plan. With Butt's help he would target the young naïf Amir, and Asif, who came with a disreputable reputation as long as his bowling arm.

Amir, who spoke for the first time in depth of the ordeal in March 2012, claimed that Majeed had blackmailed him to bowl the no-balls at Lord's. On the eve of the Lord's Test Amir received a telephone call from Majeed asking him to meet in the car park of the team hotel. They met in Majeed's car.

'All of a sudden it was as if someone launched an attack,' Amir said. 'He said to me, "You're in big trouble, bro. You're trapped and your career is at stake."'

Majeed told him that the ICC's ACSU had information that Amir had been talking about spot-fixing with a man called Ali, whom the bowler knew as a 'businessman' he had met for the first time in Dubai in 2009. Text messages between the two showed that Ali was, at the least, trying to get Amir to spot-fix for him. One, on the eve of the Oval Test, from Ali to Amir read: 'So in the first three bowl whatever you like and in the last two do eight runs?'

There is no evidence that Amir fixed a bracket for Ali in that Test match and all communication between the two had stopped after that game. Majeed is likely to have known about Amir's relationship with Ali because Butt had told the young tyro to stay away from Ali. Amir had told his captain that Ali had been 'bugging' him. 'He [Majeed] said he could help me out of my difficulties, but that I had to do a favour for him in return,' Amir said. 'I asked him: "What favour?" That's when he mentioned the two no-balls.

'I realise now that nobody is more stupid than me, that I could not see how ridiculous it was that on the one hand he should be telling me that I was in trouble with the ICC and on the other that I should bowl him two no-balls. But I was panicking and I had lost the ability to comprehend what was going on. After about five minutes, Salman joined us and he sat in the back seat, leaning over between the two front seats, just listening. He didn't say anything.

'I told him that it was impossible because my feet were always behind the line, that it was a wrong thing to do and that I was scared. He told me not to worry and to practise bowling them at Lord's during the practice sessions before the match. He said not to worry because Salman would be with me and would help me. I got out of the car and Salman, who still hadn't said anything at this point, stayed behind. I was worried now and went and sat on the team bus to go to practice, worrying about what I was to do.'

Asif needed manipulating too, but he was too wily a campaigner to fall for such a simple trick as blackmail. Asif, it is understood, was known to the ACSU as an unreliable character. In 2006 he had been banned for doping before having his suspension overturned on appeal. He had also been detained in Dubai under the suspicion of carrying drugs and he had tested positive for a banned substance when playing in the IPL.

In court Majeed said via his barrister that he had paid Asif £65,000 to 'keep him loyal' and prevent him from joining rival fixing rackets, involved elsewhere within the team. This admission backs up the belief of Dheeraj Dixit, Asif's former friend and the 'fixer' from Delhi, that Majeed had little control over the Pakistan players and that he had to keep paying out extra funds to try to prevent them from fixing with rival factions.

So we have picture of Majeed as financially broken, bungling and desperate. Someone who would blackmail an 18-year-old bowler considered the golden boy of Pakistan cricket into cheating, threatening him that his career was on the line. And then pay him a measly £1,500 for the deal. Asif, the polar opposite of Amir, and apparently a gun for hire, netted a handsome sum. Mr Justice Cooke said of Asif 'it is hard to see how this could be an isolated occurrence for you'.

Justice Cooke was, however, convinced that Majeed and Butt were perceptive designers in the fixing world. He blamed them for corrupting Amir, who he described as 'unsophisticated, uneducated, impressionable'.

He also told Majeed that he was not persuaded that the *News of the World* sting was the 'tip of an iceberg', but pointed to evidence, outside of the boasts and bluster to the newspaper's journalist, that suggested Majeed had been involved in fixing prior to the Lord's Test. 'It appears that corruption may have been more widespread than the defendants here before me and may have permeated the team in earlier days,' Justice Cooke said.

CHAPTER 17

WHAT DOES THE ACSU DO?

The ACSU was set up in 2000 in the wake of the Hansie Cronje affair. Its role was to educate players about what was right and wrong, to keep them in check if they strayed and, if they did stray seriously, to expel them. A classic teacher–pupil relationship, one might argue. And since its inception there has been much sniggering and insolence from the back row.

With corruption apparently rife in the game pre-Cronje, the ACSU has been to unruly sorts like a supply teacher drafted in at the last minute. They have been criticised for being ineffective, lacking any real power and for being reactive rather than proactive. Consider the statement from Haroon Lorgat, the chief executive of the ICC, when the *News of the World* broke the spot-fixing scandal at Lord's. 'We were already watching those players,' he said. And the cricket world threw up its collective arms, flabbergasted, and wailed: 'Why didn't you throw them out, then?'

This is a common cry whenever a match-fixing story appears in the media. The ACSU are disparaged, and not just among cricket fans. It has a poor reputation among the players in the world game. Remember that exasperated international captain asking Lorgat why more was not being done prior to the World Cup in 2011? Just like any classroom, the majority of pupils want the disruptive few removed. One international player said to me: 'They are a joke. They don't seem to do anything. We have all these rules and regulations to adhere to and yet nothing seems to get done. What are they doing to help us?'

It would appear to be an unfair statement. When the bell rings to bring the lesson to an end and the pupils collect up their belongings and rush off to enjoy leisurely pursuits, the teacher keeps working – and long hours too: paperwork, filing, meeting local police and team security managers, liaising with intelligence agencies and immigration services, attempting to spot would-be corruptors, interviewing umpires and officials.

There can be no doubt that the ACSU has helped to lessen the problem of corruption. Its Code of Conduct sees to that. To read it is to wonder at the skill, nerve and sheer front of corruptors who have managed to swerve the obstacles put in their way where many would have been put off. It is why the likes of Parthiv and Vinay do not fear the local laws, but the ACSU. Vinay said that international matches were 'hard to fix now because of the ACSU'. It is why many fixers have turned their attentions to county cricket.

Lord Condon, the retired former Metropolitan Police Commissioner, was the ACSU founder or, to stay true to our analogy, its first headmaster. Condon, who had compared cricket to US wrestling in the 1990s, with people not believing they were watching genuine contests, laid down strict rules and regulations that players had to adhere to. The ACSU's Code of Conduct is the toughest of any sporting body in the world, demanding access to bank and telephone records. Approaches must be reported, inquiries co-operated with. If a player fails, then he is disciplined. 'It's for your own good,' the headmaster might rebuke.

When the unit was set up, it was divided into parts. There were five regional security managers, each of them looking after two international teams, and then a headquarters, originally based in London before the ICC moved to Dubai in 2005, of intelligence managers who would maintain a database of the unit's workings.

When I meet Lord Condon at the House of Lords in March 2012, having pestered him for a meeting with the belligerent request to 'tell me exactly what the ACSU does', he speaks with pride at the formation of the unit, praising the 'absolute dedication' of staff he handpicked 'because I knew they were great police or intelligence officers who were desperate to see cricket sorted'. We sit across a table from one another in the Royal Gallery, a grand setting which hosts state receptions, dinners and parliamentary ceremonies.

'Those five regional security guys were on the road the whole time,' Condon says with a slight rasp to his voice, the product of a recent bout of bronchitis. 'They travelled with the teams. Their role was to deliver the education programme and provide a hotline-whistleblowing type service. Any of the players or management or anyone could contact them with information about fixing. And a lot of information we got, particularly in more recent years, came from players and management. The regional security managers were at all the matches. They did intelligence reports, they spotted known fixers, known punters, worked with the local police, intelligence services. So they were the field officers. So those five guys, that's what they do, day in and day out.

'I remember Colonel Nur, whom I recruited to be regional security man for Pakistan and Bangladesh, a very courageous former army officer. He worked tirelessly even when he was very, very ill, carried on working right up to his death. He was a very dedicated guy and part of the reason the Pakistan team went off the rails [after Nur's death], I believe, was that Nur was a father figure and they could and did tell him what was going on. He was on the road more than 200 days a year. It sounds glamorous, but he was not travelling as part of a team. He was on his own, living out of a suitcase, trying to keep the game clean.'

Information that regional security managers provide is fed into the database, an intelligence hub that Condon says is 'very sophisticated'.

'It's based on the same software that police intelligence officers use around the world, and on there are all the intelligence reports, the suspects, the bad guys, the incidents. It adheres to all the high standards of data protection. All manner of people input details: police forces, intelligence services, our own staff. Bookmakers, legitimate and unlawful, would be on there because we have memorandums of understandings with people like Betfair and they are providers of info. Also we have informants among the unlawful bookmakers, primarily in India.' Tax authorities will also be asked for their input.

'There were some players in the past who had houses or cars which they shouldn't have been able to afford,' Condon says. The database comes into its own for a major ICC tournament, like a World Cup, World Twenty20 or Champions' Trophy.

'So for the World Cup in 2003 in South Africa we worked up a list of a hundred suspects and we provided those to the South African police, intelligence agencies and immigration agency. Each of those hundred would have been turned away if they tried to enter South Africa.'

The ACSU has been added to since it was set up, but Condon still calls it a 'small team'. As well as the intelligence managers who nurture the database, the general manager of the ACSU can call on a small number of senior investigators who, although based in Dubai, work all over the world. They have backgrounds as senior police investigators, in serious crime or terrorism. It is their job to begin inquiries when reports are received, either through a regional security manager, via the email or whistle-blowing hotline or any other source. What happens next?

'In essence it could be anything from checking with the database confirmation of what we already know, it could be serious enough to generate some immediate phone calls to regional security managers, it could be serious enough to start a live operation, which could lead to people moving around the world to be in certain locations. But the first thing is the assessment, and that is modelled on what police and intelligence services do all over the world: firstly, assess the integrity of the informant, how you feel about him and, secondly, you assess the information he's provided. If it's been provided by a totally unreliable source that influences how you feel about it; if it's a reliable source and can be shown to be reliable, clearly, you take more action.'

The next step is to attempt to prove malpractice. It is no easy task.

'I can remember major tournaments where there were concerns of three or four overs when the run rate slowed down for no apparent reason,' Condon says. 'That was put before a panel of recently retired experts who couldn't agree. Some would say I can see a reason why, even though the same bowler was bowling, their line was subtly different and others who said "that's got to be moody". So, when you've got international players who can't agree, it is very hard.'

Given that anecdote, it is not surprising that the ACSU's record in bringing players to justice is not impressive. Since 2000 only two players have been disciplined: Marlon Samuels, the West Indies batsman, was banned for two years for passing on information to a punter, and in 2004 Maurice Odumbe, the former Kenya captain, was banned for five years for receiving money from bookies. In the case of Samuels, the charge was considered by many in the game to be 'trumped up'. He was a soft, slow-moving target and even some ACSU officers are understood to have felt the case was weak.

The ACSU was slow to act on the threat posed by Mazhar Majeed, too. Twice they missed opportunities. In the Asia Cup in Sri Lanka in 2010 an ACSU officer was aware that Salman Butt and another player had lied to the team management about the reason they were leaving the hotel. They said they wanted to find some Pakistani food, but instead they went to meet Majeed. Then in the early part of the summer 2010, a whistleblower emailed the ACSU with messages downloaded from Majeed's BlackBerry. The ACSU claim they did not have the manpower to react. The whistleblower instead went to the *News of the World*.

It is no wonder there are doubts surrounding the ACSU. There is a contradictory element which runs a rich seam through the match-fixing story. Have only two players been brought to book by the ACSU because they do such a good job educating and putting off the villains? Are they so toothless they are capable of only limited success? Or is cricket much cleaner than the cynics and rumour-mongers would want to believe? Condon is riled by the suggestion of a gummy bite.

'That's unfair,' he says. 'I think they are good people doing the best they can in the circumstances. They don't have police powers. They are working for an international sports governing body so they don't have the powers that police forces have. When we started we all said, right at the top of the hierarchy, that if people can be done for criminal offences then that's the best thing. It shows the seriousness of the offence, it deters others. Second best is cricket discipline. What I make a judgement of is if you look at what was happening up to 2000 and then what has happened since. I am also convinced that the majority of international cricketers over last the ten years are clean, have not been drawn into malpractice, certainly nowhere near the levels of what was taking place previously, as I think serious match-fixing of whole matches or events stopped probably around 2001 or 2002.

'As for "not doing anything", it is wrong. The ACSU have worked with the ECB and ACB and WICB so, yes, there was a lot of below-the-tip-of-the-iceberg stuff, where players would have been warned, reminded of their responsibilities. There was the [Mervyn] Westfield case [the Essex bowler convicted of spot-fixing]. The ACSU worked on that. Quite a lot of that went on.'

Condon has obvious frustrations that his unit has not received the credit it deserves. Before we met he told me he was going to stop talking about the issue in the media because of the spurious stories he was being asked to comment on and to explain why the ACSU did not take part in a sting operation. 'If I had a pound for every time ...' he sighs. If the *News of the World* could do it, why not the ACSU? For the record then, one last time: 'The deal with the players was, "Look, we're all in this together and we need to keep the game clean. If you are approached to fix, it's not going to be us playing a game. It'll be someone trying to do a fix for real, a media scam or a bit of both. Either way you will face serious consequences. Make no mistake, we are not going to try to set you up or play games as a unit. That's part of the deal".

'More importantly, in places like the UK, Australia, New Zealand, the Caribbean and, probably, India, it would be seen as *agent provocateur* and a prosecuting authority wouldn't proceed if the sport itself was setting up its own players for criminal offences. So it's only a once in ten-year media-type sting that forces the prosecuting authority to allow it to go through. They almost have no choice. Had it been set up, that Pakistan issue, internally by cricket, I don't think it would have gone to court. The prosecuting authority would have said "sorry, this is total *agent provocateur*, you've set up your own players and you've allowed all these spectators to come to the match, paying for their tickets, believing it is genuine". So that is why the ACSU doesn't do stings.'

It makes sense. What doesn't, though, is that the ACSU lacks betting expertise. During the spot-fixing trial at Southwark there was disbelief in court when Ravi Sawani, who had quit his post as the general manager of the ACSU in 2011, admitted that he didn't know what a bracket was. It was a damaging moment for the unit's credibility.

Condon and I disagree on whether it is possible in India to bet on the weird and wonderful markets that the ACSU have spoken of in the past: at which end a bowler will bowl, fielding positions, no-balls or wides of specific deliveries. I suggest to him that even a fundamental understanding of gambling in the country would raise doubts that such bets would be possible because of the way the bookmakers operate, offering odds on a limited amount of markets and prices being uniform throughout the country. Surely the ACSU know this?

'Well, if you believe what they [bookmakers] say,' Condon says. 'First of all, it's unlawful in the subcontinent so you have an uneasy stand-off with law enforcement. Everyone knows that it's a subcontinent that is passionate about cricket and gambling on cricket, so there's a sort of, at any one time, a sort of acceptance that maybe it's going on. The book-makers have a vested interest, so the more they acknowledge it, they are tempting, almost baiting the authorities to do something about it.'

But this is unconvincing in the extreme and paints the ACSU as an investigations team that seems to think it is acceptable to have expertise in education and criminal procedures but not gambling procedures. The ACSU is made up of former policeman. They are, of course, bound to be stronger in this area, but they believe in betting markets that do not exist.

If we were to give them the benefit of the doubt, it could be explained by the layman's furrowed brow when he is confronted by the vagaries of the gambling industry, legal or otherwise. It is a mysterious world inhabited by smart folk. Those outside of it reckon it is a byzantine world inhabited by fools.

But we don't have to give them the benefit of the doubt. They are supposed to be the protectors of the game. They should know the subtle-ties of the area in which they are working. For example, if a captain agrees to move the gully fielder to mid-off, that is not because there is a market on that event occurring. It is to manipulate a bracket, aiding the batsman to score runs. The same goes for a wide or a no-ball. Small incidents allow bookmakers or punters to make big profits. A batsman getting out at a pre-agreed score is not a potential bet across India, either. It is an oppor-tunity for a bookmaker or punter to make money when the odds change on the match market, bracket betting or innings runs, the 'lambi'.

The ACSU's specialist subject then, is the criminal underworld. So what has become of Dawood Ibrahim, his D-Company gang and their great rival Chhota Rajan? Their feud in the early 2000s was for control of the cricket betting underworld. Blood was spilt – Sharad Shetty, Ibrahim's betting kingpin, was murdered in Dubai by one of Rajan's henchmen. Players and administrators would quake in fear at the mention of D-Company and Rajan. Some still do. Dheeraj Dixit claims to have been threatened by D-Company in the fall-out from the Pakistan spot-fixing affair and to have survived an attempt on his life.

'D-Company doesn't fit in now,' Condon says. 'In the bad old days we had evidence of D-Company's influence in the Pakistan dressing room … picking the side virtually. But that's in the bad old days. Certainly organised crime was involved, probably at least two murders which were turf wars, one in Dubai. So what we used to say in the education programme was "we're not going to exaggerate or frighten, but be under no misapprehension if you get sucked into this, you can't say 'I'm in and now I want to be out'. You're in for life". At the top end of this there are bad people who threaten players and have threatened families. There was talk in the bad days of players' family members being kidnapped to put pressure on. It's not every day, but it has happened. This is a grubby, nasty scene and if you get drawn into this, you don't know where it will end, so best not to.'

There has to be irritation with the players then, if threats of violence from a mafia organisation have dissipated, as it is often used as an excuse for silence. Condon agrees. He admits there were times during his tenure that he had deep suspicions about individuals, but could not 'bottom them out'. The headmaster always wants to get more out of the pupils.

'We've given them such a fine education programme and yet there would be occasions when we had to hand out warnings. "We know you had dinner with X, we think X is a totally unsuitable person, you've had the education programme, so what do you think you're up to?" And particularly with young players. They say, "But he told me he was so and so." "Look, this is who he is, what he is, you're not stupid, even the most basic enquiry could have revealed who he was but no, this is your one warning. Do that again and you'll be disciplined."

'It's about raising awareness. The grooming was often "let me take you out for meal, I really admire you as a player, I can get you additional sponsorship" and the next meeting "that was a fabulous innings the last time, I'd really like you to have this watch, this Rolex" and then two or three months in, "How's the mood, anyone injured? Who will open the batting, bowling? I've been a good friend of yours, I spent a lot of money on you, it's not wrong, I'm not asking for much, we're friends." The sophisticated players can see that, but some of the players are quite young, not sophisticated, and can be steered.

'It's why I said after the Pakistan trial that I think the players, even though the majority want to keep it clean, could do more to be the eyes and ears for cricket. A lot of them know who the regular bad guys are who turn up at matches and who are fishing for bits of information. I think the arrest, charge and conviction of the Pakistan trio was another wake-up call. Things had got complacent.

'But I always say this to players, ex-players or journalists: if you have information, then put up or shut up. Don't peddle junk. If you really have the integrity of the game at heart, put up or shut up.'

CHAPTER 18

AFTERNOON TEA WITH THE COMMISSIONER

If there is one man who has 'put up' but wishes he had 'shut up', it is Lalit Modi. Modi, the cricket administrator who is either admired or abhorred for conceiving the IPL, accused Chris Cairns, the former New Zealand all-rounder, of match-fixing in a tweet in January 2010. It could be one of the most expensive 'mouse clicks' ever. Cairns sued for defamation in the first libel Twitter trail, Modi lost and in March 2012 he was ordered to pay £90,000 damages and costs of around £1.5 million.

The case had focused on Cairns' suspension and removal from the Indian Cricket League, a rival tournament to the IPL. Cairns had left the Chandigarh Lions team in October 2008 because of an ankle injury. Modi and his legal team failed to make a case that this was a cover-up to hide his involvement in corrupt activity.

Modi's lawyers had gathered evidence from former teammates of Cairns, who testified against him. The court also heard for Modi from Howard Beer, the former anti-corruption officer of the ICL. Judge David Bean, however, said that Modi had 'singularly failed to provide any reliable evidence' that Cairns was involved in match-fixing or spot-fixing or even that there were strong grounds for suspicion.

In a telephone conversation I had with Modi after the verdict was delivered, he said he was 'shocked'. I had an interest in the case as I had met with Modi previously to discuss whether I could be of any assistance to his legal team with my knowledge of the illegal betting markets in India. We met twice at the Cadogan Hotel in Knightsbridge, London, the second time with his lawyers.

On the third occasion I went to his house in Knightsbridge. 'Is he expecting you?' asked a snooty butler, who appeared to be desperate to adhere to the stereotype. 'He's in the shower.' I was shown up to a grand sitting room with two huge sofas guarded by four-foot-high porcelain Chinese dragons. On an oscillating coffee table were satsumas and a bowl of Lindt chocolates. Adjoining the sitting room was Modi's den. A heist film DVD was on the table with health pills, a packet of Dunhill International cigarettes and a Post-It note for the week's laundry. Half-an-hour later Modi, sockless with loafers, arrived.

'Tell me ... what's happening?' Modi does not waste time with pleasantries.

'I want to talk to you about match-fixing for a book I'm writing,' I told him.

'I'm only interested in Cairns.'

'OK, I know some bookmakers in India and I will be going there in February [2012]. Do you want me to see what I can find out from them?'

'You have that? What have you been waiting for? Tell me. I can have my lawyers in India in 24 hours for statements ... Hey [to the butler], I asked you ten minutes ago for tea and biscuits ... where are they?'

More meetings with Modi's lawyers followed. I was summoned to meet Rajeshwar Vyakarnam, one of Modi's team, at Fladgate Solicitors in Great Queen Street, London. The biscuits were already on the table. Vyakarnam wanted to know whether my contacts could tell him of any contact between Cairns and illegal bookmakers, the reputation of the ICL for corruption, how a fix would be set up and how to isolate these issues in a cross-examination.

It transpired that Vyakarnam and I would be in India at the same time. He travelled to Mumbai to meet former teammates of Cairns to gather evidence. While he was there I arranged for him to talk to Parthiv who, unprompted, was able to corroborate information the Modi team already had about how match-fixing works and the ICL's reputation, which was unreliable at best.

Vyakarnam and I met in Delhi at the Taj Palace Hotel on the second of the month. It was about 4pm and we were waiting for a book-maker, whom Parthiv had put me in touch with, to arrive. A segment of Vyakarnam's notes from the meeting about fixing – for obvious reasons not including the Cairns case – read as follows:

'He also said that XXXX XXXX is fixing. He told me to watch all of the videos of XXXX XXXX from 2007 to 2011 and I will see for myself how many wide balls he bowls in his last over. These are bowled on demand as per the instructions from bookies.

'I asked about the signals that a player may agree with the bookies. I explained that I had learnt that a bowler may remove his jumper, or retake his run-up. A batsman could change his bat, or take his helmet off. The bookmaker said yes, these are all the normal signals that could be made. He said that it is very easy. A bookie like him will be in touch with a lot of players, but you ideally need the captain and the opening bowlers and batsmen.

'I asked why. He said: "This is because you do 'session' betting. You will bet on the number of runs in a session, which is ten overs. So you need to know that you can control the number of runs. You can't do this unless you know which players will be playing from the start. Maybe you don't need the captain if you have a few very big players who you know will be playing at guaranteed numbers." He named XXXX XXXX.

'He told me to watch all of XXXX XXXX's games between 2002 and 2007. In those days the main format was 50-over cricket and the sessions [or bracket] would last 15 overs. He told me that if I look at those videos I will see that XXXX XXXX's run rate is huge in the first 11 overs, and then [from overs] 12 to 14 it will fall massively. This is because he is trying to make sure he falls in the agreed run total for that session.'

With regard to the ICL, the bookmaker said that teams would fix matches for $100,000 per game. 'Useful?' I asked Vyakarnam when the bookmaker had left. 'I think so, yes.'

When I returned to the UK, I telephoned Modi to ask for an interview for this book. 'No, no,' he said, 'not until after the Cairns case. I want to have the final say.'

Lalit Modi polarises opinion in the cricket world like no other. One is either for him or against him. The middle ground is barren. His rise from relative obscurity has been exponential. His fall quicker still. Today he is exiled in every respect: from the sport he loves, from his 'million dollar baby', the IPL, from his country. The only adjective that advocate or adversary may agree on is 'controversial'. He remains a man worth talking to and is rarely out of the headlines.

Lalit Kumar Modi was born into a wealthy and successful Indian business family. His father, Krishnan Kumar Modi, is chairman of Modi Enterprises, a company worth 40 billion rupees. He was educated at Asia's first boarding school, the Bishop Cotton School in Shimal, the summer capital of the British Raj. Between 1983 and 1986 he studied electrical engineering and business administration at Pace University and Duke University in the USA.

It was in the States that Modi, then a sophomore, first courted controversy. Before a North Carolina court he confessed to possession of cocaine, second-degree kidnapping and assault. A two-year jail sentence was suspended. Modi's lawyers say he did not serve the sentence because he was let off on probation and the Durham County Court did not give a final decision on the drugs charges.

But Modi had bought into the American dream. He wanted India to do the same, and it was in the States where the seeds of his empire, and ultimately the IPL, were sown. The Modi Entertainment Network was set up and in 1993 he agreed a deal with Walt Disney Pictures to broadcast their content in India. A year later Modi, convinced that the Indian television consumer would pay to watch top-quality sport at home, just like the American fan, became the pan-India distributor for ESPN in a ten-year agreement worth $975 million.

It was not until 2004 that Modi became involved in cricket administration. Election as president of the Rajasthan Cricket Association earned him a seat on the BCCI and 12 months later he became vice-president after he supported Sharad Pawar, a government minister, in a power struggle with Jagmohan Dalmiya, who was head of the ICC. Modi was perfectly placed to prove his worth.

Between December 2005 and August 2007, Modi's commercial expertise earned the BCCI $1 billion through sponsorship deals and media rights packages. So when he brought to the BCCI's attention his idea for a Twenty20 tournament that could further boost the coffers, they listened. Modi was put in charge, although he remained a speck on cricket's horizon. 'Lalit Modi, a BCCI vice-president, was named as its convenor' was how news outlets reported his role.

Soon Modi would become a household name, although it is perhaps reassuring that he, or the IPL, could not have been where they are today without some on-field success. The Indian cricket team winning the inaugural World Twenty20 Cup in South Africa in the same year ensured their compatriots fell in love with a format they had previously thought unattractive.

Modi's concept was an audacious one. The IPL would be a franchise-based league that involved cities instead of states and would include the world's best players. The winner and runner-up in the IPL would then go forward to a Champions League, meeting Twenty20 sides from around the world. Once more, Modi had been influenced by his time in America. This was NFL-style cricket. There would be bright clothing, loud music, Bollywood actors as team owners, and cheerleaders who would gyrate their scantily clad bodies on a podium every time a wicket fell or a boundary was scored. The rest of the world followed suit: New Zealand, South Africa, Australia and Bangladesh would attempt their own versions.

The BCCI, for the want of a better term, coined it. The television rights were sold for $1 billion. The sale of the eight franchises – Bangalore, Chennai, Delhi, Deccan, Kolkata, Mumbai, Punjab and Rajasthan – netted $700 million. The players coined it too. MS Dhoni was sold to Chennai Super Kings for $1.5 million in the first player auction.

Modi had changed the cricketing landscape for ever. With players desperate not to miss out on riches, the whole international cricketing calendar had to be tweaked. It was cash versus country. Players were accused of lacking loyalty to the national teams that had made them superstars, while they argued that in a short career they were being paid what they thought they were worth. Comparisons between the IPL and World Series and Lalit Modi and Kerry Packer were widespread.

Inevitably, Modi, as the commissioner and chairman, was making as many enemies as he was friends. His waspish, belligerent, dictatorial style began to vex. One IPL board member said Modi acted with 'impunity'.

Others said he was a bully. Numerous tales do the rounds about Modi's brusque style. One goes that on a visit to P Chidambaram, the Home Minister, to discuss the second season of IPL, which was threatened with postponement because of security concerns with elections taking place at the same time, Modi was at his rudest.

Instead of patiently waiting to be called to see the minister, Modi showed scant regard for the protocol and stormed in unannounced, making his demands. He was asked to leave by Chidambaram, at which point, Modi, with his mouth running away with him, spat back sparks of his own, reducing his bridges to cinders. Modi says the story is false. 'Untrue,' he says. 'Never met him for this at that point that year. All made up.' No matter, the IPL would not take place in India for that season, and had to be moved to South Africa. Modi, extraordinarily, arranged it in three weeks.

It was, however, the beginning of the end for Modi. He had made powerful enemies in the government and the BCCI and was suspended in April 2010 for 'alleged acts of individual misdemeanours'. He had overseen the bidding process and creation of two new teams, Kochi and Pune, and, not for the last time, had taken to his Twitter account to make an ill-advised statement. He tweeted the ownership structure of the franchise, which was a breach of confidentiality and led to the resignation of the Indian Minister of State for External Affairs.

Open season was declared on Modi and a raft of claims and allegations were made against him. The BCCI charged him with financial irregularities relating to the franchise bidding process, advertisement sales and theatrical rights. He was also wanted for questioning over possible foreign exchange violations relating to the IPL in South Africa. Chennai police also investigated alleged financial irregularities following a complaint by the secretary of the IPL board. There were additional claims that Modi had helped friends and family buy stakes in franchises and that he had been involved in match-fixing.

Modi's counter has been to launch a personal crusade against corruption in the game, his failed case against Cairns being a case in point. There is, however, a more disturbing reason for his action. Modi claims that attempts on his life have been made by the criminal underworld that runs India's illegal betting industry. 'I was threatened considerably by the underworld for refusing to fix IPL matches. There have been three attempts to kill me.'

This is why, he says, he cannot go back to India to face his accusers. This is why, he says, he stays in London.

Biscuit crumbs are spewed from Modi's mouth all over a pristine, shimmering oak dining table. He is incandescent. I have just told him that Lord Condon, the former chairman of the ICC's ACSU, says that the illegal Indian betting industry is no longer run by the men whom Modi claims are trying to end his life. 'Where are they living?' he exclaims, the pitch of his voice pinging the ears. 'On which planet are they living?' Modi stops and shakes his head before looking at me as if awaiting an answer. I shrug my shoulders.

'I'm serious,' he continues. 'I'm shocked to hear that. I'm in shock. I have had three assassination attempts on me for my stand on anti-corruption. That is far from the reality.'

Modi goes on to give details of the three incidents, claiming they were because he had refused to kowtow to the 'gangsters' in their attempts to fix matches in his IPL. One was in Mumbai at the end of March 2009. 'There was a shoot-out outside my house and one guy got killed and one got picked up,' he says. The other attempts came in South Africa in April of the same year and in Phuket, Thailand, in January 2010. On each occasion he was warned by the police or the intelligence agencies.

For the first moment in the short time I have known him, he becomes introspective when recalling events. His voice is softened, losing its infamous viperish tone. With thumb and forefinger he picks at the crumbs in front of him, placing them on a saucer. 'They were a problem for me and my family. In Phuket I escaped only because I had an emergency meeting in Dubai and they just happened to go to the hotel after I had left. In South Africa they got picked up by police, and in Bombay there was the shoot-out. We had a lot of security around us. We are always monitoring and checking. Fortunately, I think they have other things to do now, other people to prey on, but I am lucky.'

I suggest to Modi that it is not so lucky for cricket that there is a disparity between what a former administrator of one of the largest cricket tournaments in the world knows about a criminal influence on the game and the agency of the game's governing body attempting to deny its very presence. 'It's completely fanciful,' he says. 'It's run by it. We have an ACSU who don't know this? It's alarming. The entire underground betting system in India stops at the top of the pyramid. They are the book. Everybody else is a bookmaker, laying the bets. They are based in India, outside India, some across the border, in the Middle East.

'Their access is very well known in India into other industries. Their access into working with many people and politicians is well known. They have respectable front men. Let's put it this way: a lot of the underworld have respectable front faces. People at the front will give you no inkling of the connection at the back.'

But what of the allegations of match-fixing in IPL – that Modi, to use his words against him, was that 'respectable' front? 'Absolute fantasy,' he says. 'Malicious fantasy. Some people are out to get me and they are desperate so they make things up. It's sad.'

The IPL, however, does have a poor reputation in the game for corruption. The ACSU were alarmed that it had no official ICC anti-corruption coverage in its first two years, while bookmakers like Parthiv and Vinay expect matches to be fixed. Even bookmakers in the UK had a distrust of the tournament.

Modi does not say as much, but there is a hint of regret when he's challenged about the lack of ACSU presence during those first two years. The tournament had its own anti-corruption unit, Modi says, before scrapping it and employing the ACSU at a cost of $1.2 million. 'We put a lot of emphasis on anti-corruption when we started IPL. We had a committee that reviewed all games and we had people, ACSU people, actually, as we hired them short-term, working around the country. But it was debated upon and agreed that it was better to go with the ICC, at huge cost, although that's not an issue, but we did go out and say we should have full coverage from the ACSU.

'I was satisfied with the service I paid for. It's the best service for what they are used to doing. The multi-million-dollar question is "is that good enough?" In the world of spot-fixing is that all we can do? How are we going after all the leads? That is privy to the ICC and I don't expect them to discuss that with anyone, but we've seen few people being hauled up or taken action against and is that to assume the game is absolutely clean, to assume there is no spot-fixing taking place?'

I agree and suggest that a man of his experience in cricket administration, setting up and running a tournament valued at $4 billion, would be well placed to answer the question. 'Spot-fixing is rife in the game. And I'm talking globally. It's a Pandora's box. It's staring you straight in the face, but difficult to prove. Almost impossible to prove.

'I say that from experience in cricket: watching, broadcasting, dealing as an administrator for many years, looking at it and seeing it. I've been seeing, hearing what's been happening and that's not just from the IPL, but cricket as whole. IPL is one of the best-covered tournaments now, doesn't mean the others aren't, but are we doing enough?

'Fixing can be done in many ways; it's not just the players. It can be other than players, those associated with the game who have an impact on the game. Pitch conditions, giving out team information.'

Surely it is impossible, then, to claim that the IPL, particularly in the first two editions without ACSU protection, was clean? 'I think it was clean, but I could never, sitting here today, categorically tell you that we picked up everything for spot-fixing, and that goes for all games, not just IPL. It's extremely difficult to spot. We had to warn players from time to time. We found undesirable elements in the stadium and removed them. We found them touring with players or managers of players who were in touch with bookmakers and we removed them.'

On a previous meeting with Modi he had given me the names of players who he believed were involved with 'undesirables'. It was pre-Cairns so his tongue was looser. 'I have to be careful now,' he laughs. 'I don't want another libel case, nor do I want to get shot.' The players he named included superstars. The jaw would drop.

'Yes,' he says. 'They are big names. And I know a lot of players today globally who fraternise with big bookmakers, legal or illegal, and I don't see any reason why that should be [allowed].

'I had to speak to the players myself sometimes. Of course, the conversation would go, "We haven't done it, it's not true, it's circum-stantial, me? How's it possible? Me?" And that's how it went. I would say: "This is where the conversation ends. We know what we know, and we know what you know, so get it out of the game. Let there not be another incident." To everything there was an explanation. They had an answer for everything.

'This is a shame, because the players have to be the ones who take responsibility. It's their game. The game is by them, for them and of them. They need to be speaking out instead of pushing it under the carpet, which is normally the case. They need to come out and tell the truth. No one will know better if it is happening than the teammates. If they won't talk or give information it's difficult for anyone else to know.'

Modi has the bit between his teeth now. He leans forward in his chair and furiously gets through another biscuit, chain-slurping his tea. It could be considered comical, but that would be harsh. There is inherent passion here for the good of the game. It is rare indeed in the course of researching these pages to hear someone speak so forthrightly. No one from the ACSU has matched this and definitely no other administrator.

'I think people like to blame me. So what? I don't care. But I know the truth and that will come out one day. You know people say the IPL globalised fixing in one sentence and the next they say that fixing is rife because players don't get paid enough?

'In IPL players were paid so well that there was no incentive to fix. If anything, we took it out of the game. The amount of money young players are making today, they don't need a secondary income. They make more by playing a clean game.

'If a player is a soft target, he is a soft target, and there is not much anyone can do about that. IPL is not to blame for that. Twenty20 is not to blame for that. The ACSU have blamed Twenty20 in the past. Whether it's T20, ODI or Test match, the same players play all formats of the game. Once the bookmaker makes you taste the money he will extract his pound of flesh, he'll ensure he gets the co-operation he needs, in any format.'

Modi is right, but one gets the sense that the cricket world would balk at anything that now comes from his mouth. Here in London, he is a soft target himself. He has been disparaged and his reputation is in shreds as his enemies have taken aim from the other side of the world and unerringly found the target.

In his defence, and to return to a previous theme, Modi has 'put up' and that is a first in a sport which – despite clearly suffering from a problem that threatens its validity – too readily buttons its lip. Modi, of course, has got in trouble for speaking his mind but, if he is serious about ridding the game of this bane, that sharp tongue might actually achieve something.

'These allegations [about me],' he says, 'Get them out there in the public domain. Everyone knows about them, which is good because when I prove that they were all false – and remember that not a single charge has come to fruition, despite inquiries – these people will remember. The truth will come out.

'Everyone has this misconception I got into the game for the money. I got into the game because I wanted to clean up the bloody game. I am serious about doing that. I'm biding my time, deciding when to go back to India and strike again.'

CHAPTER 19

THE ENGLISH DISEASE

It is the sort of bright, fresh spring day at Lord's on which one cannot help but be optimistic before a new cricket season. The grand old ground is preening itself in preparation with fresh licks of paint, repairs to the boundary fence and a trim to the hallowed turf. Even the keepers of the Grace Gates have smiles on their faces.

Looking down on all of this, from the home dressing room, are the Middlesex players. With Middlesex tenants at Lord's, arguably the finest ground in the world, the club are the cricketing equivalent of a raffish, ever-sprouting homeless family being housed in a stucco-fronted mansion in leafy, luxurious St John's Wood. The gaggle of players seem a jovial, expectant bunch, as well they might after last season claiming the second division title of the County Championship.

They are joined by a Sky Sports camera crew, Ian Smith, the legal director of the Professional Cricketers Association, Angus Porter, the chief executive, Jason Ratcliffe, the assistant chief executive and, on the famous balcony making a phone call, Chris Watts, the ECB's anti-corruption operational executive, who has been in the role for less than six months. It is not an ordinary gathering for these vaunted rooms. This is the one guaranteed chance a season the PCA and ECB will have to address the group of players about the threat of corruption in the county game.

It is a relevant topic with the sound of the judge's gavel still echoing through the corridors of the nearby offices of the ECB after Mervyn Westfield, the Essex bowler, became the first English cricketer to be convicted of spot-fixing. Westfield was paid £6,000 to concede at least 12 runs in his first over against Durham in a televised one-day match in 2009. It was following an anti-corruption briefing such as this in spring 2010 that the Essex coach Paul Grayson and the captain Mark Pettini were informed that Tony Palladino, a teammate, had been shown bundles of cash by Westfield in his flat, who said it was from fixing matches. Westfield emptied out a bag full of notes that he kept in his bedroom cupboard.

The Middlesex players wait patiently for the presentation to begin. They sit on padded benches which hug the walls. Six or seven, including the captain Neil Dexter, sit beneath the board displaying the names of England players who have scored a Test match century at Lord's. Some are reading newspapers, others drink from mugs of tea and try on this season's new kit while the rest seem bewitched by their mobile phones. The monotony is broken by Jason Ratcliffe, who begins the session. 'It can be dull, but it's very pertinent to know.'

Ratcliffe, who played as a batsman in 136 first-class matches for Warwickshire and Surrey, runs through the topics that will be discussed. They are varied: the PCA Benevolent Fund, financial advice, agents, player surveys, the spirit of the game, disciplinary procedures, social networking, and the Morgan review, undertaken by former ECB chairman and one-time ICC president David Morgan into the structure of the county game. 'It's a whistlestop PCA tour,' Ratcliffe says.

But it is corruption that is the thrust, particularly the cajoling of the players to complete the PCA's online tutorial, a 30-minute quiz that takes the form of an old-school comprehension. Today's session is the bulk of the syllabus, if you will, for an education programme crafted to cut out more Westfield incidents.

Ian Smith 'names and shames' the Middlesex players who have yet to complete the tutorial. There is much giggling and ribbing when the names are read out, including that of Andrew Strauss, the England captain. There are mitigating circumstances. 'We sent the link to the wrong email address for Straussy,' Smith says. There is a serious point, however. If players do not complete the online tutorial – it must be done on their own – by the time their county sends off their list of players for registration for the forthcoming season, they will not be allowed to play.

Michael Vaughan, the former England captain, delivers the online introduction. 'You'll learn the rules and what will happen if you get caught breaking those rules,' he says. 'But most importantly you'll learn the methods people will use to try to corrupt you and how to resist that and report it.'

The use of Vaughan, of course, adds kudos, but it is a slightly clumsy choice, considering question number five, which asks: 'A well-known licensed betting company offers you a job predicting the outcome of each week's cricket fixtures for their members-only subscription website. Can you accept the job?' Vaughan, now retired, works for a well-known licensed betting company predicting the outcome of each week's cricket fixtures.

Overall there are 14 questions spread across three modules. The first module rams home that players should not bet on cricket, and the meaning of inside information, like team news, weather reports, pitch forecasts or form of players. These are exactly the sort of details that have Parthiv and Vinay salivating, and the kind of subjects that crop up in the everyday chat that players have with supporters as they walk back from the nets or lounge by the pool, just like an innocent Ian Bell did at the Taj Hotel in Mumbai.

'If your opening bowler was injured the night before a match and nobody outside the squad knew that, would that information be useful to someone thinking of placing a bet on your match the next day?' reads the tutorial. 'Of course it would, so don't tell anyone outside the squad. Simple. If you get caught, you can be banned for anything between six months and five years.'

In the second module, the tutorial heavy-handedly puts the fear of God into players when discussing how match-fixers attempt to control them. 'There are great similarities between the activities of fixers in corrupt gambling and the activities of paedophiles,' it says. Surely the comparison of fixers and paedophiles is emotive scaremongering?

'There are four basic ways in which a match-fixer will try and get you to do something for him. First, he may just ask. It may seem too simple, but we have had instances in the game where strangers have approached players directly and openly with a proposition: "I will give you £8,000 if you bowl two no-balls in your first over."

'Second, there is entrapment. This is your classic "mafia"-type tactic. It's where a player gets into trouble – usually debt, but sometimes women or family troubles – and in order to get out of that trouble you have to do something unlawful. The high-risk category here are gamblers –

players or officials or anyone, for that matter, who gambles will, almost inevitably, get into debt and debt is what a match-fixer looks for.

'Third, a common tactic is to use a trusted intermediary – someone you've known for a long time – to approach you with a proposition. Fourth is what we refer to as the "grooming" process, which is to take time to build a long-term relationship based on trust.'

When meeting previously with Ian Smith, when the PCA were based in offices in celebrity-packed Primrose Hill, he told me the story of a player who had been photographed by his corruptors in a compromising position with a female and they threatened to go to the newspapers. 'Do your worst,' he told them. 'I'm not married, I don't care if those appear anywhere.' His blackmailers were blunted by his brusque response.

In the third section, players are told how to report information about teammates or the opposition and the consequences if they do not. It has been one of the problems for the ACSU that players are worried they will face sanction, by the letter of the law, if they do not immediately report something. The ACSU has struggled, and it continues to do so, to reassure players on this front. As one player has argued to me previously: 'What is immediate? Five minutes, one hour, as soon as the lunch break, the next day, next week?' The ACSU are still wrestling with this issue.

Smith reminds the Middlesex players one more time about their responsibility to the game and to each other (this will become a common theme) to complete the tutorial, before moving on to the topic of inside information. It is a smart move to focus on this particular area when the PCA has so little time to get their point across. It is key because it is right that corruptors would first try to hook players by asking for what are seen as soft facts.

'The first element of inside information is what you know by virtue of being here in the dressing room, which is not known out there,' Smith says. 'In effect secret, confidential to the team. The second element is that it's got to be useful to someone in a gambling context. Something someone can use to give them an advantage, a jump on the opposition, whether that be a bookie or another gambler.

'So if you think about what you know as a cricketer from inside the dressing room, you've got to consider what you can reasonably say outside the dressing room. There will no doubt be team rules as what you can say about selection. I'll give you a good example from the World Cup [2011]: Stuart Broad tweeted one morning that he was too sick to play. That was several hours before the team was released. He had clearly breached a Team England rule about inside information from the dressing room because he pre-empted the announcement of the team, so he was in trouble for that. Unfortunately, the ICC took a view that he was in breach of the anti-corruption code for disclosing inside information, but we quickly shut that down. Why? Because it's public. Broady had about a quarter of a million followers at the time. And Twitter is a completely open source. Anyone can look at it. So he wasn't disclosing information that was an advantage in a betting context because everyone knew or had access to it, so the ICC were wrong. But please, if you've got any doubt, don't say it rather than say it.'

Chris Watts has the tougher task of making players bend to his will. He must convince them to report anything suspicious about their teammates or opponents, breaking dressing room omertà. He has experience, though. Before taking the role of the ECB's anti-corruption chief, he worked for 30 years in the Metropolitan Police, rising to senior detective working on homicides and counter-terrorism. He also specialised in managing informants. One of his first acts at the ECB was to set up an amnesty for players to make reports. He will not reveal the number he has received through the confidential telephone line and email address, but admits the Westfield case has been a 'wake-up call' and that there is 'a big threat out there'.

'Corruption is a jigsaw,' he says. 'We know we've got a picture, but we don't know if it's a 50-piece puzzle, 500-piece or 5,000-piece. We need more pieces to get an idea of what the problem is and what we can do about it.'

Holding up a copy of the ECB's Anti-Corruption Code of Conduct, a 20-page document of small-print articles and sub-articles, Watts asks the Middlesex players: 'Anyone ever seen that? Is that a nod? Yes? Great. Has anybody actually looked it up and looked inside it? No. Of course not, because you're cricketers and your focus is going out there and doing what you do best. But you've all signed up to this and you are bound by it. This is why it's so important you complete the online tutorial. If you come across anything you think is corrupt, a breach of the code, you must report it without delay, quote unquote. If you don't, you're in breach.

'We don't want that to happen. That's why we've brought in the amnesty reporting window. Anyone heard about that? ... Some nods some shakes. So some have heard about it. The ECB has put in place a reporting window that runs until the end of April for you to report anything that you have come across historically without fear of sanctions for late reporting, because that is one of the breaches of the code. However, if you come across and say "actually last year I got involved in a nice bit of spot-fixing and made a decent wedge" it doesn't apply to that. It only applies to late reporting.

'What happens if you do make a call or email? We'll talk it through, how best to deal with it. It doesn't mean to say that if you make a report it will end up with one of your colleagues in prison. That is one scenario. The worst case. Mervyn did what he did, he pleaded guilty at court. It doesn't mean to say every case ends like that. It might be just a warning.'

Porter takes over from Watts and asks the group, who have been quiet but attentive throughout: 'We haven't gone into the rights and wrongs, the morality of it, so if someone is stupid enough to give you £5,000 to bowl a no-ball? What is the harm?'

Ollie Rayner, the spin bowler, pipes up. 'You're affecting the game.'

'Of course,' Porter says. 'But does it lead anywhere?'

'They've got you by the balls,' Rayner replies.

'Exactly,' Porter says. 'Next time, God knows what they'll ask. It could be something worse.'

To witness the PCA and the ECB working together to try to counter corruption is admirable. Just like a counsellor might say to an alcoholic, the greatest step is recognising that you have a problem. The English game knows this and is doing something about it. It has not always been this way. In the summer of 2010 news broke of the arrest of Mervyn Westfield and Danish Kaneria, his Essex teammate, who was eventually released without charge by police, but latterly banned from playing in England for life by the ECB. The ECB – typical of a sporting body faced with such a crisis – scoffed at the idea of something serious, something deep-rooted.

With Westfield's and Kaneria's mug shots barely back from the developers, I interviewed a high-ranking ECB official about the potential for an epidemic. It was too soon. When using the analogy that if you see a mouse running around in your living room it is certain that there are many more under the floorboards, I was accused of trying to scandalise the county game to boast a journalistic reputation. 'English cricket [does] not have a major issue,' came the haughty retort. Asked if that was naive, the incredulous response was 'it would be naive to think otherwise'. It was a foreign problem, blustered the source.

'People can make allegations about all sorts of things,' he said. 'In other parts of the world there are frequent allegations. I don't think we're dealing with a huge problem because it's educational. Saying it is a problem is gross exaggeration. There's no hard evidence of anything of the sort. You only have to watch the games; they're being played at pretty major levels of intensity. People are not *not* trying.'

At the time, such beliefs up high in the administration of the English game were understandable. Naive, but understandable. It is rare indeed for an official to express worry about the integrity of his sport for fear of the views being heard by potential sponsors. Besides, such men take their lead from what the ICC's ACSU tells them and they had been consistent in their belief that county cricket would be unaffected.

In 2001, in his first report as head of the ACSU, Lord Condon said that the risk to domestic cricket all over the globe was 'patchy, anecdotal and not compelling'. And in 2009, during the World Twenty20 in England, the very summer that Westfield was misbehaving, a senior ACSU figure ruled out any match-fixing in the domestic game. 'There's not enough interest in county cricket in the illegal markets,' he said. 'It is the international tournaments that get the focus because that is where the most money can be made.'

So what changed? A switch was flicked. The one-day county game became a target for the fixers when matches started to be televised in India in 2008. They filled a gap in the television schedules. The Indian domestic season does not start until August and the national team rarely plays at home during the English summer. In 2011, Sky Sports televised at least 68 games. In 2012 an early television schedule for Sky slated 37 matches in the 40-over domestic competition and 23 in the Twenty20 competition. More would be announced later in the season. If they are on Sky Sports, they are on in India too, with the channel ESPN Star Sports picking up the feed.

When a county match in England is televised in India the bookmakers – providing a game that they would consider to be more profitable, like the IPL or, of course, an India international match, is not televised at the same time – have the potential to take bets on it. The Indian market, as huge and organised as it is, is still only capable of taking live bets on one match at a time. When there is the potential to make money, there is the potential for corruption.

When the ECB signed a seven-year contract worth more than £100 million with ESPN Star Sports in June 2012 for exclusive rights in Asia, the Middle East and Africa, starting from 2013, the threat increased.

Television, however, is just one of the four cornerstones which make county cricket so appealing to the punters and bookmakers. Players' wages, a bloated schedule and, until the appointment of Chris Watts, no anti-corruption unit completed a structure which could have been designed by an architect of greed.

The average county player earns between £40,000 and £50,000 a year. Mervyn Westfield, who was banned for five years by the ECB, was believed to have a salary of £20,000. Some county players can earn as little as £15,000 a year. In a short career which, if they are lucky, will last ten years, the temptation is clear. It would take a strong-willed individual indeed to turn down more than a third of his salary for bowling badly in one over. One measly over to boost a measly wage. It is no wonder that cricketers may say 'what is the harm?'

This is as it has been since the days of *The Cricketer's Fields*, the account of corruption written by Reverend Pycroft in 1851. 'The temptation was really very great – too great by far for any poor man to be exposed to.'

What is the harm, too, when one considers the number of meaningless fixtures county players appear in, often in front of sparse crowds. In five months in 2009 Essex played 43 matches in four different competitions (16 four-day matches in the County Championship, eight in the 40-over league, nine in the Friends Provident Trophy one-day competition and ten in the Twenty20 tournament). They were promoted from the second flight of the four-day game, but did not win any silverware that season. Weary bodies and minds are more vulnerable to considering an approach from a fixer.

Certainly there would have been no real deterrent for agreeing a fix. Unlike international matches, where the ICC's anti-corruption officers patrol the hotels looking for known fixers, county games are not policed. Anyone can walk up to a county player and start a conversation, either in the hotel or at the ground. At some grounds it is even possible to chat to players as they sit in the pavilion and it is not unusual for players to take a stroll around the boundary if they have already batted. They are easy targets.

So consider this scenario: a player who may not have many years left in the game and who is fretting about what career to try next is approached by a businessman who claims to be a huge fan and wants to buy him dinner. The player, staying in a hotel with his teammates as they are playing a four-day game away from home, thinks it will make a decent change from the same old faces, the same old conversations. So he goes. The businessman takes him out a few more times during the season. They become friends. One evening, the player is asked to do a small favour for his new pal in the match tomorrow, which is televised on Sky Sports. His county have no hope of promotion from the second division of the one-day league and they are not expected to win. 'Can you concede more than ten runs in your first over? I can pay £10,000.'

Of course the player knows it is wrong. But £10,000 for bowling poorly, when he could quite easily be hit for more than that amount anyway, in the umpteenth meaningless game of the season? What is the harm? His team don't need to win. They probably won't win. That one over won't make much of a difference either way. But what a difference £10,000 would make. Bills could be paid, credit cards paid off, a nagging spouse becalmed, a holiday for the whole family every year for the next ten years. It takes a strong individual indeed to say 'no', let alone to report such an offer.

If the average county player is of concern, more so are the stellar performers from overseas that counties sign in a desperate attempt to increase gate revenue. These are the type of freelance cricketers that populate the Twenty20 tournaments that have sprung up over the world. Cricketers for hire who parachute into a team for a few months, sign a hefty contract, play a few games and then pack their bags and leave. They have no loyalty to that club or their teammates. They are only there for the money. It is big money, too. One such player was paid £3,000 a week for five months.

There is a feeling around the county circuit that it is these types who are giving the English game a bad reputation for corruption. While the homegrown, relatively impoverished player may be tempted by the opportunity of a fast buck for a fix which might not affect the result, the 'backpacker', as they are often called, has no qualms about bowling a few wides in his first few overs or making sure he is hit for runs in an attempt to fix the session market. What does he care? In a few months he will have left this club behind and be plying his trade in the IPL, or perhaps the Bangladesh Premier League, a tournament scarred by fixing claims in its inaugural season in 2012.

Rattan Mehta, the punter from Delhi, laughed at my feigned wide-eyed innocence when I balked at his suggestion that county cricket was fixed. It was all the prompting he needed. 'They are coming live in India now,' he laughed. 'Twenty20 matches, 40-over matches. All 40-over matches are live. Every match you watch how much the odds swing. I know one county player who had £100,000 deposited into a Dubai account. He had a big party.'

Vinay, too, had warned of corruption in the county game, revealing that in 2008 he had been offered the results of three matches in the 40-over league before they happened for three lakh (£3,800) by a Delhi-based bookmaker. 'I thought this was too much, too much of a sum to pay ... it could go wrong. So I said no. He said I could have the information for free. He was right. And he was right for the next three games in England.'

On my first trip to see Vinay he alleged that a 40-over match between Sussex and Kent at Hove in August 2011 was fixed. 'It was fixed,' he said. 'I can bet on that. Kent won the match, 40-40 domestic. That was a fixed match. One of our bookmakers called me in the match telling me to leave it, don't bet on it, don't take bets. I ask if there was a problem with the police. He said: "It's a fixed match. Kent will surely win."' Kent won by 14 runs. The match was televised, although it was far from irrelevant for Sussex, who would have guaranteed qualification for the semi-finals of the tournament with victory.

It is understood that a bookmaker from Mumbai was involved in the 'fixing' of this match. He has now left the bookmaking industry, trying his luck in the casinos of America after he was arrested by police in India under the foreign exchange and regulatory act.

The ECB, it is known, had started investigations into this match in the summer of 2012. The PCA are understood to be aware of the reports surrounding this game, which attracted almost £14 million of turnover on Betfair when a televised county match may average normally half that. So, too, are Sussex, who are believed to have informed those two bodies about the potential of corruption. They did not, however, at that time inform the ECB or PCA of the names of the players who were alleged to have been involved.

Such stories give credence to the suspicion that the Mervyn Westfield incident was the tip of the iceberg. Tony Palladino, labelled county cricket's whistleblower for exposing Westfield, has spoken only once of his involvement. In an interview with the *Sun* newspaper in January 2012 he said spot-fixing was common. 'You'd be a fool to think spot-betting wasn't happening at Essex before, and at other counties,' he said. 'It must have been. They've chosen county cricket because it is not as high profile as international cricket. What worries me is there might have been other cases that have been swept under the carpet. I've spoken to international players who've been approached several times in Asia. It's rife out there.'

Palladino looked a haunted man in the picture that accompanied that interview. When I phoned him to ask whether he would discuss Westfield and the scam in more detail, he politely declined, saying he 'wants to forget all about it and concentrate on my sport'. It would appear, though, that Palladino is the victim. Before the story surfaced, Palladino was loaned to Kent as he had become a scapegoat at Essex. 'There were whispers I was trying to get rid of a bowler to make it easier for myself in the team.' Palladino joined Derbyshire at the end of the 2010 season.

The conduct of Essex was called into question in court. When Westfield was sentenced to four months in prison in February 2012, the judge at the Old Bailey said it was his teammate Danish Kaneria who had acted as the fixer, or go-between, for the deal and that Kaneria's management and teammates had turned a 'blind eye' to his offers to fix matches (Kaneria was later banned for life by the ECB).

Paul Grayson, the Essex coach, told the court that he had heard that Kaneria, who was a Pakistan international spinner, had asked players if they wanted to meet bookmakers. Mark Pettini, captain at the time, added that Kaneria had spoken of potential deals in front of him, James Foster, the vice-captain and David Masters, a veteran bowler. He said that Kaneria knew people who would 'pay considerable money to influence matches'. Westfield's QC, Mark Milliken-Smith, said it was 'startling' that no one in the Essex dressing room reported Kaneria to the ECB, and said teammates had possibly kept quiet because Kaneria was an important match-winning bowler.

One former county player said that he was not surprised at all by an apparent 'lack of leadership' at Essex. 'There was a poor culture there and a lot of teams knew about that,' he said. 'They were a nasty, niggly side and you always felt they were playing outside the spirit of the game. They were weakly led, I felt. Those sorts of conversations that Kaneria was supposed to have been having in the dressing room wouldn't have happened under a [Adam] Hollioake at Surrey, or a [Matthew] Fleming at Kent. He'd have been thrown out that very week and not been allowed back.'

This twist to the tale is why the PCA and ECB are at pains to encourage players to report approaches, but it also leaves Chris Watts in a difficult position. According to the code of conduct, Grayson, Pettini and Foster could all be considered in breach and be susceptible to bans. The conundrum is familiar to the ACSU. If the Essex trio were to be punished for tardiness in reporting, what message does that send to other county players?

Indeed, perhaps the only straightforward aspect of the sordid affair was the historic hearing at the Old Bailey, during which Westfield joined the Pakistan spot-fixing trio in the annals of cricketing villainy. The anatomy of the fix, if indeed there was one, was complicated.

Westfield was paid £6,000 to concede 12 runs off his first over. Immediately, one might jump to the conclusion that corruptors would use that information to bet on the exact number of runs that would be scored off that over on the illegal Indian market.

It is not that simple, though, as Vinay and Parthiv have made clear in previous chapters. The Indian system is vast, but remember that it is uniform in so far that it is controlled by a number of powerful syndicates who set the odds on only four markets: match odds, session runs (brackets), innings runs (lambi) and lunch favourite. Only small-time individual bookmakers, who limit a customer base of fewer than 50 to stakes of no more than 25,000 rupees (£306), might (although it is highly unlikely) accept a request from a customer for a bet on the number of runs scored off an over. The market is minute.

Consider the amount Westfield was paid and the sum that the corruptor, latterly named as Kaneria, must have received. Then think about the large number of bets that would have needed to have been struck with a large number of bookmakers. They would not have been easy to find.

It is more likely that a syndicate was behind the ploy and this rings true when it transpired that a Delhi bookmaker, Arun Bhatt, had been Kaneria's contact. With Westfield's first over being the eighth, the timing was perfect to fix the bracket market, the first ten overs of a one-day innings. As we know, bookmakers ask customers to bet over or under on the number of runs to be scored, say 63–67. With inside information on how many runs are to be scored off the eighth over, they could manipulate the runs quote to deceive customers, of which the syndicate has tens of thousands.

A second possibility is that there was no fix at all and that Westfield was being 'groomed'. It could have been a test and the corruptor was merely proving that he had Westfield under his command.

Such vagaries are what Watts must come to terms with in his role. The ECB argue that his appointment and the setting-up of the anti-corruption unit, known as ACCESS, had been planned since Lord

Condon recommended in his 2001 report that each country would replicate the ICC's ACSU. Something that had been put off for years suddenly became a pressing concern as soon as the Westfield fix was revealed.

Watts is hopeful that the former Essex player will talk to him and, possibly, help educate players in the future. Over a cup of tea in his office following his introduction to the Middlesex players, I ask him how he intends to go about trying to find more pieces to that jigsaw he was talking about. 'I can't be in every hotel, at every match. There are 18 first-class counties. I need eyes and ears. I need people to come with me on this journey and that can be anyone who knows what's going on, or has suspicion about what's going on. Hence you keep going back to this jigsaw. I'm trying to build a picture. Players are particularly vulnerable. I need to get out there and talk to them and tell them they can trust me.'

It is a daunting task. Yet the one-man-band is relishing the challenge. One suspects down the line he may need an extra pair of hands. 'I don't know about that at the moment,' he says. 'In the future, who knows? I'm working hard at the moment though, I can tell you. I've got plenty to do.'

CHAPTER 20

THE FIX THAT WAS?

> Bookie update ... India will bat first and score over 260, 3 wickets
> fall within the first 15 overs, pak will cruise to 100, then lose 2
> quick wickets, at 150 they will be 5 down and crumble and lose
> by a margin of over 20 runs*

After the spot-fix that wasn't, the Pakistan cricket team became a byword
for corruption. They were looked upon with narrow-eyed mistrust. For
that reason, if there was any team to be suspected of wrongdoing at the
2011 World Cup, it was always likely to be them.

During the Southwark trial, Kamran Akmal and his brother Umar,
the wicketkeeper and batsman respectively, were named as potential
fixers. An ACSU officer told me 'if I wanted to rid a team of corruption I certainly would not want brothers playing together'. Wahab
Riaz, the Pakistan fast bowler, was also spoken of at the trial. According to Aftab Jafferjee, the prosecutor, his role was one that 'raises deep
suspicions'.

Another Pakistani who was the subject of unsubstantiated allegations
was Younis Khan. Younis resigned the captaincy in 2009 after he was
accused by the Pakistan government of leading a side that threw a match
in the Champions Trophy. Intikhab Alam, who was the manager during
that tour and the World Cup, was also questioned. Both Khan and Alam
denied any wrongdoing and were never charged.

---

* Of allegations about corruption in this match, Haroon Lorgat, the ICC chief executive, stated: 'The ICC has no reason or evidence to require an investigation into this
match. It is indeed sad for spurious claims to be made which only serve to cause doubt
on the semi-final of one of the most successful ICC Cricket World Cups ever.'

Further back still, Waqar Younis, the coach, was in 2000 the subject of a number of allegations in the Qayyum Report – Pakistan's investigation into corruption – with the following conclusion: 'All the allegations taken together warrant some action against Waqar Younis. Two of Waqar's own managers and someone reputed to be his friend have alleged wrongdoing against him. These appear sufficient grounds for recommending a censure. Moreover, that Waqar should be kept under observation and investigated. Further, during proceedings it was felt that Waqar has been reluctant to help this commission and even when prompted was not fully forthcoming.'

It is easy for a conspiracy theorist with Mohali on his mind to join the dots with such circumstantial evidence. But what of proof? The smoke and mirrors of the *News of the World* sting aside, and the absence of a betting opportunity, the newspaper's demand for no-balls at specific times was vital. Benedict Bermange, the Sky Sports statistician, was called on by the court to explain the mathematical probability of predicting the exact moment when Mohammad Asif and Mohammad Amir would bowl the three no-balls. It was one in 1.5 million. That figure did as much to condemn the Pakistan three as any hidden camera or retrieved text message.

Those three no-balls were peculiar. There was plenty that was quirky, too, about the match in Mohali. By trawling through the history books and past scorecards, it is possible to work out just how quirky.

Specialist help is required, though. It comes in the form of Jatin Thakkar, a Mumbai-based statistician, who was co-founder and developer respectively of two statistical analysis tools which have demanded that cricket puts less store in the old-fashioned value of batting and bowling averages.

Chance of Winning, which Thakkar helped found, is a system built to predict, at the end of each over, the chances each team has of going on to win a match. It takes into account all the variables – strength of the teams playing, resources lost, resources remaining, pitch conditions – and distills it down to a single percentage and summarises the past, present and future of the match in question.

While Chance of Winning is a tool to assist in predicting match outcomes, the role of Impact Index is to decipher how a player will perform. It determines the accurate worth of a player's performance, in a match, team and career context. Since every match has its own fingerprint based on the context of the performances during the game, this finds a way to measure the ratio of each of the 22 performances in the match. Thakkar, using his database, which would make your eyes boggle, ran a check on that Mohali afternoon, comparing it with the previous 2,434 one-day internationals.

The first task was to analyse the validity of 'the script'. Ever since the arrival of that message from Parthiv into my Twitter inbox I have fretted over whether, despite its accuracy, it could have been a lucky guess. Thakkar searched his database, which stretched back to 7 December 1992, to reveal the likelihood of predicting the progression of Pakistan's innings to such detail.

His results proved that if Parthiv, or someone else, had made it up, then they were on the kind of lucky streak which demanded the purchase of a lottery scratchcard. Such a sequence – 'Pakistan cruise to 100, lose 2 quick wickets, at 150 they will be 5 down and crumble and lose by a margin of over 20 runs' – is rare over the study period.

Jatin explained his method: 'I [took] matches in which a team was chasing 250 to 280 and then applied the match situations that Pakistan's chase went through in the exact manner – 90–110 for 2–3 wickets in 20–25 overs (this has happened 30 times), 140–160 for 4–6 wickets in 30–38 overs (this has happened 14 times) and then to have lost the match from thereon with a margin of more than or equal to 20 (this has happened 6 times). All the counts are including Pakistan's match.'

Including the semi-final, it has happened six times in the 2,434 matches. As a percentage this is 0.24650780608052586. Translated into odds – the currency of this book, if there is one – it is a 405–1 against shot. To put this into context, a hat-trick is a 106–1 chance, a five-wicket haul is 8–1 and a century 11–2. Not impossible, by any stretch of the imagination, and not as unlikely as the ordered no-balls, but a long chance nonetheless.

Of course this does not prove that the match was fixed. Far from it. It is safety in numbers, if you will, in terms of the confidence that Parthiv and his associate in Dubai were not spinning a yarn. It means it can be considered worth investigating.

There are other incidents in the match which can be examined with statistics to determine how 'quirky' it was. Analysing a match in such a way is a process which the ACSU do not subscribe to. Instead they rely on a report from the umpires at the end of play. It is worth mentioning that after the semi-final the ACSU officer who was present at the meeting with the two officials, Ian Gould and Simon Taufel, and the television and third umpires, said that there was 'nothing suspicious about the game'. A Pakistan supporter may beg to differ, at the very least mentioning the five dropped catches.

The rational point of view is that such mistakes were down to the pressure and enormity of the occasion. Human beings under stress behave strangely and that is an argument which would stand up in any court in the land. Still, it is worth looking at the behaviour of three Pakistan players in particular who were criticised for their performances.

The first is Misbah-ul-Haq, the No 5 batsman who scored 56 runs at a strike rate of 73.68 (runs per 100 balls). He was tagged 'Mysterious Misbah' for his go-slow as Pakistan attempted to chase, or should that be crawl, after a target of 261.

Misbah played out 42 dot balls, which was the most among Pakistan's batsmen, and over the first 42 deliveries he faced, he scored only 17, failing to score off 27 balls. When Indian bookmakers or punters are asked whether the semi-final was fixed, they always bring up Misbah.

The statistics suggest this is grossly unjust. Misbah has had a strike rate of fewer than 74 (minimum 15 balls faced) in his one-day international career 45 per cent of the time. In other words, there is nothing untoward. Moreover, when he reduces his strike rate to such a level, the records say that Pakistan win 59 per cent of matches.

Misbah's innings, and Younis Khan's 32-ball 13, were collectively described by Azhar Mahmood, a former teammate of the duo, as 'terrible'. When Misbah and Younis were at the crease for 74 balls, the two scored 30 runs, with no boundaries. The run rate climbed from 6.07 to 8.45. If Misbah could be excused for playing poorly, Younis is not so fortunate. His strike rate of 40.62 was uncharacteristic. Younis has scored at a rate of 41 (facing a minimum of 15 balls) in a shade fewer than 15 per cent of his one-day international innings. That is odds of 9–2. One cannot consider those to be unusually high or evidence of a player deliberately underperforming. Pakistan won only 29 per cent of matches when Younis has delivered such a performance.

It is also possible to quantify how unusual Pakistan's struggle was between the 20th and 29th overs, when they could only progress their score from 89 to 118. It was the exactly the sort of ponderous scoring rate that Lord Condon alluded to during our discussion at the House of Lords. Again, it was rare, having occurred in only 23 per cent of chases. In each of those matches the team batting second was beaten.

There were other performances that could be considered anomalies and could comfortably, of course, be explained away by stress. Such a study could be considered subjective. For every player who has under-performed, no matter how alarmingly, there could be two or three who have overperformed. The purpose of picking out the above examples is not to point the finger at individual players, but to assess behaviour that at the time was considered uncommon and to decipher whether those accusations were fair.

No doubt there would have been examples from India's batting card that could have been picked on, for better or worse. After all, Parthiv had predicted that India would score 'more than 260'. He was wrong. India posted exactly 260. It needs to be clarified that there is no evidence that suggests India were 'in on it'. Yet Thakkar, who spent two days crunching the numbers, wrote in an email that the research had strengthened his view that there was 'something not quite right' about the game.

'It was truly compelling and interesting to work on this,' he wrote. 'The low possibilities of senior players all underperforming that way in one match, plus those drops of Tendulkar! It just puts down on paper why all of it was so impossible.'

In addition to the semi-final, I asked Thakkar to study – using the same parameters of 2,434 matches – the two 'fixes' that Parthiv had notified me of during the group stages of the tournament. His findings were equally interesting:

Pakistan v. New Zealand – 'My sources in Dubai say NZ win'*
Batting first, New Zealand scored more than 90 runs in the last four overs. They won by 110 runs. 'As per the records from the fall-of-wickets table (which records scores and over number at various stages when the wickets fall), New Zealand's stands the highest run rate – at over 22 runs per over – in the last four to six overs for a first innings. It is better than the second highest on the list by 36 per cent.' This was an unprecedented event.

Sri Lanka v. Zimbabwe – 'Sri Lanka to score fewer than 350'**
'Seems al [sic] planned to not pass the innings runs of SL ... it was around 350.' Sri Lanka were not supposed to score more than 350. They scored 327 as the run rate slowed noticeably when they would have been expected to accelerate. 'From the stage that Sri Lanka were in (around 270–280 runs in 43–45 overs with top-order still batting in the first innings of the match), 67 per cent of teams have scored at a faster rate than Sri Lanka did and 48 per cent have crossed 340–360 at the end of the innings.' There is nothing untoward about these figures.

Statistics too often are used for support rather than illumination, but in the case of the Pakistan v. New Zealand match, the numbers would at least provide backing to an argument that the ACSU should consider an investigation into this match. It is understood that they have received no reports or intelligence of anything suspicious from either group game,

---

* The PCB were told of Pathiv's claims and asked to comment. Spokesman Nadeem Sarwar said: 'Regarding your queries on corruption in the ICC Cricket World Cup 2011, the ICC has already dismissed all such allegations. You can find the ICC statement on its corporate site.'
** The Sri Lanka Cricket Board did not reply when asked to comment about the World Cup group match.

so one should not hold one's breath. In the future, though, investigations could be launched if statistics and intelligence are at hand, the two planets coming into line.

A third planet could be betting patterns. The ACSU has an agreement with Betfair, the betting exchange, that they should be notified of any suspicious activity. In practice, this memorandum of understanding is inefficient, with Betfair only looking into matches if they are asked to by the ACSU. A two-way street with both organisations alerting the other would be desirable.

The ACSU have not asked Betfair for information about the World Cup semi-final or the two group matches. The betting exchange are reluctant to provide the betting patterns to journalists, so I contacted Global Sports Integrity (GSI), a consultancy which works with regulators, participants and other stakeholders to maximise their understanding of the modern betting environment and to best prepare for and manage the threat of corruption. Previously they had worked on a case for the Australian Rugby League which resulted in the conviction of Ryan Tandy, a Canterbury-Bankstown Bulldogs player, who attempted to manipulate the first scoring play of a match against the North Queensland Cowboys in 2010.

Mark Phillips, a director of GSI and former principal betting investigator for the British Horseracing Authority as part of their intelligence unit, watched the Mohali semi-final in 'real time' and matched the action with software called Fracsoft, which replays the Betfair match odds market.

Perhaps predictably, there was no smoking gun from the betting patterns. There were some noticeable moves, like the £25,000 gambler who staked at regular intervals, but this could be explained as a professional gambler trading the match. To discover who the £25,000 gambler is and where he hails from would be interesting, but Betfair are unable to reveal the identity of individual customers.

The main problem encountered during the study was that the match was such a huge betting event that suspicious patterns were difficult to spot. The match attracted turnover of more than £40 million. 'Either the match wasn't fixed, Betfair wasn't used or it was used subtly enough so the match odds were not thrown out of line,' Phillips said. 'With such liquidity that's not too difficult, especially considering the "fixers" would have eight hours [the length of the match] minimum to place their bets. My opinion is that the game was clean.'

'Fixers' failing to leave a paper trail is not unusual. If it was India's live-match odds syndicate who used Betfair with knowledge of the fix or a group of gamblers, savvy and powerful enough to influence a match of such magnitude, the probability of them making such a basic error as exposing a money trace straight back to their door is small. It is perfectly possible that bookmakers or punters needed only to manipulate the vast and unregulated Indian market to make their wedge on this game, if indeed it was blackened.

'This is a subtle art,' Vinay said in Nimbahera when discussing the potential for the bracket being manipulated in the Twenty20 match between Australia and India in Melbourne.

What the analysis of the statistics and betting patterns do prove, however, is the near-impossible task of uncovering evidence which cannot be discounted as circumstantial. 'The script' is tantalising and, at odds of 405–1 against, compelling. But it is not proof. Nor is the statistical analysis of the Pakistan players. Nor is the irregular scoring pattern at a key time of the Pakistan innings. Ditto the £25,000 gambler.

Together these are not enough for prima facie. As the *News of the World* proved, *res ipsa loquitur* (literally, 'the thing speaks for itself') is required. That means evidence gathered from secret video recordings, telephone conversations or text messages. The odds of acquiring such information are long, too.

CHAPTER 21

SPY

'You are under surveillance,' Karim says. 'I'm under surveillance. This is the way it has to be for this kind of project. They will want to run checks on who you are, what you are up to and me also. This is not to scare you, my friend. Then, one day, you will get the answers you need.'

Karim is a lawyer from Karachi, Pakistan. Our paths crossed as we have a mutual distrust of the World Cup semi-final in Mohali. He, too, claims to have known that Pakistan would lose the match before a ball was bowled. Ever since he has been trying to understand why, if at all, it was fixed and by whom. Bookmakers? Punters? The Indian lobby? Collusion between the governments of India and Pakistan?

Progress has been slow but, apparently, effective. In April 2012 it was understood that an investigation into the semi-final had been launched by a Pakistan intelligence agency, either the Federal Investigation Agency (FIA), the chief investigative agency of the government, or the Inter-Service Intelligence (ISI), the infamous independent group of spooks that was established in order to strengthen the sharing of military intelligence between the three branches of Pakistan's armed forces in the aftermath of the Indo–Pakistani War of 1947. Karim, bursting with pride that 'the Mohali disgrace will be exposed', said that the match would be 'nailed'.

Whether the spies and plotters will be able to prompt an inquiry by the Pakistan Cricket Board, public or otherwise, remains to be seen. It is possible that such things will be dealt with 'in house'. It is the way such agencies operate, probing, prompting in the caliginosity, deeper and darker than any shadowy mafia goon or bookie.

The spy was not easy to contact. It took almost weekly Skype contact between Karim and a go-between to set up a 'meeting'. Then there were the 44 emails that were sent with more than 900 conversation threads.

Most of these were discussing the theories and possible reasons as to why a game of such importance would be rigged. There are many. Some appear to be utterly far-fetched, others more prosaic in the context of this book: a good, old-fashioned gambling scam, for example.

The justification for any fix is the same, however, for every story one hears. That is that India could not countenance Pakistan playing in a World Cup final in Mumbai, the city which was hit by a terrorist attack in 2008 orchestrated from within Pakistan and by Pakistanis. The shame for Indians would be too much to bear, they say. And imagine the reaction if Pakistan had won the final? Parading and dancing with the trophy on soil which had previously been scarred by Indian blood would have been torment.

So the conspiracy theorists claim that one of two plots was hatched. Firstly, that the Indian business lobby, powerful and unimaginably rich, pooled cash to buy off the Pakistan team and ensure no ignominy. The other that the two governments, recognising the state of peril the region could find itself in with Pakistan playing a World Cup final in Mumbai, struck a deal. For the victory, India would reinvigorate trade between the two countries. It is claimed that 400 memorandums of understanding (MOUs) with regard to trade were signed in the wake of Mohali. MOUs, of course, mean nothing on their own, but there has been an improvement in relations. The two signed Favoured Nation Status agreements and a new terminal was opened in April 2012 at the Wagah–Attari border, where previously the only goods going south was limestone and the only goods going north were tomatoes. There are also rumours of the Pakistan Cricket Board being paid US$1 million for their co-operation.

It is noteworthy that Lalit Modi, powerful and connected as he is in Indian business, rejected the first theory out of hand. Lord Condon said government involvement was 'absolute fantasy'.

The point of talking to the spy was to gain more clarity surrounding the rumours. 'He will speak with you,' said the go-between. But, of course, there is the quid pro quo. For talk time, the spy would need the details of Parthiv's script. It was despatched.

The go-between, throughout our conversations, would never refer to his contact as a 'spy'. He was, somewhat amusingly, called the Leather

Trader. 'He is the best leather trader in all of Pakistan,' said the link-man. 'I can guarantee you he will get you some very nice shoes as a gift from Pakistan for your help in ridding our country of corruption.' By shoes, he meant information, such as transcripts or mobile phone records. 'And by the way,' he said, 'he thought the script was very, very interesting.'

On the first occasion we were due to speak, the Skype call had to be cancelled because 'the trade union has sent the leather trader up to our troublesome border, someone needs some new shoes up there'. For 'trade union' read the investigation agency; for 'troublesome border' read Afghanistan.

Eventually, the spy was online and ready to speak on Skype. 'I'm still alive,' he laughed as I asked him how his visit had been to the border. It was, however, quickly down to business as he said 'not much time here ... these shoes don't make themselves'.

The spy said he had no proof that the semi-final was fixed and spoke only of rumours in Pakistan high society. 'Before the semi-final there were a lot of rumours that the bookies were very hot and there was a lot of gambling going on before that match. This was being discussed every-where, in the restaurants and coffee shops people were talking of this.'

Did he know who fixed the match, and what of claims of a govern-ment conspiracy? 'I wouldn't say that [government conspiracy] this can be proved or that I know this happened,' he says. 'I assume that probably what would have happened was that the Pakistan government would have agreed to this principally and give India a bye through to Mumbai and in return they [received] trade, or leniency, they were looking for. I look at it from that perspective. It's always possible that sort of thing can filter through to the players. The board might also be knowing and instructed players. It is a possibility. This is the political aspect.'

I ask him whether he, or another leather trader, or trade union, are able to pass on any information which might help to prove one way or another, whether the Mohali match was wrong. 'What evidence do you require?' he asks. 'In a digital shape? In a voicemail message?'

Anything that has been sourced by agencies and accurate, I tell him.

'I think I can get you much more than this if I can get connected to the right people. The only thing I'm interested in is that if I get some voice message, communication between two individuals, surely you would recognise one of them, but the other guy would not be known to you, he would be a source. That voice will have to be kept "mum". It will have to disappear from that evidence.'

That evidence, unsurprisingly, has yet to materialise. The Skype contacts still take place and email conversations flow back and forth. It was one such mail that revealed the 'investigation' had begun. 'The matter was taken up at the highest level of the leather trader's association, and the corporate heads agreed to pursue this business venture all the more vigorously,' wrote the go-between. 'They may send a few decent leather shoes your way.'

Karim waits patiently. 'Not long now,' he says. 'They have your contact details. You will get a tap on the shoulder, a telephone call. In person this information will be handed to you.' It is likely to be a fruitless wait.

CHAPTER 22

FIX IT

With every step, email, text message, telephone exchange, handshake and conversation on the long trip to cricket's corrupt core, my confidence in the sport eroded. Weaving all of those together word by word into this book has meant it has now ceased to be. I have caught the whispers and claims of too many teams, matches and players to be able to sit in a stadium or in front of a television and not, in the words of Lord Condon, exclaim 'that must be moody'.

During this investigation into cricket's gambling problem, there has not been a recognised international team I have not heard some sort of corruption gripe against. It is Pakistan who have been the main thrust of the research, India and Sri Lanka less so. But Australia, Bangladesh, West Indies, New Zealand and South Africa have had their moments. England too. In a now battered notebook I have the names of 45 international and domestic players who have been mentioned to me as being up to no good. This is not a problem exclusive to the subcontinent and it is a regret that it was not possible to devote more time to each and every allegation.

It was not the intention to grow weary, but it was an obvious consequence of spending too much time with such a sick patient. It was, however, always the plan to ruminate on potential revival remedies, no matter how bleak the prognosis.

If there is to be a new beginning, then it must be ushered in by the digestion of the most bitter of medicines. And that is an ACSU investigation into the World Cup semi-final played between India and Pakistan at Mohali.

This would be mightily uncomfortable for the ICC, probably too much so, given the status of that match and the tournament or the consistent rumbling that the BCCI would not tolerate having the competition they joint-hosted and won to send a nation into delirium, tainted. But the evidence that something was awry in that most combustible of matches is growing. The ACSU have been notified of each piece of evidence garnered in the process of writing this book, including Parthiv's script and the two suspicious World Cup group match 'fixes'.

In addition, they were handed a dossier by the *Sunday Times* that was written by a certain Mazher Mahmood, he of Fake Sheikh and Pakistan 'spot-fix' scandal fame, which included information that the semi-final was rigged. In March 2011 the newspaper published claims by a man called Vicky Seth, who they said is a Delhi-based bookmaker. Seth is, in fact, a rogue punter who attempts to conceal his identity and places several bets with several bookmakers in an effort to make as much money as possible on inside information. He is, as Vinay would say, 'behind the curtain'.

The *Sunday Times* also reported that the ACSU had begun an investigation into the match. This was not correct, according to Haroon Lorgat, the ICC chief executive. He said the article was 'baseless and misleading'. 'The ICC has no reason or evidence to require an investigation into this match,' Lorgat insisted. 'It is indeed sad for spurious claims to be made which only serve to cast doubt on the semi-final of one of the most successful ICC Cricket World Cups ever.'

Prior to the World Cup, the Indian magazine *Sports Illustrated* gave the ACSU details on India and Pakistan players they had sourced from bookmakers. These bookmakers said that more than £400 million was shunted between bookmakers and gamblers in the two countries.

When I met with an ACSU officer and suggested the ICC would rather keep schtum about the semi-final, he said: 'I'm all for fighting corruption, I don't want to hide it. Historically there have been people in cricket who want to hide it. I'd much rather get everything out in the open and have five bad years and then get it straight.'

Getting it straight will not be easy. The ACSU need to get themselves straight too. They are the domestic cats of the world game. As soon as something goes wrong in the household, they feel a sharp boot to the backside. This, largely, is unfair, but there needs to be a far greater understanding of the issue they are dealing with.

The ACSU were embarrassed when Ravi Sawani, their former boss, admitted in the Southwark trial that he did not know what a 'bracket' was. They should also be pilloried for failing to grasp the nuances of spot-fixing, wrongly believing that there are manifold markets for book-makers or gamblers to exploit. It is a quick and easy lesson to learn how a corruptor might pay a captain to adjust the field or two batsmen to fiddle the scoring rate so a bracket or the lambi can be manipulated.

As the police force for the game, the ACSU is guilty of not knowing the nature of the crimes taking place on its beat. This filters through the rest of the sport, as affiliate associations, administrators, managers, coaches and players all take their lead from the ACSU on corruption.

This has to change. The ACSU may cite a lack of manpower – so much to do, so few to do it – as a reason for their inertia and that is a justifiable gripe if we cast minds back at how they did not have the staff to follow up on the claims of the Pakistan whistleblower. More staff are required for the unit, which consists of a general manager, YP Singh, an information manager and only two senior investigators (one based in Dubai and one in India). This is a pathetically feeble core for a sporting body well aware of its troubled past. It is also wrong that there should be only five regional security managers for ten international teams. Pres-ently Arrie de Beer must look after South Africa and Zimbabwe, John Rhodes Australia and New Zealand, Ronald Hope England and West Indies, Dharamveer Singh Yadav India and Sri Lanka, and Hassan Raza Pakistan and Bangladesh.

How the ACSU expects a regional manager like Hope to be effec-tive when he has to work across two continents is extraordinary, not to mention his four colleagues who have been handed assignments because of geographical 'proximity'. Consider that on 2 July 2012 England and Australia met in a one-day match at the Oval, while on the other side of the world on the same day New Zealand were hosting West Indies in a Twenty20, and it is clear that it is an archaic structure commissioned before the international fixture list had a growth spurt.

On that July day, what did a West Indies player, who may have only felt comfortable talking to Hope, do when he wanted to report an approach from a bookmaker, point one out in the team hotel or raise a concern about a teammate's behaviour? If he was told 'sorry, Ron's in London', he probably stayed quiet and the opportunity was missed. There needs to be a dedicated regional manager for each international team and, while we are at it, give him an assistant too. There can never be too many hands.

But enough of deprecating the ICC and the ACSU. That is too easy. A cheap shot. Our ire and vilification should be saved for one group only: the players. Innocent or guilty, each of them has their hands stained with the colour of the dirty money that swills through the illegal markets.

This is because since the bad old days of the 1990s a culture has been allowed to fester and develop in the dressing rooms around the world, which dictates that what happens in-house, stays in-house. Teammates will not rat on teammates, they won't 'grass', despite the game that they supposedly love and which pays them a living being at stake.

This is shameful because there is no more powerful regulatory force than the players. They could do more than any sting operation, ACSU officer or administrator to rid the game of corruption by reporting every approach by a corruptor or informing on teammates or opponents of whom they have inside knowledge. But clearly they choose not to and it infuriates the ACSU, which has a pristine record in protecting the identity of informants.

'It's down to the players to take ownership,' said an ACSU source. 'I have had a line from a few players who say "there should be more ACSU people". No, we should have 22 guys on that field and that are telling us, or 20, who the two are who are at it.

'They know far more about cricket than I ever will. That's where it should come from. I can watch a game, I know cricket, but the player on the field will have a far better feel. A player will know when a batsman plays a shot which is not right or when a captain moves a fielder to an odd position. We do get some feedback, but it could increase tenfold.'

If the culture is to change, the lead must come from the Professional Cricketers Association, the Federation of International Cricketers' Associations and the individual cricket boards. There is an unpalatable tendency, certainly on the behalf of the latter group, to attempt to humiliate anyone who makes an allegation against a team or player.

This does not foster an environment in which it is OK to speak. Quite the opposite.

Hashan Tillakaratne, the former Sri Lanka Test captain, was attacked by his own board for daring to pipe up about fixing that took place during his days as a player and his fears over the current team. Zulqarnain Haider, the Pakistan wicketkeeper who said he was threatened with violence for not playing along with the fixers, had his intelligence and mental faculties questioned by players and the Pakistan Cricket Board, who for good measure fined him when he left a tour of Dubai because of fears over his safety. Tony Palladino, the Essex whistleblower, was made to feel an outsider. The BCCI refused to take seriously the claims of Mazhar Majeed, a convicted fixer, that he had access to India players. The New Zealand Cricket Board balked at the *Sunday Times* article which questioned some of their players.

It is not to be expected that as soon as an allegation is made a cricket board holds up its hands and says 'yes, you've caught us, we've got a major problem', but a more measured approach would be an uncommon tonic. 'Yes, everyone is innocent until proven guilty and we trust our players, but we will be investigating.' Would that not encourage more players to come forward instead of the witch-hunts?

The battle to cleanse the sport is as much of minds as it is of hearts. Legal minds that is. Debate has been lukewarm over whether India should legalise gambling. Some say cricket cannot be clean without it; others stress that, with India home to the third largest Muslim population in the world, the potential for a volatile religious reaction is not worth the risk.

Ladbrokes made a presentation to the Maharashtra government in 2008 about the benefits of legalising gambling. They said 'we will consider it'. Nothing has happened since and there are only sporadic mentions of legalisation, prompted when a scandal breaks.

The indifference is strange. If gambling was legalised, the tax benefits would be enormous and on day one of legalisation the threat of corruption in cricket would be reduced by half. Well, half of the perpetrators at least.

If India's bookmakers were to be above board, they would have to operate exactly like a Ladbrokes or William Hill. That would mean an end to the credit system, where bookies accept customers on trust. They would have to have money in their account to wager. To have an account they would have to give their personal details. When accounts are kept and verified, you have a paper trail. If you have a paper trail you have no rogue punters setting up fixes with their 'friends' in cricket teams. This is why there is no sizeable (noticeable) corruption orchestrated by gamblers with traditional, legal bookmakers. They know that bookmakers are able to spot a suspicious betting pattern and the accounts which are driving it. An illegal, unregulated market – which has no such safety catch – is a necessity for fraud.

The bookmaker syndicates – Jayanti Malad, Shobhan Mehta, the Shibu et cetera – could still manipulate the odds, of course, just as any high-street bookmaker in the UK is capable of doing, but the worry that their first-tier, second-tier or third-tier franchisees are accepting bets from punters with inside knowledge of a fix would be eradicated. Another plus would be that they would not have to pay off the police. No more skulking around. No more brutal beatings. So where's the problem?

Most probably it is with the mafia figures who control the syndicates. The men who give the orders, significantly Dawood Ibrahim. Ibrahim would most certainly not want to pay tax. He is not a man of legal business. He would also have the financial clout, and, shall we say, persuasive patter to ensure that any move by ministers to put gambling on a straight and narrow line is halted.

Still, the law chamber can stifle the problem as we wait, maybe interminably, for the mob influence to wane. India must make match-fixing illegal. It is implausible that, years on from the Mohammad Azharuddin affair, no player, bookmaker or gambler can be put on trial for such a serious crime. It is no wonder India is the cradle when, nowhere in black or white, scribbled or printed in statutory law, does it state that match-fixing is wrong.

Australia, recognising such a flaw in their law-making, has begun the process of making match-fixing illegal. Proposed legislation was accepted in November 2011 by states and territories, agreeing a ten-year maximum jail term for offenders. If India followed suit, players and corruptors would at least be forced to think twice.

It is that kind of law change which is first needed in India to try to correct the country's obsession with money – as brilliantly described by K Madhavan – which spurs the problem in cricket. 'Greed is good' shouted one memorable Mumbai billboard. The quest to better oneself is, seemingly, never-ending. There is nothing wrong with that per se. In a country where one sees appalling poverty with regularity, who could begrudge the desire to make sure one does not slip into the gutter, particularly if a fast buck can be made without breaking the law?

Cricketers, just like everyone else, reflect the society they live in. It is why Parthiv and Vinay are constantly on the make. Parthiv was in Sri Lanka in March 2012 trying to make friends with players during England's two-Test tour. Vinay's new scheme is to come to London to set up a restaurant. He wants me to find him a business partner. It is why Dheeraj Dixit briefly attempted to become a politician before realising he didn't have the money muscle. When he is not taking pictures of himself and posting them on his Facebook page, he is for hire as a family portrait photographer.

Of course, the pessimist that I have become will never truly believe the game is pure. It cannot be. That is because as human beings we are different: moral, corrupt, courageous, yellow-bellied, foolish, smart, generous, greedy. In a cricket match there could be 21 players who all possess the most appealing of those traits, yet it would only take one of them to spoil it for the rest. So we have come full circle, back to where the journey began. The words of Billy Beldham resonate still: 'What has been will be again, what has been done will be done again; there is nothing new under the sun.'

GLOSSARY OF TERMS AND KEY NAMES

ACSU: the Anti-Corruption and Security Unit of the ICC. Set up in in 2000 under the retired Commissioner of the London Metropolitan Police, Lord Condon. The ACSU monitors and investigates reports of match-fixing and has an officer present for every series: Test, ODI or Twenty20, to 'spot' potential corruptors.

Pradeep Agarwal: accused of attempting to fix matches in the 2008 edition of the IPL, and filmed sitting on the balcony of the India dressing room in the 2011 World Cup match against the Netherlands. An ICC investigation ratified his presence as an official liaison officer and confirmed that his 'status' as a bookmaker was media speculation.

Kamran Akmal: Pakistan wicketkeeper, who was named as a potential fixer in the Southwark spot-fixing trial.

Umar Akmal: Pakistan batsman, and brother of Kamran, who was named as a potential fixer in the Southwark spot-fixing trial.

Wasim Akram: Pakistan all-rounder fined and barred from captaining his country by Justice Qayyam's enquiry in May 2000.

Mohammad Amir: Pakistan bowler banned and later jailed for bowling predetermined no-balls during Lord's Test in 2010.

Mohammad Asif: Pakistan bowler banned and later jailed for bowling predetermined no-balls during Lord's Test in 2010. Friend of Dheeraj Dixit.

Mohammad Azharuddin: former India captain banned for life following CBI report into match-fixing in 2000. The high court in Andhra Pradesh ruled that the ban on the cricketer was 'illegal and unsustainable'.

Cherrene Balasanthiran: London barrister who watched 'the script' unfold in the 2011 World Cup semi-final with me. Niece of Uncle Percy.

Barrish chalu: ('rain is falling') cry from bhao line operator or commentary line operator.

BCCI: Board of Control for Cricket in India.

Billy Beldham: Surrey batsman who in 1997 was named as one of the hundred greatest cricketers of all time by John Woodcock, the esteemed former cricket correspondent of *The Times*. Died in 1862 having revealed the scourge of corruption to Reverend Pycroft, author of *The Cricketer's Fields*.

Ian Bell: England batsman who chatted to me on the morning of one-day international in Mumbai in October 2011.

Betfair: the world's largest person-to-person betting exchange, which allows gamblers to offer bets and place bets. Indian bookmakers use the site to trade their wagers and are capable of moving odds in their favour by weight of money. Betfair was set up in 2000 and claims to have more than four million customers. A one-day international match averages a turnover close to £15 million.

Bhao line: the telephone line bookmakers' customers call to listen to the odds being continuously shouted by the bhao line operator while a match is on. The odds are provided by the syndicate.

Arun Bhatt: Delhi bookmaker believed to have been in contact with Danish Kaneria, the Pakistan and Essex bowler, to set up the Mervyn Westfield fix.

Big G: Parthiv's boss and associate of Shobhan Mehta. Claimed fixing would be rife in 2011 World Cup group matches.

Bowler chalu: cry made by the bhao line operator to let customers know that the bowler has started his run-up.

Bhopal: capital of Madhya Pradesh and the city where Vinay lives.

Bracket: also known as session betting, one of the four markets the Indian industry offers. A batting team will be given a runs spread for a ten-over segment at the start of an innings, and updated ball-by-ball, and customers decide whether to bet over or under that run spread at odds of 9–10 (bet £10 win £9). Most popular in ODI and Twenty20 matches.

Stuart Broad: England bowler who the ACSU tried, and failed, to charge for a breach of the anti-corruption code for a tweet during the 2011 World Cup.

Salman Butt: the Pakistan captain banned and later jailed for ordering predetermined no-balls during Lord's Test in 2010.

Chris Cairns: New Zealand all-rounder who successfully sued Lalit Modi for libel after an accusation of match-fixing.

CBI: India's Central Bureau of Investigation, an agency for investigation and collection of criminal intelligence information. Responsible for the 2000 report into match-fixing and illegal bookmakers that ended careers of, among others, Mohammad Azharuddin.

Sanjay Chawla: London-based bookmaker who was recorded by Delhi police fixing matches with Hansie Cronje, the disgraced South Africa captain, in 2000.

Chocolate: Indian bookie slang for four, either size of bet or boundary.

Commentary line: not to be confused with the bhao line, this is purely a commentary line, which Vinay runs to provide ball-by-ball information to bookmakers, who subscribe to the service.

Completed match: the fifth market punters can bet on in India, but only if there is bad weather.

Lord Condon: the first director of the ICC's ACSU.

Mr Justice Cook: judge who presided over the Pakistan 'spot-fixing' trial at Southwark.

Hansie Cronje: disgraced South Africa captain banned for life in October 2000 following South Africa's King Commission, which investigated match-fixing claims by Delhi police. Known to have fixed matches including the 2000 Centurion Test against England. Associated with Sanjay Chawla. Died in a plane crash in 2002.

Crore: a unit in the South Asian numbering system equal to 100 lakhs.

Cut: a share of the total amount of money placed at a first-, second- or third-tier bookie who works under a syndicate.

Dabba: a cellphone with modified SIM-cards which do not receive calls and only make calls out to one pre-programmed number: the bhao line. Hired by customers for around 780 rupees a month (£10).

Decimal odds: the Indian market uses a decimal system, which is favoured because almost all customer accounts are credit accounts. The formula is stake x decimal odds = payout. Betfair uses a decimal odds system. Traditional UK bookmakers use fractional odds. For example, India were .86 to win the first one-day international against England in October 2011. That equates to 5–6 in fractional odds.

Dheeraj Dixit: former cricket photographer who I met in October 2011. Accused by the Indian media and Veena Malik of being a match-fixer, a charge he denies.

Double: Indian bookmaker slang for when two runs are scored.

ECB: England and Wales Cricket Board. Governing body of cricket in England and Wales. Responsible for English national side and county cricket.

Federal Investigation Agency: the chief investigative agency of the Pakistan government.

First-tier bookmaker: A rung down from the syndicate. Usually has more than 200 customers. Vinay is a first-tier bookie. Number of customers decreases the further down the chain from second-tier to third-tier.

MA Ganapathy: Author of the 2000 CBI report into match-fixing and interrogator of Mohammad Azharuddin.

Herschelle Gibbs: South Africa batsman banned for six months for his part in the Hansie Cronje scandal.

The Green Man and Still: pub on Oxford Street in London where cricketers in the 19th century would meet bookmakers to arrange match-fixing.

GSI: Global Sports Betting Integrity – consultants who advise sporting bodies on anti-corruption investigations and prevention.

Mukesh Gupta: Indian bookmaker who would furnish India's CBI with damaging information on the depth of corruption. Gupta was clared of criminal charges by the Delhi High Court in 2011.

Yasir Hameed: Pakistan batsman whose complaint against Mazher Mahmood for a similar 'sting' operation in the summer of 2010 was upheld by the Press Complaints Commission.

Zulqarnain Haider: Pakistan wicketkeeper who refused to be involved in corruption and who went AWOL from his team's tour of Dubai in 2011 after receiving death threats from fixers.

Hawala system: the method by which bookmakers transfer money to one another, customers and corrupt players. Money can be paid across continents and countries without it actually moving. A customer approaches a hawala broker in one city and gives a sum of money to be transferred to a recipient in another city. The broker calls another broker in the recipient's city and organises the payment, promising to settle at a later date. No records are kept of such transactions.

Michael Holding: Former West Indies fast bowler and television commentator. Advised me about dangers of Indian underworld.

Dawood Ibrahim: head of the organised crime syndicate D-Company in Mumbai. Believed to control India's syndicate bookmakers. Dheeraj Dixit claims to have received death threats from his gang. He was No 3 on the *Forbes'* World's Top 10 list of most dreaded criminals list in 2011.

ICC: International Cricket Council – responsible for the administration of the world game.

Indian Cricket League: preceded the Indian Premier League. Launched in 2007, but lasted only two seasons. Had a reputation for corruption among Indian and UK bookmakers.

Inter-Service Intelligence: independent Pakistan intelligence agency, better known as the ISI.

IPL: Indian Premier League – a Twenty20 tournament launched in 2008, bringing together players from all over the world who were bought by eight city franchises in an auction. Blamed by the ACSU for globalising spot-fixing.

Ajay Jadeja: former India all-rounder banned for five years following the CBI report into match-fixing in 2000. The ban was later quashed by the Delhi High Court in 2003. Linked to Rattan Mehta, the Delhi-based punter.

Jain/Jainism: Religion which Vinay claims 80 per cent of bookmakers follow. Known for being intolerant of violence and harm to humans or animals.

Danish Kaneria: Pakistan spin bowler who was charged with corruption by the ECB for his involvement in the Mervyn Westfield case. Later banned for life by the ECB who regard him 'as a grave danger to the game of cricket'.

Karim: Pakistani lawyer who helped to put me in contact with Pakistan intelligence agency spy.

Khali: dot ball.

Khana: to lay, to bet on a team to lose. Customers will phone bookmakers and say 'khana India'. Khana translates literally as 'to eat'.

Younis Khan: Pakistan batsman who played in the World Cup semifinal against India. In 2009 he attempted to resign as Pakistan captain in protest after a government committee accused the team of match-fixing during that year's Champions Trophy.

King Commission: South Africa's 2000 inquiry into the match-fixing allegations against Hansie Cronje.

Tipu Kohli: a bookmaker who alleged that Rattan Mehta had paid Pakistan to lose a series in Sri Lanka in 1997.

Murali Krishnan: esteemed Delhi-based investigative journalist who has been tracking the match-fixing story for more than 20 years.

William Lambert: 19th-century cricketer accused of match-fixing.

Lambi: The innings runs betting market, one of the four markets the Indian industry offers. A batting team will be given a runs spread at the start of an innings, and updated ball-by-ball, and customers decide whether to bet over or under that run spread at odds of 9–10 (bet £10 win £9). For example, India's run spread was set at 276–280 in the first one-day international against England in October 2011.

Lakh: a unit in the South Asian numbering system equal to 100,000.

Lagana: to back, to bet on a team to win. Customers will phone bookmakers and say 'lagana India'.

Brian Lara: named in the CBI report as having associated with MK Gupta, the bookmaker. Was cleared by the West Indies Cricket Board and has never been charged.

Haroon Lorgat: chief executive of the ICC who took office in 2008. Claimed that the World Cup of 2011 would be free of corruption.

Lunch favourite: the lunch favourite is offered as a forward bet, or pre-match bet, so it is not available when the match is in play. A customer betting on the lunch favourite is not selecting one team over the other, instead selecting a pre-determined price for whichever team is considered favourite at the innings break in a limited-overs match or lunch break.

K Madhavan: former joint director of CBI who in 2000 was appointed by the BCCI to conduct an inquiry into the match-fixing report authored by MA Ganapathy.

Salim Malik: former Pakistan captain banned for life by Justice Qayyam's enquiry in May 2000. His life ban was lifted following a court appeal in Lahore on 23 October 2008.

Veena Malik: Bollywood actress of Pakistani origin and former girlfriend of Mohammad Asif who accused Dheeraj Dixit of being a fixer. The ACSU spoke to her about her allegations.

Match odds: the most popular of the markets available in the Indian market. Backing or laying a team to win or lose respectively.

Rattan Mehta: one of India's most notorious punters, who I met in TGI Friday's in Delhi. Mehta placed bets on India v. New Zealand Test at Ahmedabad in 1999. Claims fixing is rife in county cricket.

Lalit Modi: Conceived the IPL and was commissioner of the Twenty20 tournament. Was replaced for alleged impropriety. Lost libel case to Chris Cairns, who he accused of match-fixing. Has suffered death threats from the Indian underworld. Now resides in London.

Mazher Mahmood: The former *News of the World* journalist who exposed corruption in the Pakistan team in the summer of 2010 with the 'spot-fixing' scandal.

Mazhar Majeed: Pakistan players' agent who was exposed, and later jailed, for setting up the spot-fixing scandal in the Lord's Test match.

Jayanti Malad: Renowned as Delhi's biggest bookmaker. Associate of Vinay. Malad runs the pre-match betting syndicate. Also known as Jayanti Shah.

Shobhan Mehta: Mumbai's biggest bookmaker. Associate of Big G and Parthiv. Mehta runs the live match betting odds syndicate. The CBI report of 2000 said he had 'connections with the cricketers in one way or the other'. Also known as Shobhan Kalachowki.

Nimbahera: small city in Rajasthan where Sumer, a partner of Vinay, operates as a bookie.

Nagpur syndicate: organised by a bookie called Jeetu Nagpur, the syndicate provides live match odds to bookmakers.

Graham Onions: England bowler who chatted to me on the morning of one-day international in Mumbai in October 2011.

Party: a group of bookmakers who form a partnership to share bets they have taken so one is not overexposed.

Tony Palladino: teammate of Mervyn Westfield who blew the whistle on his fellow bowler's corruption. Claimed spot-fixing was rife in the English county game.

Pandrah: a 15-lakh rupee (£18,000) stake.

Parthiv: Mumbai-based bookie who provided details to me of fixes in World Cup, including the World Cup semi-final script. Took me to the one-day international v. Engand in Mumbai in October 2011.

Trevor Penney: India fielding coach who chatted to me on the morning of the one-day international in Mumbai in October 2011.

Mark Phillips: director at GSI. Analysed betting patterns for me in World Cup semi-final between India and Pakistan. Former principal betting investigator for the British Horseracing Authority as part of their intelligence unit.

Punter: a gambler and the new breed of fixer, taking over from the bookmakers who previously arranged the majority of fixes. Will attempt to get to know players and then ask them to do favours on the pitch. A punter will place several bets with several bookies so to hide his identity, often using agents or friends. Rattan Mehta is one of India's most notorious punters and was being watched by the ICC's ACSU.

Qayyum Report: led by Justice Qayyum Pakistan's version of the CBI report. Published in 2000. Laid bare extent of fixing within national team, banning Salim Malik and Ata-ur-Rehman for life and carpeting Wasim Akram (Malik's ban was lifted in 2008 by a local Lahore court).

Manoj Prabhakar: former India bowler banned for five years following the CBI report into match-fixing in 2000.

Reverend Pycroft: author of *The Cricketer's Fields*, published in 1851, which included the first account of corruption in cricket and coined the term 'it's just not cricket'.

Chhota Rajan: rival Mumbai gang leader to Dawood Ibrahim's D-Company. Admitted ordering killing of Sharad Shetty, D-Company's main fixer, in 2003.

Ata-ur-Rehman: former Pakistan player banned for life by Justice Qayyam's enquiry in May 2000. The ICC cleared him to play again in 2007.

Ravi Sawani: former general manager of the ACSU. Told the South-wark spot-fixing trial that it was possible to bet on a no-ball, but also admitted he didn't know what a bracket was.

Ajay Sharma: India batsman banned for life following 2000 CBI report.

Sharad Shetty: fixer for Dawood Ibrahim. Murdered by rival Mumbai crime gang in Dubai in 2003.

The Shibu: syndicate group run by Labu Delhi which provides the odds for the session, or brackets, betting.

Harbhajan Singh: India spin bowler to whom Mazhar Majeed claimed he had access. Majeed's claims were dismissed by the player, who said he had never met him, and by the BCCI.

Yuvraj Singh: India all-rounder to whom Mazher Majeed also claimed he had access. Majeed's claims were dismissed by the player, who said he had never met him, and by the BCCI.

Spot-fixing: fixing of an element of a match other than the result, most commonly the brackets or session betting or the lambi.

Alec Stewart: former England captain who was named in the 2000 CBI report for taking money from MK Gupta for information. Stewart was cleared by the ECB and has never been charged with an offence.

Syndicate: syndicates set and provide the odds for the illegal industry in India. First-, second- and third-tier bookmakers subscribe to the service and they are fed constantly changing odds via mobile telephone while a game is on. Can have links to players and are able to set up fixes. There are four syndicates in India. The live match betting odds are provided by Shobhan Mehta, the Mumbai-based bookie; Jayanti Malad offers the pre-match betting odds; session betting (the brackets) come from a group known as the Shibu (the top bookie is Labu Delhi); and a fourth, a 'rival' to Mehta's live odds, are the Nagpur syndicate, organised by a bookie called Jeetu Nagpur.

Jatin Thakkar: Mumbai-based statistician who analysed the World Cup semi-final for irregularities in scoring rates and player performances.

Trade/trading: the act of hedging bets. Bookmakers ensure profits by backing high and laying low; a stockbroker would guarantee profits in exactly the same way.

Transparency International: the global civil society organisation, which claims to lead the fight against world corruption. Its 2010 Corruption Perception Index ranked India 87th out of 178 countries.

Teen: three.

Sachin Tendulkar: godlike India player who was questioned and exonerated by KA Madhavan in investigation into India v. New Zealand Test at Ahmedabad in 1999.

Hashan Tillakaratne: former Sri Lanka captain who alleged in April 2011 that the national team had been fixing matches since 1992.

Vinay: Bhopal-based bookie who met me in October 2011 and invited me to his home. I stayed with him in February 2012.

Rajeshwar Vyakarnam: one of Lalit Modi's legal team who worked on the Chris Cairns libel case. Vyakarnam met with me in a Delhi hotel to interview a bookmaker.

Mark Waugh: former Australia batsman fined by the Australia Cricket Board for passing information to an Indian bookmaker in 1998.

Shane Warne: legendary leg-spinner who was fined by Australia Cricket Board for passing information to an Indian bookmaker in 1998.

Chris Watts: ECB anti-corruption head who for 30 years worked in the Metropolitan police, rising to senior detective working on homicides and counter terrorism.

Mervyn Westfield: Essex bowler who became the first county cricketer to be convicted of spot-fixing after receiving £6,000 to concede at least 12 runs in his first over against Durham in a televised one-day match in 2009.

Wicket gaya: ('It's a wicket') cry made by the bhao line operator or commentary line to tell customers that a wicket has fallen.

Henry Wiliams: South Africa bowler banned for six months for his part in the Hansie Cronje scandal.

YP Singh: former CBI joint director of anti-corruption, who took over from Ravi Sawani as head of the ICC's ACSU in June 2011.

Waqar Younis: former bowler who was coach of the Pakistan team during the 2011 World Cup. The 2000 Justice Qayyum report into match-fixing recommended that he 'be kept under observation and investigated'.

Hussain Zaidi: investigative reporter from Mumbai.

BIBLIOGRAPHY/SOURCES

(not including sources quoted in text)

1. 'There is nothing new under the sun'

Fixing games is nothing new – cricket lost its innocence years ago, *Guardian*, 8 November 2011

Gambling: A story of triumph and disaster, Mike Atherton, Hodder & Stoughton, 2006

2. Fear

Dawood aide Shetty killed, www.mid-day.com, 20 January 2003

Match-fixers see chance of a killing, *Guardian*, 7 February 2003

From Jogeshwari shawls to five-star suites, *Indian Express*, 21 January 2003

Transcripts of Cronje's alleged talk with bookie, *Indian Express*, 8 April 2000

No Holding Back, The Autobiography, Michael Holding, Weidenfeld & Nicolson, 2010

3. 'You wanna fix a match?'

Betting scandal as Australia report bookmaker suspicions to ICC, *Daily Telegraph*, 18 August 2009

Legalise cricket gambling in India: Lorgat, *Indian Express*, 7 February 2011

ICC probes Australia–Zimbabwe World Cup match, *Times of India*, 1 March 2011

Did Dawood's men fix Australia–Zimbabwe match? *Times of India*, 20 March 2011

4. Script

Politics and cricket collide for India and Pakistan's summit, *Guardian*, 29 March 2011

Cricket relegated to a distraction in frenzied build-up to World Cup semi-final, *Daily Telegraph*, 29 March 2011

Only a match in Mohali, Cricinfo, 29 March 2011

An encounter to stop a subcontinent, Cricinfo, 30 March 2011

The first 15 overs and mysterious Misbah, Cricinfo, 30 March 2011

Is this really patriotism? Cricinfo, 1 April 2011

5. Bookie

The Phrase Finder web site ('Hedge your bets')

Who is Shobhan Mehta? Rediff.com, 3 June 2005

Bookies arrested, kingpin on the run, www.mid-day.com, 7 October 2011

7. Bookie v. punter

Sri Lankans pay price for management scandals, *The Times*, 15 December 2011

Tillakaratne alleges match-fixing in Sri Lanka, *Times of India*, 29 April, 2011

8. Punter

CBI report into match-fixing, 2000

'I met Warne at five-star parties', *Outlook*, 12 July 2004

Plumb in the middle, *Outlook*, 16 February 2004

9. 'Fixer'

Veena and Dixit play he-said-she-said match, Despardes.com, 2 September 2010

'Bookie' Dixit to pen tell-all book, *Hindustan Times*, 2 September 2010

13. Road to Nimbahera

India has highest number of road accidents in the world, DW news agency, 29 April 2010

14. Wicket gaya!

The world's ten most wanted fugitives, *Forbes* magazine, 14 June 2011